Mastering the VIC-20™

THE ELLIS HORWOOD SERIES IN
COMPUTERS AND THEIR APPLICATIONS
Series Editor: BRIAN MEEK
Director of the Computer Unit, Queen Elizabeth College, University of London

INTERACTIVE COMPUTER GRAPHICS IN SCIENCE TEACHING
Edited by J. McKENZIE, University College, London, L. ELTON, University of Surrey,
R. LEWIS, Chelsea College, London.
INTRODUCTORY ALGOL 68 PROGRAMMING
D. F. BRAILSFORD and A. N. WALKER, University of Nottingham.
GUIDE TO GOOD PROGRAMMING PRACTICE: 2nd Edition
Edited by B. L. MEEK, Queen Elizabeth College, London, P. HEATH, Plymouth Poly-
technic, and N. RUSHBY, University of London
**CLUSTER ANALYSIS ALGORITHMS: For Data Reduction and Classification of
Objects**
H. SPÄTH, Professor of Mathematics, Oldenburg University.
DYNAMIC REGRESSION: Theory and Algorithms
L. J. SLATER, Department of Applied Engineering, Cambridge University and
H. M. PESARAN, Trinity College, Cambridge
FOUNDATIONS OF PROGRAMMING WITH PASCAL
LAWRIE MOORE, Birkbeck College, London.
PROGRAMMING LANGUAGE STANDARDISATION
Edited by B. L. MEEK, Queen Elizabeth College, London and I. D. HILL, Clinical
Research Centre, Harrow.
THE DARTMOUTH TIME SHARING SYSTEM
G. M. BULL, The Hatfield Polytechnic
RECURSIVE FUNCTIONS IN COMPUTER SCIENCE
R. PETER, formerly Eötvos Lorand University of Budapest.
FUNDAMENTALS OF COMPUTER LOGIC
D. HUTCHISON, University of Strathclyde.
THE MICROCHIP AS AN APPROPRIATE TECHNOLOGY
Dr. A. BURNS, The Computing Laboratory, Bradford University
SYSTEMS ANALYSIS AND DESIGN FOR COMPUTER APPLICATION
D. MILLINGTON, University of Strathclyde.
COMPUTING USING BASIC: An Interactive Approach
TONIA COPE, Oxford University Computing Teaching Centre.
RECURSIVE DESCENT COMPILING
A. J. T. DAVIE and R. MORRISON, University of St. Andrews, Scotland.
PROGRAMMING LANGUAGE TRANSLATION
R. E. BERRY, University of Lancaster
MICROCOMPUTERS IN EDUCATION
Edited by I. C. H. SMITH, Queen Elizabeth College, University of London
STRUCTURED PROGRAMMING WITH COMAL
R. ATHERTON, Bulmershe College of Higher Education
PASCAL IMPLEMENTATION: The P4 Compiler and Compiler and Assembler/Interpreter
S. PEMBERTON and M. DANIELS, Brighton Polytechnic
PRINCIPLES OF TEXT PROCESSING
F. N. TESKEY, University of Manchester
ADA: A PROGRAMMER'S CONVERSION COURSE
M. J. STRATFORD-COLLINS, U.S.A.
REAL TIME LANGUAGES
S. YOUNG, UMIST, Manchester
SOFTWARE ENGINEERING
K. GEWALD, G. HAAKE and W. PFADLER, Siemens AG, Munich
INTRODUCTION TO ADA
S. YOUNG, UMIST, Manchester
COMPUTERIZATION OF WORKING LIFE
E. FOSSUM, Norwegian Computing Centre

Mastering the VIC-20™

A. J. JONES
Department of Mathematics
Royal Holloway College
University of London

E. A. COLEY
Senior Microcomputer Sales Engineer
Dynaland Limited
Reading

and

D. G. J. COLE
Microprocessor Applications Engineer
Pro-Bel Limited
Reading

ELLIS HORWOOD LIMITED
Publishers · Chichester

JOHN WILEY & SONS INC.
New York · Brisbane · Chichester · Toronto

First published in 1983
Reprinted in 1983 by

ELLIS HORWOOD LIMITED
Market Cross House, Cooper Street, Chichester,
West Sussex, PO19 1EB, England

The publisher's colophon is reproduced from
James Gillison's drawing of the ancient Market
Cross, Chichester

Distributors:

Australia, New Zealand, South-east Asia:
Jacaranda-Wiley Ltd., Jacaranda Press
JOHN WILEY & SONS INC.
GPO Box 859, Brisbane, Queensland 4001, Australia

Canada:
JOHN WILEY & SONS CANADA LIMITED
22 Worcester Road, Rexdale, Ontario, Canada

Europe, Africa:
JOHN WILEY & SONS LIMITED
Baffins Lane, Chichester, West Sussex, England

North and South America and the rest of the world:
JOHN WILEY & SONS INC.
605 Third Avenue, New York, NY 10158, USA

©1983 A. J. Jones, E. A. Coley, D. G. J. Cole/
Ellis Horwood Limited

British Library Cataloguing in Publication Data
Jones, A. J.
Mastering the VIC-20
1. VIC (Computer)
I. Title II. Coley, E.A. III. Cole, D.G.J.
001.64'04   QA76.8.V5

Library of Congress Card No. 82–24165

ISBN 0–85312–585–6 (Ellis Horwood Limited, Publishers)
ISBN 0–471–88892–3 (John Wiley & Sons Inc.)

ISBN 0–471–88852–4 (John Wiley & Sons Inc. – Cassette)
ISBN 0–471–88909–1 (John Wiley & Sons Inc. – Disk)

Typeset in Press Roman by Ellis Horwood Limited.
Printed in Great Britian by R. J. Acford, Chichester.

VIC–20 is a registered trade mark of
Commodore Business Machines

Table of Contents

6 **Table of Contents**

Disk directory for main programs

2	"BIT PATTERNS"	PRG	1	"M/C COUNTER"		PRG
10	"MINISYN"	PRG	1	"M/C TESTSTOP"		PRG
2	"SHUFFLES"	PRG	2	"TESTSTOP LOADER"		PRG
6	"TEST CARD DISP"	PRG	1	"M/C TINCOPY"		PRG
13	"PONTOON"	PRG	1	"M/C COPY"		PRG
3	"PLAY UFO TUNE"	PRG	2	"M/C PLOTSUB"		PRG
3	"DECIMAL TO HEX"	PRG	1	"PLOTSUB TEST"		PRG
2	"RENUMBER"	PRG	22	"(3K)STARSHIP"		PRG
4	"GRAPHICS DEMO"	PRG	8	"(3K)HI-DRAW"		PRG
3	"SINE CURVE"	PRG	1	"M/C HI-DRAW"		PRG
6	"3K HI-RES"	PRG	5	"HI-DRAW LOADER"		PRG
4	"CASS DATA FILES"	PRG	12	"HI-DUMP+M/C"		PRG
6	"SEQ FILES"	PRG	14	"HSC0"		PRG
3	"LO-DUMP"	PRG	14	"HSC1"		PRG
1	"PRINTER DOT ADD"	PRG	14	"HSC2"		PRG
3	"PICTURES"	PRG	14	"HSC3"		PRG
1	"LIGHT PEN DEMO"	PRG	479	BLOCKS FREE.		

Cassette tapes or floppy diskettes containing these programs are available from:

USA − John Wiley & Sons Inc., 605 Third Avenue, New York, NY10158, USA.

UK/Europe − Ellis Horwood Limited, Cooper Street, Chichester, West Sussex, PO19 1EB, England for further details.

Preface

In this book we have tried to lead the reader along the path which we ourselves followed after acquiring a VIC-20. We do hope you, the reader, will gain as much pleasure from using our book as we have had in writing it.

Our efforts have been supported by many people. In particular we would like to thank: Peter Raybaud and his colleagues at Adda Computers Ltd, Ealing; John Collins, Malcolm North and the amazing Nick Green of Commodore Business Machines (UK) Ltd, Slough; our publisher Ellis Horwood for all his essential support and Mike Horwood for his patience and foresight.

Liz would also like to thank Douglas Milnes of the Personal Computer Palace (Dynaland Ltd), Reading, for fortitude in the face of unreasonable time sharing. Dave especially wants to thank Mary Considine for similar reasons in a different context!

A very special vote of thanks is due to Graham Carpenter. From subjecting Starship to extensive field testing to unflinching doggedness when battling with hostile machine code, Graham has helped us every step of the way. By unanimous acclamation we hereby award him the Galactic Empire Medal (GEM), First Class.

Finally we should all like to express our appreciation to Marion and John Brooker for speedy and accurate typing and careful artwork.

In the words of Lewis Carroll just 'start at the beginning, continue to the end and then stop'.

A.J.J.
E.A.C.
D.G.J.C.
Wokingham, Berkshire
September 1982

To our parents

1
VIC BASIC

.1 Introduction

To work through this chapter you should have a VIC-20 available and have studied the booklet *Personal Computing on the VIC-20* which is supplied with the microcomputer. We assume that you have encountered most of the BASIC commands, statements and functions listed in Appendix C of the booklet and that they have entered and RUN programs. Thus the reader is presumed to already possess a modest knowledge of BASIC programming.

The aim of Chapter 1 is to review some aspects of particular commands such as PRINT, PEEK ( ), POKE, and GOTO, and to amplify some useful techniques in string handling, arrays, and logical operators. We also want to set you thinking about how to structure programs sensibly and what things look like from the machine's point of view. This last we regard as important, for to become really adept in the use of a microcomputer your knowledge of how the machine actually gets things done must progress hand in hand with your programming skill. Given persistence and knowledge virtually anything is possible.

By the end of this chapter you will be able to view any part of VIC-20 memory and to change any individual bit, if it can be changed.

.2 Variables and strings

Granted that a microcomputer is a device for manipulating data, one can reasonably ask what *kind* of data can a microcomputer manipulate? Although all data is evenutally expressed in terms of zeros and ones, at BASIC programming level there are three types of data which can be distinguished.

Integer variables. Whole numbers such as $0, \pm 1, \pm 2, \ldots$ etc. in the range -32768 to $+32767$.

Real number or floating point variables such as

$$3.14159265E - 20.$$

In this particular example the number represented is 3.14159265 multiplied by 10 to the power -20 (shift the decimal point left 20 places), and -20 is called the *exponent* of 10. Thus every real number variable may be represented as a decimal part multiplied by 10 to some exponent. The range of usabl exponents is -38 to $+38$, a VIC counts $10\uparrow -39$ as 0 and gives an overflow error for $10\uparrow 39$.

An integer variable is defined by a statement like $X\% = 10$ and a real number of floating poin variable by $X = 10$. Strictly speaking $X = 10$ means LET $X = 10$ but LET takes up precious space and i semantically redundant if one realizes that $=$ is *not* symmetric in BASIC, that is $X = 10$ is not the sam as $10 = X$. To illustrate this, the program

$$100\ X = 10 : PRINT\ X$$

will run and print the number 10, but the program

$$100\ 10 = X : PRINT\ X$$

will give a SYNTAX ERROR.

When using single variables there is no space-saving advantage in using an integer variable as oppose to a real number variable, in fact each occupies 7 bytes of memory (see 1.5). However, when usin variables as *array elements,* discounting the space used by the array header, there is a saving of 3 byte per element using integer rather than real number variables; for large arrays this gain is significant.

Up to two characters can be used to identify variables, you can use more but only the first two wil be recognized. Labels which contain BASIC keywords as a subword should be avoided. Variable name to avoid are ST, TI, and TI\$ as these are assigned by the operating system: ST is the status variabl which reports the status of the last I/O operation, TI is the time in Jiffys (1/60 secs) since the machin was turned on and TI\$ is TI expressed in hours, minutes, seconds. The variable TI\$ may be reset by th user whereas TI may not

String or character variables such as

" ABCD0123 "

which is a string of length 8. A string is set by a statement like $X\$ = $ "AB" and consists of a sequence o characters of any length up to 255. The characters of a string may include color control or curso control characters.

Whereas manipulating integer or real number variables is a straightforward matter of specifying th arithmetic operations you want VIC to perform, string manipulation is somewhat more subtle and has it own set of specialized functions such as:

ASC(X\$) which gives the ASCII code of the first character of X\$, e.g.
      ASC("AB") equals 65.

CHR\$(N) which gives the string character whose ASCII code is N, e.g.
      CHR\$(65) equals "A".

LEFT\$(X\$,N) which gives the N left-most characters of X\$, e.g.
      LEFT\$("ABC",2) equals "AB" .

MID\$(X\$,M,N) which gives a string of N characters starting from the M*th* character in X\$, e.g.
      MID\$("ABCDE",3,2) equals "CD".

STR\$(X) which gives a string which corresponds to the printed version of the number X, e.g.
      STR\$(32.2) equals " 32.2".

Note the string comes complete with the initial space which always precedes a positive number. For a negative number this space is used for the minus sign.

VAL(X\$) which converts the string X\$ into a number, e.g.
      VAL("32.2") equals 32.2.

This is a useful function to use with INPUT. If INPUT is expecting a number and receives any other kind of character a REDO FROM START message occurs, this can spoil a carefully set up screen format and is avoided if a string is INPUT and then converted to a number using VAL, e.g. VAL("AB") equals 0 because 'A' is not a numeric character.

LEN(X$) which gives the length of the string X$, e.g.
LEN("AB") equals 2.

Example

Suppose we wish to PRINT a tidy column of integer numbers three spaces from the left of the screen. The numbers may be positive or negative and of any length. If we simply display the I*th* number X%(I) by

PRINT SPC(3) X%(I)†

a very untidy column will result, as the numbers are of varying length. To right justify we can instead use

PRINT SPC(3)RIGHT$("   " + STR$(X%(I)),6)   [4 spaces]

The explanation is as follows. Strings can be concatenated with + e.g. "A" + "B" equals "AB". Thus if X%(1) = −2 we have

"   " + STR$(−2) = "   −2"

whereas if X%(I) = − 65535 we have

"   " + STR$(−65535) = "   − 65535"

If RIGHT$(,6) is used on both of these with the first printed above the second, the result is

− 2

− 6 5 5 3 6

as required.

In answer to the possible next question: no, you cannot subtract strings, try it and see. However, strings do have a defined order. It is true that "A" < "B", because ASC("A")=65 < ASC("B")=66. Longer strings are compared by successive comparison of character ASC codes, thus "AAA" < "AAB". This is useful on two accounts. Firstly it enables us to compare two strings and see if they are equal or not equal. Secondly, since the ASC codes for alphabetic characters run sequentially up from 65 it means that alphabetic strings are ordered just as they would be in a dictionary (the word is "lexico-graphically'), this can be useful in various text-handling procedures.

Another lesson to be drawn from the previous example is that getting PRINT to do exactly what you want can be frustrating process. For example, using a semicolon after the character or number to be printed will leave the cursor in the next screen position and suppress a carriage return, *unless* the last position printed to was at the end of a row, in which case a carriage return will occur come what may. This carriage return can be effectively undone by using a cursor-left at the end of the string printed, followed by a semicolon of course, *unless* the last position printed to was the final screen position (bottom right). In this you cannot pretend the carriage return did not happen because the whole screen scrolls up! Moral: do not PRINT to the final screen position if you do not want the screen to scroll.

---

†SPC(3) does *not* actually PRINT 3 spaces, it merely skips forward 3 spaces.

1.3 Arrays and FOR loops

One of the most powerful BASIC commands is the FOR ... TO ... STEP ... NEXT ... loop. It can be used for repetitive computation or condition checking, and used in conjunction with arrays FOR loops can move whole blocks of data from one place to another. The syntax of FOR is FOR I = A TO B STEP C and the loop counter I is incremented by the command NEXT, from A, in steps of C, until I is greater than B. If STEP C is omitted it is assumed C = 1, in computer jargon C defaults to 1. Once the loop has been set up changes in A, B or C have no effect unless the loop is re-entered later in the program; thus, for example, you cannot change the STEP value C midway in the loop and expect the change to be acted upon for the next value of I. You can, however, change the value of I, although this should be done with care.

Example
Suppose a previously dimensioned array A%(I), $0 \leqslant I \leqslant 100$ has been filled by computation and we wish to check that no element of the array is equal to zero.

```
100 FOR I = 0 TO 100
110 IF A%(I) = 0 THEN PRINT "ZERO FOR I = ":I:I = 100
120 NEXT
```

If the conditions A%(I)=0 is found to be true then execution of line 110 continues, otherwise execution proceeds directly to line 120.

IMPORTANT NOTE. If an IF statement *fails* to be true then execution proceeds directly to the *next program line*.

If A%(I)=0 is found to be true for some I then the PRINT command is executed, I is set to 100 and when NEXT is next encountered the FOR loop decides it is finished. Incidentally avoid jumping out of a FOR loop without going through NEXT. BASIC will let you do this but nevertheless don't. It is poor technique and can create all kinds of weird problems in a long program.

Frequently when manipulating an array the following problem arises. An element, say the A*th* element, has been selected from the array. We now wish to 'close the gap' either by moving every element of the array below A one place to the right, or by moving every element of the array above A one place to the left. An example of this situation is the card shuffle given in Chapter 2. There is an important rule of thumb to cover this situation.

IMPORTANT NOTE. When moving array elements to the *right* do it from the *top down*. When moving array elements to the *left* do it from the *bottom up*.

Example
Moving array elements to the right. Suppose we want to select the A*th* element of an array, close up the array to leave a gap at the bottom, and insert the selected element as the new first element.

```
10 DIM A%(100)
20 FOR I = 1 TO 100 : A%(I) = I: NEXT
30 REM ARRAY NOW SET UP
40 REM SELECT A(TH) ELEMENT
50 A = INT(100*RND(1)) + 1 : REM RANGE 1 TO 100
60 A%(0) = A%(A) : REM STORE IN SPARE ELEMENT
70 REM MOVE-RIGHT UP TO A
80 FOR J = A TO 1 STEP −1
90 A%(J) = A%(J − 1)
100 NEXT.
```

If line 80 were replaced by FOR J = 1 TO A the move would be wrong. Can you see why? For J = 1 we would replace A%(1) by A%(0) which is correct, but for J = 2 line 90 then replaces A%(2) by *the new* A%(1) which is wrong. Moreover it is wrong all the way up. Notice that by using A%(0) as a temporary store we avoid having to worry about what happens if A = 1. If A = 1 we do not actually want to move anything at all, but rather than use an IF statement to make A = 1 a special case we let the J loop make one move anyway. In this program there is no particular gain in doing this, but if the J loop were within another loop, say an I loop, as is the case for the card shuffle in section 2.1, we should then have to check the IF statement for every value of I, which would slow the procedure noticeably.

FOR loops are also useful for comparing the time taken to do some operation in one or more different ways. For example to find $\sqrt{2}$ we could use SQR(2) or 2↑.5; which is faster? In human terms they are both so fast that we cannot tell the difference with one operation. However, the following program easily shows up the difference.

```
10 T = TI : REM TAKE THE TIME
20 FOR I = 0 TO 1000
30 X = SQR(2)
40 NEXT
50 PRINT (TI − T)/60
60 T = TI : REM TAKE THE TIME AGAIN
70 FOR I = 0 TO 1000
80 X = 2↑·5
90 NEXT
100 PRINT (TI − T)/60
```

We find that the first FOR loop takes about 43.37 secs and the second 45.6 secs, hence 2↑.5 takes about 5% longer than SQR(2).

There is an important underlying idea behind the last program.

IMPORTANT NOTE. If you want to know what is going on, *ask the microcomputer*.

Naturally you have to ask the right questions but this comes with practice. For example, if a program is not behaving as planned, put a STOP just before the place where you think things are going wrong. When you RUN the program and BREAK IN LINE so-and-so occurs, use direct commands to PRINT to the screen or printer all the values of the important variables. In this way you will greatly speed the debugging process. The important point is that the answer to virtually every question which arises about what is going on is there in the machine, you only have to ask.

The great trade-off in nearly all complex computer programs is *time* versus *space*. One reason whc the VIC-20 is an excellent machine to learn on is that (without a RAM pack) space, that is usable memory, is limited. Yes, we know that sounds silly, but it is true. If you are tight on space then you will be *forced* to do only exactly what is needed and to do it as concisely as possible. Think what driving standards would be if everyone learnt to drive in a Lamborghini. . . .

RULE OF THUMB. Long is wrong.

Nowhere is the great trade-off more apparent than in the use of arrays. Arrays eat space, the only thing which compares with the appetite of arrays for space is lots of text. On the other hand, given the index I, accessing the value A%(I) is *fast*.

Example

This problem arises in connection with MINISYN the program discussed in section 1.6. Given that one of 25 particular keys has been pressed, and ignoring all other keys, we want to set the three tone oscillators to the frequency which corresponds to the key pressed. If you glance forward to MINISYN the ASCII codes of the relevant keys are the DATA statements of lines 340 to 380. These are read into the array K%(I) in line 390. Similarly the corresponding frequencies are in the DATA statements of lines 400 to 470 and are read into the array M%(I) in line 490.

The desired sequence of events is this. A key is pressed, picked up by GETA$ and the corresponding ASCII code found by taking ASC(A$). Next we want to find if ASC(A$) is one of the numbers in K%(I) and if so which one. This one could do with a routine like

```
1000 FOR I = 0 TO 24
1010 IF ASC(A$) = K%(I) THEN X = I
1020 NEXT
```

We could then turn the oscillator on with, say POKE 36874,M%(X). Now there is one major drawback to this idea, it is that the response time is unacceptable. When you hit a key on a keyboard instrument you do not expect to wait an appreciable time whilst it makes up its mind what note you want! The required frequency must go straight into 36874 virtually immediately.

Since the function of MINISYN is relatively simple, space is not a major factor, whereas speed is. (The instruction page set up in lines 250 to 335 is just icing on the cake and could be omitted if necessary.) Can we trade-off space for speed and take out the keycheck routine?

Now the highest ASC code likely to be encountered is 140, this can be determined by a study of the CHR$ table on p. 168. Suppose we set up an array F%(I) of length 140 and use the value of ASC(A$) as an offset to access the correct frequency. In all but 25 of the elements of F%(I) we put the number 0. If 0 is put in 36874 it will merely turn the oscillator off which is what we want. On the other hand suppose ASC(A$) = 95 and we arrange that F%(95) = 225, then POKE 36874,F%(ASC(A$)) will have exactly the desired effect. Thus lines 1000 to 1020 and POKE 36874,M%(X) can be replaced by the single command

```
POKE 36874,F%(ASC(A$))
```

The array F%(I) can be set up before keyboard play commences, at a time when fractions of a second do not count, and then used subsequently to provide the appropriate value for 36874 virtually immediately. The problem is solved at the cost of introducing an array of length 140.

Where relatively slow computations have to be executed frequently it is often advantageous to use an array as a look-up table. For example, every time the PLOTSUB of the last program in Chapter 4 is used the function $2\uparrow I$ is needed for some I in the range 0 to 7. If at the beginning of the program we set up an array C%(I) with

```
10 FOR I = 0 TO 7 : C%(I) = 2↑I : NEXT
```

then every time $2\uparrow I$ is needed we can substitute C%(I), which is far faster.

1.4 Structuring programs[†]

You may be interested to know that something like 90% of professional programming time is spent updating or modifying existing programs. This strikes us as an absurd state of affairs, just think of all the new programs that never get written.

[†] In this brief account of structured programming we follow the treatment given in L. A. Leventhal, *6502 Assembly Language Programming,* Osborne/McGraw-Hill, 1979.

The reasons are not hard to see. Updating an earlier program, generally written by someone who is no longer available, need not be time-consuming but often is because of (a) poor documentation, (b) lack of ordered program structure. Lack of structure usually involves one major flaw in programming technique: over-use of GOTO.

The GOTO statement is simultaneously the most powerful and most dangerous of all BASIC commands. If GOTO is not strictly necessary, avoid it. If your program reeks of GOTOs it is *wrong*. To put it another way, if the program is sensibly structured GOTO will rarely be needed. With GOTO hiding in every other line, debugging or modifying a program can become like wrestling with an octopus; every time you think you have things under control there is this nasty wet feeling around your throat!

Any program can be assembled out of three basic modules.

1. A *linear sequence of steps* executed consecutively: S1, S2, S3, etc., where S1, S2, S3 may be single instructions or an entire program.

2. A *conditional structure* of the type if C then S1 otherwise S2. Here S1 is executed if C is true and S2 if C is false.

3. A *loop structure* of the type do S until C, where S is an instruction or sequence of instructions and C is a looping condition which is tested before continuing the loop. Note that this has the effect of guaranteeing that the loop is always executed at least once.

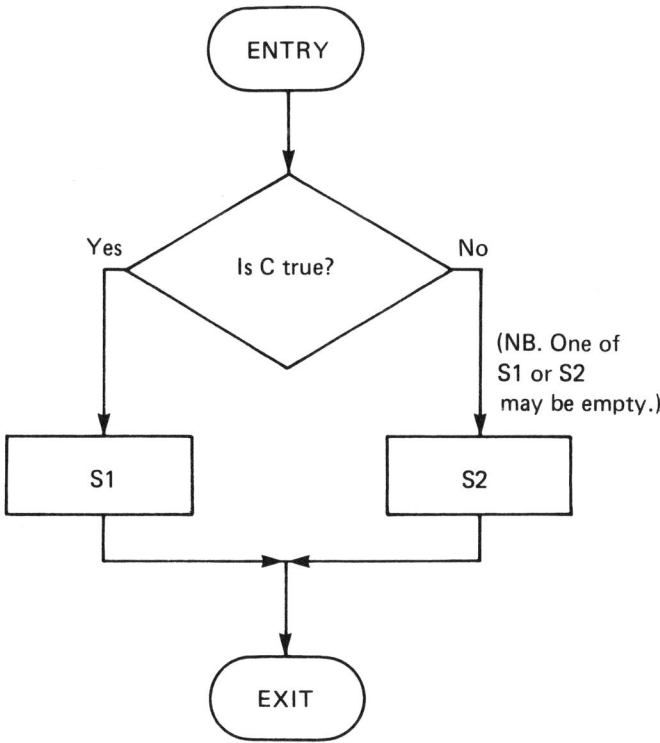

Figure 1.1 – Flow chart of the
'If-then-otherwise' structure.

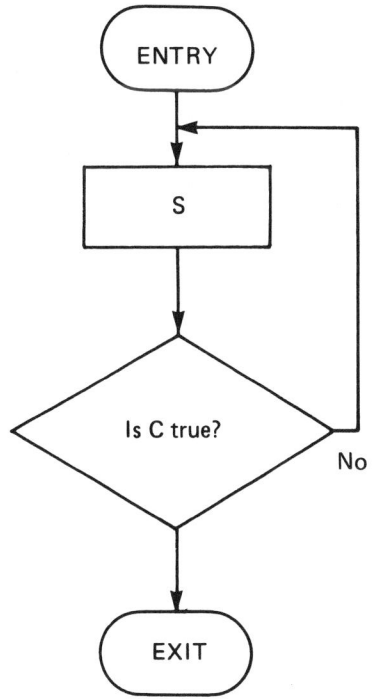

Figure 1.2 – Flow chart of the
'Repeat-until' structure.

A glance at figures 1.1 and 1.2 will show immediately that both conditional and loop structures have a single entry and a single exit.

We can characterize the principal features of structured programming as being:

I. Only the three basic structures, and possibly a small number of auxiliary structures, are necessary.

II. Structures may be nested to any level of complexity so that any structure can, in turn, contain any of the structures.

III. Each structure has a *single entry* and a *single exit*.

The advantages of structured programming are that: the sequence of operations is easy to trace which allows easy testing and debugging, the structures can easily be made into modules, the structured version of a program is partly self-documenting and generally easy to read, and consequently structured programs are easy to document.

The disadvantages are that: structured programs are sometimes slower and can use more memory than unstructured programs, the three basic structures are not always efficient or convenient for a given implementation, structured programs consider only the sequence of program operations, not the real-time flow of data, and therefore structures may handle data awkwardly.

Still, the fact remains that memory space is getting cheaper and if even a moderate proportion of existing programs were properly structured an enormous saving would result.

The occasional GOTO may be perfectly placed and acceptable, but we should like to register the plea that Frankenstein be given a monopoly in creating monsters!

1.5 Bytes, PEEK ( ), POKE and binary

The memory of a fully extended VIC-20 consists of 65536 'cells'. So that each cell can be identified it is given a number which is called its *address*, valid addresses lie in the range 0 to 65535.

The command PEEK(Address) enables us to look at the contents of any cell given its address. For example the command

PRINT PEEK(65535)

will return the value 255. Thus PEEK( ) gives us a window through which we can view any part of VIC memory.

Each address can contain a number between 0 and 255. Why 255, you may ask? The answer to this question lies in the way that computers count. Human beings count in multiples of 10, thus 64035 really means

$$6*(10\uparrow4) + 4*(10\uparrow3) + 0*(10\uparrow2) + 3*(10\uparrow1) + 5$$

(by convention $10\uparrow0$ is 1). In this way we can represent any number using only the digits 0,1,2,3,4,5,6,7,8,9. Notice 9 is one less than the magic number 10. We say that human beings do arithmetic to *base* 10. Now in reality there is nothing magic about 10, any other whole number greater than 1 could serve just as well as the base for an arithmetic. In fact computers do arithmetic to base 2. Thus the number 129, which in human terms means

$$1*(10\uparrow2) + 2*(10\uparrow1) + 9,$$

is remembered by the computer as

$$1*(2\uparrow7)+0*(2\uparrow6)+0*(2\uparrow5)+0*(2\uparrow4)+0*(2\uparrow3)+0*(2\uparrow2)+0*(2\uparrow1)+1,$$

or more briefly as 10000001. Notice we are still talking about the *same* number, namely 129, but the *representation* of that number is different; think of 10000001 as a synonym for 129.

Since computers do arithmetic to base 2 they need only use the digits 0,1. A switch is either on (1) or off (0), a pulse is either present (1) or absent (0). It is easy to see why base 2 makes sense for computers. Arithmetic to base 2 is, for obvious reasons, called *binary* arithmetic, and the digits 0,1 are called *bits*.

Let us return to the question, why does each address contain a number in the range 0 to 255? The answer is quite simple: each memory cell contains exactly 8 bits. Therefore the biggest binary number which can live at any address is 11111111, that is

$$1*(2\uparrow7)+1*(2\uparrow6)+1*(2\uparrow5)+1*(2\uparrow4)+1*(2\uparrow3)+1*(2\uparrow2)+1*(2\uparrow1)+1$$

or in human terms $128 + 64 + 32 + 16 + 8 + 4 + 2 + 1 = 255$.

The following program will display the decimal contents and equivalent binary bit pattern of any valid address. If the contents change then the displayed information will also change, but not necessarily as quickly. You can use the program to wander around in VIC memory and see what is going on. Interesting areas to look at are the *stack,* addresses 256 to 511, the VIC chip registers, addresses 36864 to 36879, and the I/O registers, addresses 37136 to 37167. You can speed the rate at which the contents are scanned by reducing the delay loop in 130. Hit RETURN to end the program and the space-bar to enter a new address.

BIT PATTERNS

```
10 PRINT"◻":D$="◼00000000"
20 INPUT"ADDRESS";A$:A=VAL(A$)
30 IFA<0ORA>65535THEN10
40 PRINT"◻◻◻◻CONTENTS  BIT PATTERN"
50 PRINTSPC(13)"76543210"
60 IFPEEK(A)<>PTHENPRINTD$+"     "
70 P=PEEK(A)
80 FORI=7TO0STEP-1
90 BI=(PAND(2↑I))/(2↑I)
100 PRINT"◻"+D$SPC(20-I)RIGHT$(STR$(BI),1)
110 NEXT
120 PRINTD$+RIGHT$("      "+STR$(P),4)
130 FORI=0TO2000:NEXT
140 GETB$
150 IFB$=" "THEN10
160 IFB$=CHR$(13)THENEND
170 GOTO60
```

Eight bits equals one *byte,* the contents of any address. On power up the (unexpanded) VIC-20 displays the message 3583 BYTES FREE which tells the user that there are this number of bytes available for his use.

For some memory on the VIC-20 the contents cannot be changed, and remain intact even when the machine is turned off. This kind of memory is called Read Only Memory or ROM. The remaining memory can have variable content but this information is lost when the machine is turned off. This second kind of memory is called Random Access Memory or RAM. A description of which blocks of memory are ROM and which are RAM is given in Chapter 3.

Assuming that the address we are looking at corresponds to RAM the contents can be set to be whatever we want, some number in the range 0 to 255 of course, by means of POKE. For example try

POKE 7680,1 : POKE 38400,2

A red 'A' should appear in the top left hand corner of the screen. Here we put the number 1, the screen code for A, in address 7680 and the number 2, the color code for red, in address 38400. It happens that 7680 is the first location of the block of memory devoted to the screen display, and 38400 the first location of the corresponding block of memory devoted to the color display. Notice PEEK( ) takes brackets but POKE does not.

Plainly PEEK( ) and POKE are fairly fundamental commands. The first gives us the ability to read any part of VIC memory and the second gives us the power to alter the contents of any address, provided that this is possible.

1.6 The program MINISYN

This program uses the three tone oscillators of the VIC chip and sets up the VIC-20 as a two octave keyboard with sustain; that is, a note sounds as long as the key remains pressed. To add educational and visual interest a color bar display appears simultaneously as each note of the scale selected is played. The colors progress in the same sequence whichever scale is selected, even though the notes which com--promise the scale change. If a note is played which is not part of the scale selected the screen goes black.

In order to fit a reasonable facsimile of a two-octave keyboard into the VIC-20 keyboard it proves necessary to turn the VIC-20 around. Thus if the VIC-20 is facing *away* from you the nearest row of keys correspond to the white keys of a piano and the second row to the black keys, with gaps where appropriate; see Figures 1.3 and 1.4.

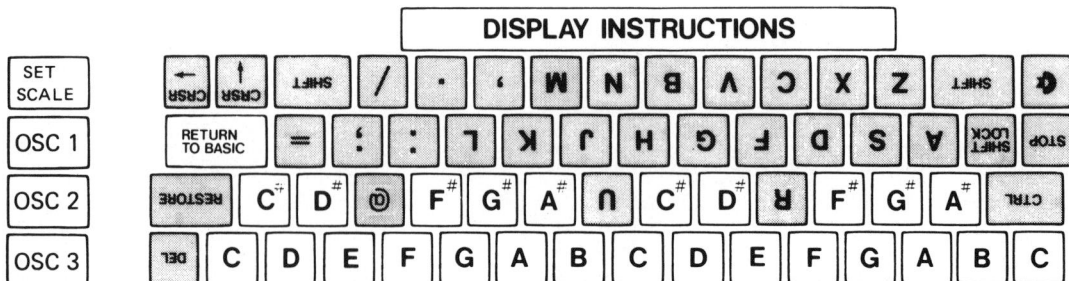

Figure 1.3 – MINISYN keyboard layout.

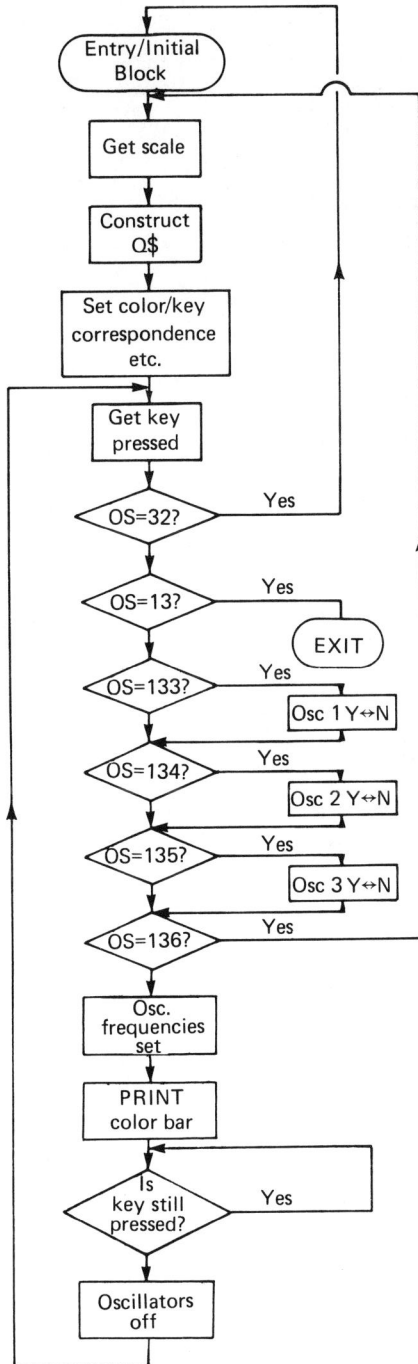

Figure 1.4 – Flow chart of MINISYN.

The three oscillators can be turned on and off with the F1, F3, F5 keys, and F7 is used to select a new scale. The program is terminated by hitting the return key. Since the function keys are used the program cannot be run with the Super Expander cartridge or the Programmers Aid.

```
10 REM*MINISYN*
20 GOTO210
30 REM*COLOUR GOSUB*
40 CC=C%(OS):IFCC=255THENRETURN
50 ONCC+1GOTO60,70,80,90,100,110,120,130
60 POKE36879,15:RETURN
70 PRINTLEFT$(D$,19)"◀"+Q$;:RETURN
80 PRINTLEFT$(D$,15)"◸"+S$;:RETURN
90 PRINTLEFT$(D$,12)"◤"+S$;:RETURN
100 PRINTLEFT$(D$,9)"◼"+S$;:RETURN
110 PRINTLEFT$(D$,6)"◈"+S$;:RETURN
120 PRINTLEFT$(D$,4)"▦"+S$;:RETURN
130 PRINTLEFT$(D$,1)"◫"+S$;:RETURN
140 REM*OSC GOSUBS*
150 IFX=0THENS=36874:X=1:RETURN
160 IFX=1THENS=1016:X=0:RETURN
170 IFY=0THENT=36875:Y=1:RETURN
180 IFY=1THENT=1017:Y=0:RETURN
190 IFZ=0THENU=36876:Z=1:RETURN
200 IFZ=1THENU=1018:Z=0:RETURN
210 REM*PROGRAM*
220 DIMM%(24),K%(24),Z%(13),F%(140),C%(140)
230 P$="                        ":D$="▨▨▨▨▨▨▨▨▨▨▨▨▨▨▨▨▨▨▨▨":T$="             "
240 S$="◀"+P$+P$+P$+P$:V=36878:POKE36879,170
250 PRINT"◼▸◼◼◼ ◼INSTRUCTIONS"
260 PRINT"COLOURS ARE DISPLAYED  IN SEQUENCE IF THE"
270 PRINT"  CORRECT NOTES ARE    PLAYED.ALL OTHER NOTESDISPLAY A ◼BLACK◼ SCREEN
"
280 PRINT"       ◼◼ ◼ ◤ ◼◼ � ◼ ◼ ◼"
290 PRINTCHR$(13)"       SCALES ARE     ◼C  C# D  D# E  F  F# G  G# A  A# B
  C  ◼"
300 PRINT"◼F1◼F3◼F5◼ SELECT VOICES"
310 PRINT"◼F7◼ SELECTS A NEW SCALE"
320 PRINT"◼RETURN◼ ENDS PROGRAM   "
330 PRINT"◼SPACE◼ SHOWS THIS PAGE  "
335 PRINT" ◼    PRESS ANY KEY    ◼"
340 DATA95,49,81,50,87
350 DATA51,69,52,53,84
360 DATA54,89,55,56,73
370 DATA57,79,48,80,43
380 DATA45,42,92,94,19
390 FORI=24TO0STEP-1:READK%(I):NEXT
400 DATA225,223,221
410 DATA219,217,215
420 DATA212,209,207
430 DATA203,201,199
440 DATA195,191,187
450 DATA183,179,175
460 DATA167,163,159
470 DATA151,147,143
480 DATA135
490 FORI=24TO0STEP-1:READM%(I):NEXT
500 FORI=0TO24:F%(K%(I))=M%(I):NEXT:REM NOTES/KEYS
```

Listing continues next page

```
510 REM*SCALE*
520 DATA0,2,4,5,7,9,11
530 DATA12,14,16,17,19
540 DATA21,23
550 FORI=0TO13:READZ%(I):NEXT
560 FORI=0TO140:C%(I)=255:NEXT:REM NO COLOUR
570 GETA$:IFA$=""THEN570
580 PRINT"█"LEFT$(D$,10)
590 INPUT"SCALE";K$:Q=255
600 IFK$="C"THENQ=0
610 IFK$="C#"THENQ=1
620 IFK$="D"THENQ=2
630 IFK$="D#"THENQ=3
640 IFK$="E"THENQ=4
650 IFK$="F"THENQ=5
660 IFK$="F#"THENQ=6
670 IFK$="G"THENQ=7
680 IFK$="G#"THENQ=8
690 IFK$="A"THENQ=9
700 IFK$="A#"THENQ=10
710 IFK$="B"THENQ=11
720 IFQ=255THEN590
730 IFLEN(K$)=1THENK$=K$+" "
740 Q$="█"+P$+T$+K$+T$+P$+P$
750 REM**SET COL/KEY**
760 FORI=0TO24:C%(K%(I))=0:NEXT:REM*SET TO BLACK*
770 FORL=0TO13
780 W=Q+Z%(L)-24*INT((Q+Z%(L))/24)
790 C%(K%(W))=L-7*INT(L/7)+1
800 NEXTL
810 C%(K%(24))=C%(K%(0))
820 PRINT"█":POKE36879,239:POKEV,15
830 GETA$:IFA$=""THEN830
840 OS=ASC(A$):P=PEEK(197)
845 IFOS=32THENRUN
850 IFOS=13THEN940
860 IFOS=133THENGOSUB190
870 IFOS=134THENGOSUB170
880 IFOS=135THENGOSUB150
890 IFOS=136THEN580
900 POKES,F%(OS):POKET,F%(OS):POKEU,F%(OS):GOSUB30
910 IFPEEK(197)=PTHEN910
920 POKES,0:POKET,0:POKEU,0:PRINT"█":POKE36879,239
930 GOTO830
940 POKEV,0:POKE650,0:PRINT"█":POKE36879,27:END
```

The color bar and oscillator select GOSUBs have been placed at the beginning of the program to facilitate speed of response. Thus the program really begins in line 210.

The initial block, consisting of lines 220 to 570 performs the following functions

Dimension all arrays.

Initialize strings and variable V, volume.

Set screen/border color for instruction page.
Print instruction page.
Read ASCII codes of keys needed, K%(I).
Read frequencies of notes needed, M%(I).
Read scale intervals (tone, tone, semitone, etc.), Z%(I).
Initialize key/color array C%(I) for no color.
Wait, while instruction page is read, until key pressed.

Lines 590 to 720 input a valid scale and set the scale parameter Q. This could be done more compactly using a string array, but has been left in the above form to make the program easier to understand.

We thought it would be helpful if the colour bar of the base note of the scale selected, always a white bar at the bottom of the screen, also contained the symbol for the scale, that is C, C# etc. To this end lines 730 and 740 construct Q$, a block of reverse field spaces with K$ in the centre.

Line 760 sets the color associated with every key in K%(I) to black. Lines 770 to 800 then associate with each note in the scale selected one of seven colors. Conceptually these lines are a bit tricky. Although a scale is called an *octave* it really only consists of *seven* notes, the eighth note is the same *note* as the first but doubled in frequency. Thus progressing up through scales really means working up in multiples of seven, even though they are called octaves, amazing isn't it? Similarly although our music keyboard has 25 keys the 25*th* key, in actual fact the note C, corresponds to the 0*th* key which is also a C. Therefore we need to wrap colors in multiples of seven around a keyboard in multiples of 24. The 25*th* key, K%(24), corresponding to the top C, we take care of separately in the line 810. Understanding exactly what is going on here will be much easier after reading the section on division with remainder in Chapter 2.

The rest is pretty straightforward except for the way sustain is arranged. This is done by exploiting the fact that address 197 always contains the code of the current key pressed. Therefore as soon as we collect the key pressed in line 840 we make a note of the contents of 197. After the appropriate oscillators have been set to the correct frequency and the associated color bar displayed, in line 900, we look to see if the contents of 197 have changed. If the contents of 197 are unchanged we look again, and keep looking until it does change. When the contents of 197 change the oscillators are turned off in line 920 and we return to line 830 to determine the next key pressed. Note that line 900 is always executed, to make it conditional would slow things up, and if an oscillator is not selected the POKE is to a harmless address in the cassette buffer e.g. S = 1016.

1.7 Logical operators

Apart from arithmetic and string manipulation the VIC-20 can also perform logical operations. Like everything else the VIC-20 does, logical operations are expressed in terms of zeros and ones.

The logical operators are AND, OR and NOT. Although we have never found much reason to use NOT, the operators AND and OR are extremely useful; they enable the microcomputer to take quite complex decisions on the basis of several numeric or string parameters. For example

$$\text{IF } X < 10 \text{ OR } Y > 9 \text{ AND } A\$ <> \text{``B'' THEN } 100$$

In this case program execution will jump to line 100 if the condition is met; that is, if the compound logical statement is *true*, otherwise execution will continue on the next line.

Try the following program

$$10 \; X = 10$$
$$20 \; PRINT \; (X < 10).$$

When RUN it should print 0. This is because $X < 10$ is false. If you change line 10 to $X = 9$ the program will print -1 because then $X < 10$ is true.

NOTE : $0 = $ FALSE, $-1 = $ TRUE.

Now try ANDing and ORing various combinations of -1 and 0. The results can be summarized in two little tables

AND	0	−1
0	0	0
−1	0	−1

OR	0	−1
0	0	−1
−1	−1	−1

Note both operators are symmetric, e.g. 0 AND $-1 = -1$ AND 0. We can interpret these *truth tables,* as they are called, along the following lines. If you take a statement which is false (0) AND a statement which is true (-1) the result is a statement which is false 0, that is 0 AND $-1 = 0$.

In the line

IF $X < 10$ OR $Y > 9$ AND A$ $<>$ "B" THEN 100

each relational operator $X < 10$, $Y > 9$, A$ $<>$ "B" returns the value 0 or -1 according to whether it is true or false. Thus if $X = 9$, $Y = 10$ and A$ = $ "A" we get the values $-1, -1, -1$ for these operations. To decide the truth or falsity of the compound logical statement the operating system merely works out

$(-1$ OR $-1)$ AND-1 $(= -1)$

using the truth tables given above.

However, this is only half the story on logical operators. It is pretty neat being able to base decisions on the outcome of a compound logical statement, but AND and OR have another equally important yet quite different application. Try the following program

$$10 \; X = 32767 : Y = 1024$$
$$20 \; PRINT \; (XANDY), (XORY)$$

When RUN it should print

1024   32767

Here X and Y can be integer values in the range -32768 to $+32767$, other values will give a SYNTAX ERROR. Integers in this range can be represented by a 16-bit binary number as in Table 1.1.

Table 1.1 – How positive and negative integers are stored.

Integer	Bit pattern as stored in two addresses															
	15	14	13	12	11	10	9	8	7	6	5	4	3	2	1	0
. . .																
−3	1	1	1	1	1	1	1	1	1	1	1	1	1	1	0	1
−2	1	1	1	1	1	1	1	1	1	1	1	1	1	1	1	0
−1	1	1	1	1	1	1	1	1	1	1	1	1	1	1	1	1
0	0	0	0	0	0	0	0	0	0	0	0	0	0	0	0	0
1	0	0	0	0	0	0	0	0	0	0	0	0	0	0	0	1
2	0	0	0	0	0	0	0	0	0	0	0	0	0	0	1	0
3	0	0	0	0	0	0	0	0	0	0	0	0	0	0	1	1
. . .																

$$(\text{NOT } X = -(X+1))$$

What AND and OR are actually doing in this program is matching the bit patterns of X and Y in two different ways. Let us look first at the bit patterns.

	15	14	13	12	11	10	9	8	7	6	5	4	3	2	1	0
32767	0	1	1	1	1	1	1	1	1	1	1	1	1	1	1	1
1024	0	0	0	0	0	1	0	0	0	0	0	0	0	0	0	0

For AND if *both* of corresponding bits are 1 we get a 1, otherwise we get a 0. Similarly for OR if *either* of corresponding bits is a 1 we get a 1, otherwise we get a 0.

Examples

$$63 \text{ AND } 16 = 16 \qquad 1\,1\,1\,1\,1\,1 \text{ AND } 0\,1\,0\,0\,0\,0 = 0\,1\,0\,0\,0\,0$$
$$17 \text{ AND } 7 = 1 \qquad 0\,1\,0\,0\,0\,1 \text{ AND } 0\,0\,0\,1\,1\,1 = 0\,0\,0\,0\,0\,1$$
$$63 \text{ OR } 16 = 63 \qquad 1\,1\,1\,1\,1\,1 \text{ OR } 0\,0\,0\,1\,1\,1 = 1\,1\,1\,1\,1\,1$$
$$17 \text{ OR } 7 = 23 \qquad 0\,1\,0\,0\,0\,1 \text{ OR } 0\,0\,0\,1\,1\,1 = 0\,1\,0\,1\,1\,1$$

−1 AND 8 = 8   1 1 1 1 1 1 1 1 1 1 1 1 1 1 1 1 AND 1 0 0 0 = 1000
−32768 OR 8 = −32760   1 0 0 0 0 0 0 0 0 0 0 0 0 0 0 0 OR 1 0 0 0 =
                        1 0 0 0 0 0 0 0 0 0 0 0 1 0 0 0

X AND 7 = The remainder when X is divided by 8.
X AND 15 = The remainder when X is divided by 16.

If you managed to get this far relax, the nasty part is over and we now come to the useful part. In section 1.5 we concluded that PEEK( ) and POKE were fairly fundamental commands, and in the BIT PATTERN program we were able to view the bit pattern in any byte of VIC memory. Notice how the I*th* bit of P is obtained in line 90 of the program.

$$\text{If } P \text{ AND}(2 \uparrow I) = 2 \uparrow I \quad \text{then bit I is 1}$$

$$\text{If } P \text{ AND}(2 \uparrow I) = 0 \qquad \text{then bit I is 0}$$

Either way the I*th* bit of P is given by

$$\text{BI } = \text{ (PAND}(2 \uparrow I))/(2 \uparrow I)$$

This tells us how to look at any particular bit of any byte in the entire VIC memory. But it does even more than that, it changes POKE from a hammer which knocks bytes in, to a scalpel which can insert or excise any bit of any byte in memory provided the byte is not in ROM.

Examples
(a) To set the I*th* bit of address A to 1, without changing any other bit.

POKEA, PEEK(A) OR $(2 \uparrow I)$

(b) To set the I*th* bit of address A to 0, without changing any other bit

POKEA, PEEK(A) AND $(255 - (2 \uparrow I))$

(c) To change the I*th* bit of address A whatever its value, without changing any other bit

$B = 1 - (\text{PEEK(A)AND}(2 \uparrow I))/(2 \uparrow I)$
POKEA,PEEK(A)AND$(255-(2 \uparrow I))$OR$(B*(2 \uparrow I))$

2
Longer programs

2.1 More about arrays and speed

The Program MINISYN illustrates that arrays are a powerful tool for organizing data and speeding up program execution. In essence the concept of an array is quite simple. We can view the array $A(I)$, $1 \leqslant I \leqslant N$ as a sequence of boxes into which we can place data.

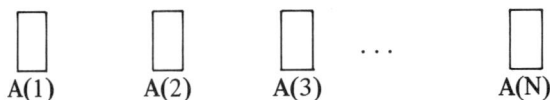

$$A(1) \qquad A(2) \qquad A(3) \qquad \cdots \qquad A(N)$$

If $A(I)$ is a real number array then each box is actually 5 bytes of memory in the user BASIC program area, if it were an integer array then each box would be 2 bytes of memory.

The data to be inserted into an array frequently consists of integers in the range 0 to 255, for example, screen codes or ASCII codes. In this situation using an integer array is very wasteful since each byte that we store will use 2 bytes of memory. Remember, an integer array is designed to store integers in the range -32768 to $+32767$. Where speed is not the over-riding consideration but we do not want to pass up the organizational advantages of an array, there is a better solution. The symbol A could just as well stand for 'Address' and the 'boxes' could be consecutive locations in memory. Integers in the range 0 to 255 can be made elements of such an 'array' using POKE and read back using PEEK. The only question to be answered before implementing this idea is, which block of memory should be used?

When a program is running the whole of the user BASIC program area above the program is potentially usable, by the operating system, as memory space in which to store the values of the various variables, arrays and strings needed during program execution. Whether the *whole* area is in fact used depends on how many variables, arrays and strings the program actually needs. However, a further complication is that this allocation of storage is a dynamic process. For example, arrays are stored above single variables and when a new variable is encountered during program execution the operating system shifts the entire array storage area up 7 bytes in memory to create space for the new variable. Plainly, POKEing our 'array' into the user BASIC program area is a bad idea.

There are two reasonable solutions to this problem. The first is to reduce the user BASIC program area by lowering the top of memory, as explained in Chapter 3. The 'array' can then be POKEd into the space created, with no possibility of being overwritten by the operating system or interfering with its memory-juggling activities. The second solution is even simpler and this is to use the one substantial block of memory which is normally free during program execution, namely the cassette buffer, addresses 828 to 1020. Naturally, if the cassette is used during program execution the data in our 'array' will be lost, but provided this is not the case there will be no problems. Using this approach we can now create an 'array' of integers in the range 0 to 255 with length up to 193 at *no cost whatsoever* to the user BASIC program area.

Example

In this program a card shuffle is done firstly by using an array D%(I), $1 \leqslant I \leqslant 52$ and secondly by using a POKE/PEEK 'array' in the cassette buffer. The shuffles are timed so that the times for each routine can be compared. A card is represented as an integer in the range 1 to 52 and these numbers are first stored consecutively in the array. The shuffle proceeds along the lines sketched in section 1.3. To begin with a random integer, A, in the range 1 to 52 is selected and the A*th* element of the array is placed in a temporary store Z%. Every element up to the $(A-1)th$ is then moved one position to the right and Z% inserted as the first element. Next time around a random integer, A, in the range 2 to 52 is selected and the A*th* element of the array is stored in Z%. Every element from the second to the $(A-1)th$ is then moved one to the right and Z% inserted as the second element. The process continues until all 52 elements are exhausted. You should confirm that the routine correctly handles the case $A = I$ and the extreme case $A = I = 1$.

SHUFFLES

```
5 PRINT"J":PRINT"USING ARRAYS IT TAKES..."
10 DIMD%(52):T=TI
20 FORI=1TO52:D%(I)=I:NEXT
30 FORI=1TO52:A=I+INT((53-I)*RND(1)):Z%=D%(A)
40 FORJ=ATOISTEP-1:D%(J)=D%(J-1):NEXTJ
50 D%(I)=Z%:NEXTI
60 PRINT(TI-T)/60"SECS"
70 PRINT:PRINT"USING PEEK AND POKE IT TAKES..."
80 T=TI
90 FORI=1TO52:POKE828+I,I:NEXT
100 FORI=1TO52:A=I+INT((53-I)*RND(1)):Z%=PEEK(828+A)
110 FORJ=ATOISTEP-1:POKE828+J,PEEK(828+J-1):NEXTJ
120 POKE828+I,Z%:NEXTI
130 PRINT(TI-T)/60"SECS"
140 END
```

When the program is RUN we find that the first shuffle takes around 8 seconds and the second around 12 seconds. Therefore using POKE/PEEK is around 50% slower than using a standard array. If the program is RUN several times another interesting point emerges, namely, in both shuffles the time taken varies from RUN to RUN: we leave you to work out why this is so.

2.2 Division with remainder

In BASIC there are three types of one-dimensional arrays: real number arrays like A(I), integer arrays like A%(I), and string arrays like A$(I). BASIC also allows the possibility of higher dimensional arrays, for example in a two-dimensional array the (I,J)*th* element could be specified as A(I,J).

For the time being we shall take the word *array*, in a general sense, to mean any block of data which is organized so that an individual piece of data can be accessed by a single integer parameter, I, say. In this sense both methods of storing the numbers 1 to 52 in SHUFFLES could be said to use arrays.

Another example of an array in this more general sense is the area of memory devoted to the screen display. Normally this area of memory begins at address SC = 7680 and extends to address SC + 505, a total of 506 possible screen locations. Each of these 506 addresses contains a byte which is the screen code of the corresponding character displayed on the screen. Addresses SC to SC + 21 contain the first row of the screen display, SC + 22 to SC + 43 the second row, and so on for all 23 rows. Thus, if we index the screen row by U, $0 \leqslant U \leqslant 22$ and the column by V, $0 \leqslant V \leqslant 21$ the address of the character cell in row U, column V in screen memory is SC + SL where

$$SL = 22 * U + V \qquad (0 \leqslant V \leqslant 21),$$

and SL lies in the range $0 \leqslant SL \leqslant 505$.

Conversely we may pose the question: given a screen location SL, $0 \leqslant SL \leqslant 505$, how do we find the correponding row and column, that is the corresponding values of U and V? Notice that there are many solutions of the equation SL = 22*U + V in integers U,V, for example if SL = 208 we have

$$208 = 22 * 11 - 34 = 22 * 10 - 12 = 22 * 9 + 10 = 22 * 8 + 32, \text{ etc.}$$

Nevertheless only one of these representations, namely $208 = 22 * 9 + 10$, corresponds to a value of V in the range $0 \leqslant V \leqslant 21$. For any integer SL there is a unique representation SL = 22*U + V, in multiples of 22 plus a remainder in the range $0 \leqslant V \leqslant 21$, and we can find U and V with the following BASIC code

$$U = INT(SL/22) : V = SL - 22*U$$

There is a very useful general principle at work here. If we want to express any integer N in multiples of a positive integer M, plus a remainder V in the range $0 \leqslant V \leqslant M - 1$, that is

$$N = M * U + V \qquad (0 \leqslant V \leqslant M - 1),$$

then this can be done in only one way, and the BASIC code

$$U = INT(N/M) : V = N - M * U$$

will do it. The idea goes back to Euclid who used it to devise a method of finding the highest common factor of N and M. (Note that if an integer divides N and M it must also divide V, which is smaller than M.)

Example

An integer N in the range 0 to 65535 can be expressed as a 16-bit binary number which we can consider as being made up of two bytes, a Hi-byte and a Lo-byte. Remember, a byte is 8 bits. A single byte represents an integer in the range 0 to 255 and 256 * 256 = 65536. Therefore to find the Hi-byte and the Lo-byte we should work in multiples of 256. Applying division with remainder we have

$$\text{Hi-byte} = INT(N/256), \quad \text{Lo-byte} = N - 256 * (\text{Hi-byte}),$$

result which we shall use many times when finding an address, for example see the last program in this chapter.

The technique of division with remainder finds many applications in computing since it enables us to label the data in an array in more than one way. For example, in the case of the screen memory, given SL we can find the corresponding row and column, or conversely given the row and column we can readily compute SL.

Other examples arise in dealing with the character matrix (see Chapter 4) where we need to work in multiples of 8 or possibly 16.

2.3 Displaying cards

In section 2.1 two routines for shuffling cards were discussed. We now turn our attention to displaying all 52 cards of a standard deck. In the program a card is represented by a number CD in the range 1 to 52. To display a card we first need to know its suit and value. Each suit contains 13 cards so we can assign the values of CD as

$$1 \text{ to } 13, \quad \text{Spades} \quad, \text{CH\%}(0) = 65, \quad S\% = 0,$$
$$14 \text{ to } 26, \quad \text{Hearts} \quad, \text{CH\%}(1) = 83, \quad S\% = 1,$$
$$27 \text{ to } 39, \quad \text{Clubs} \quad, \text{CH\%}(2) = 88, \quad S\% = 2,$$
$$40 \text{ to } 52, \quad \text{Diamonds}, \text{CH\%}(3) = 90, \quad S\% = 3,$$

where the array CH%( ) contains the screen code for the spade symbol, heart symbol, etc., and S% denotes the suit.

Given a value CD we would like to know the suit and value of the card. It seems sensible to assign the values 1,2,3,4,...,13 to the cards Ace, Two, ..., King respectively. We can compute the *suit* S% and the *value* V using division with remainder, but there is a slight snag since remainders which are 0 should really be 13 to give a King. Taking this into account we have

$$S\% = \text{INT}(CD/13) : V = CD - 13 * S\% : \text{IF } V = 0 \text{ THEN } V = 13 : S\% = S\% - 1$$

where the conditional statement is a 'fix' to take care of the fact that for multiples of 13 both the value and the suit would otherwise be incorrect.

Having found the suit and value we next consider the steps which are needed to display the card. The first decision to be taken is, how many cards might we want to display simultaneously?

Given the size of the VIC-20 screen and requirement that each card displayed should be of a reasonable size, the number 6 was chosen for the maximum number of cards to be displayed at any one time. The position of a card on the screen is therefore specified by a *position* indicator PI which takes values in the range 1 to 6. The numbers CD and PI must be specified before the CARD GOSUB is called.

From PI we can compute the offset DD% of the *top left corner* of the card from the base SC of screen memory, see Figure 2.1.

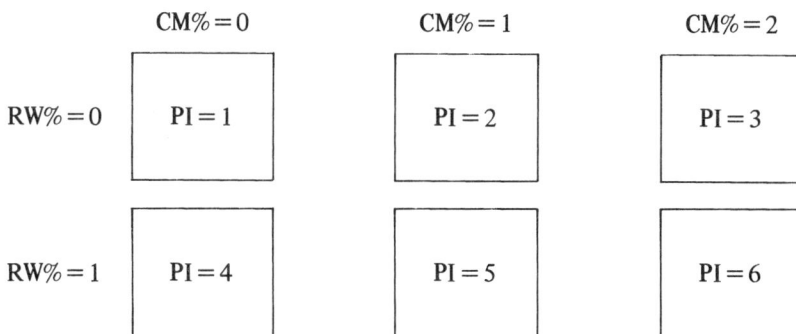

Figure 2.1 – Card positions.

To find DD% we give each card position a 'row' RW% and a 'column' CM%; since we are working in multiples of 3 these are computed by division with remainder as

$$RW\% = INT((PI-1)/3) : CM\% = PI-1-3*RW\%$$

The top left corner of the first card position corresponds to the screen location 45 and the difference between successive top left corners in the same row is 6. Finally, the offset between corresponding screen locations having RW% = 0 and RW% = 1 is 198. This gives

$$DD\% = 45 + 6*CM\% + 198*RW\%$$

As a safeguard against the possibility that the CARD GOSUB might be called with a value of PI greater than 6 we AND the number RW% with 1, which effectively wraps the hypothetical card position 7 back to overprint position 1. Defensive programming requires that one should never POKE to a location outside the area of memory intended, and the CARD GOSUB will involve a lot of POKEs! So our final formula for DD% is

$$DD\% = 45 + 6*CM\% + 198*(RW\%AND1)$$

If the base of screen memory is SC and that of color memory is CO then top left corner of the card position PI corresponds to screen address B and color address C, where

$$B = SC + DD\% : C = CO + DD\%$$

Having decided where in memory the top left hand corner of the card to be displayed is actually located we can now proceed to display the card frame. A program which tests the whole CARD GOSUB is listed below.

```
10 DIMCH%(3):CH%(0)=65:CH%(1)=83:CH%(2)=88:CH%(3)=90
20 A=PEEK(36866)AND128:SC=4*A+64*(PEEK(36869)AND112):CO=37888+4*A
30 FORCD=1TO52:PI=1
40 PRINT"*":GOSUB1040
50 GETA$:IFA$=""THEN50
60 NEXT
70 END
1040 REM**CARD GOSUB**
1050 S%=INT(CD/13):V=CD-13*S%:IFV=0THENV=13:S%=S%-1:REM SUIT&VAL
1060 RW%=INT((PI-1)/3):CM%=PI-1-3*RW%:DD%=45+6*CM%+198*(RW%AND1):REM FRAME OFFSE
T DD%
1070 B=SC+DD%:C=CO+DD%
1130 REM*CARD FRAME*
1140 POKEB,85:POKEB+1,64:POKEB+2,64:POKEB+3,64:POKEB+4,73
1145 POKEC,5:POKEC+1,5:POKEC+2,5:POKEC+3,5:POKEC+4,5
1150 POKEB+22,93:POKEB+44,93:POKEB+66,93:POKEB+88,93:POKEB+110,93
1155 POKEC+22,5:POKEC+44,5:POKEC+66,5:POKEC+88,5:POKEC+110,5
1160 POKEB+26,93:POKEB+48,93:POKEB+70,93:POKEB+92,93:POKEB+114,93
1165 POKEC+26,5:POKEC+48,5:POKEC+70,5:POKEC+92,5:POKEC+114,5
1170 POKEB+132,74:POKEB+133,64:POKEB+134,64:POKEB+135,64:POKEB+136,75
1175 POKEC+132,5:POKEC+133,5:POKEC+134,5:POKEC+135,5:POKEC+136,5
1190 IFZ%=DP-2ANDPI=2THEN1400:REM DOWN CARD
1195 REM*PATTERN*
1200 A=CH%(S%):CC=2*(S%AND1):REM CHAR&COL
1210 ONVGOTO1220,1230,1240,1250,1260,1270,1280,1290,1300,1310,1320,1330,1340
1220 GOSUB5000:POKEB+23,1:POKEC+23,0:GOTO1400
```

Listing continues next page

```
1230 GOSUB5010:GOTO1400
1240 GOSUB5010:GOSUB5000:GOTO1400
1250 GOSUB5030:GOTO1400
1260 GOSUB5030:GOSUB5000:GOTO1400
1270 GOSUB5030:GOSUB5050:GOTO1400
1280 GOSUB5030:GOSUB5050:GOSUB5000:GOTO1400
1290 GOSUB5030:GOSUB5060:GOTO1400
1300 GOSUB5030:GOSUB5060:GOSUB5000:GOTO1400
1310 GOSUB5030:GOSUB5060:GOSUB5010:GOTO1400
1320 GOSUB5000:POKEB+23,10:POKEC+23,0:GOTO1400
1330 GOSUB5000:POKEB+23,17:POKEC+23,0:GOTO1400
1340 GOSUB5000:POKEB+23,11:POKEC+23,0:GOTO1400
1400 IFV>10THENV=10
1410 RETURN
5000 POKEB+68,A:POKEC+68,CC:RETURN
5010 POKEB+46,A:POKEB+90,A:POKEC+46,CC:POKEC+90,CC:RETURN
5030 POKEB+23,A:POKEB+25,A:POKEB+111,A:POKEB+113,A
5040 POKEC+23,CC:POKEC+25,CC:POKEC+111,CC:POKEC+113,CC:RETURN
5050 POKEB+67,A:POKEB+69,A:POKEC+67,CC:POKEC+69,CC:RETURN
5060 POKEB+45,A:POKEB+47,A:POKEB+89,A:POKEB+91,A
5070 POKEC+45,CC:POKEC+47,CC:POKEC+89,CC:POKEC+91,CC:RETURN
```

In displaying the frame we have the option of using FOR loops for the two horizontal lines and for the two vertical lines or, alternatively simply POKEing every screen and color location individually. In fact the second alternative is adopted, because although using FOR loops saves approximately 200 bytes of program space the resulting routine is rather slow. The factors affecting the speed of GOTOs, GOSUBs and FOR loops are worthy of a brief digression.[†]

When BASIC executes a GOTO or a GOSUB the operating system has to search for the line number referred to by the instruction. If this is greater than the current line number the search starts from the current line, if it is less then the search starts at the beginning of the program. For this reason, in a large program the commonly used GOSUBs are often placed at the beginning of the program to reduce the search time.

When a FOR loop is encountered the operating system first locates the address in which the value of the loop counter is stored. It does this by searching a list of variables, previously set up as the variables were encountered. This list is located in memory after the end of the BASIC program. (If the loop counter is a new variable then array storage is moved up and space created.) It therefore pays to initialize FOR loop variables, before other variables, near the beginning of a long program: this is especially true where speed is critical. The operating system next checks that no *current* FOR loop has the same variable name. If it finds one, this and all inner loops are aborted and replaced by the new one, havoc then ensues.

IMPORTANT NOTE. Nested FOR loops should always use distinct variable names
for their loop counters.

Assuming no such current loop is found the FOR statement then stores the following information which will be used by NEXT: the TO and STEP values, the address of the FOR variable and the address of the start of the loop. Thus execution of NEXT does not involve a search of the variable list nor a search for

---

†See the article 'Be a better BASIC buff' in *VIC Computing,* 1, 5, June 1982.

the line number of the start of the loop. If, however, the loop variable is specified in order to make the program easier to read, as for example in NEXT I, then the loop will run considerably more slowly. The programmer can take one further precaution to speed the execution of FOR loops:

IMPORTANT NOTE. Wherever possible put long loops inside short loops rather than the other way round.

Returning now to the CARD DISPLAY routine, after setting up the card frame in lines 1140 to 1175 we next have to insert the pattern. For this we need the suit symbol from CH%(S%) and the color (black = 0, red = 2), which can be computed from S%; both are set in line 1200. The subsequent pattern is now determined by the value of V. In line 1210 V is used to select one of 13 pattern display sub-routines. Thus line 1220 displays an Ace, line 1230 displays a Two, and so on until line 1340 which displays a King. Rather than using 13 blocks of POKE statements, one block for each pattern, these routines call upon just 5 such blocks from which all number cards can be assembled. The court cards, including the Ace, are essentially a modified One (line 5000) and a Five, for example, is an overlay of a One (line 5000) and Four (line 5030).

Having assembled the CARD DISPLAY routine the next, and with any luck final, step is to test it before incorporating it as a single GOSUB in a longer card game program. The program TEST CARD DISPLAY first sets up the array CH%( ) needed for the suit symbols, and then in line 20, checks the VIC control registers to determine the start of screen memory SC, and of color memory CO. A full explanation of line 20, which enables the program to run whatever RAM packs are used, is given in Chapter 3. Any VIC-20 program which uses POKEs to the screen or color should always use this routine. The program displays each card in the first position, moving to the next card when any key is pressed. The value of PI should also be varied during the testing procedure to ensure that all six positions can correctly display a card.

2.4 Pontoon

Now that card-shuffle and card-display routines are available it becomes possible to construct a program to play a card game. The game selected is Pontoon (Blackjack), being reasonably simple and quite well known. The program listed at the end of this section will run on an unexpanded VIC-20 provided it is entered as listed; there is not much space to spare, around 4 bytes actually, so avoid superfluous spaces.

A schematic for Pontoon is given in Figure 2.2, this relates to lines 40 to 500 of the program. The key variable is DP, the deck pointer, which normally points to the next card in the deck D%(I), $1 \leqslant I \leqslant 52$. Before any cards have been dealt DP is set equal to 1 in line 90. In lines 100 to 160 four cards are dealt, alternately to the player and computer, and displayed on the screen, the second computer card being displayed 'face down' (decided by line 1190). The player's cards are stored in an array P%( ) and the computer's cards in an array C%( ). The variable P is used to juggle the card positions so that the player's cards are displayed in positions 4 and 5, whilst the computer's cards are displayed in positions 1 and 2. Since DP has been selected as the FOR loop counter in this routine, when line 170 is reached DP has been incremented from its initial value by 4, which is correct since 4 cards have been dealt. For the remainder of the current game DP will always be incremented by 1 whenever a card is dealt, consequently DP will always point to the next available card.

Note that in line 1400 after a court card has been displayed its value V is set to 10 so that V can be used for scoring. The player can always decide the value of an Ace, after it has been displayed (lines 200 and 270).

From line 180 the program is largely self-documenting. The remaining significant variables are

- V1   player's score,
- V2   computer's score,
- PW   player's wins so far,
- CW   computer's wins so far.

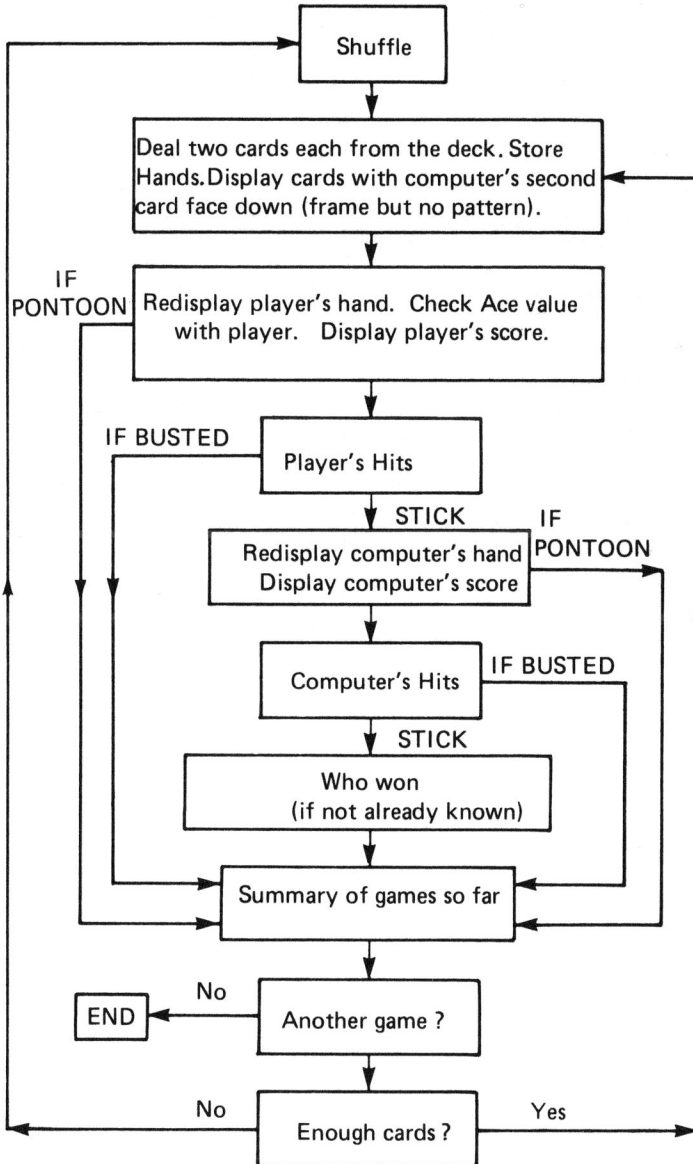

Figure 2.2 – Schematic for Pontoon.

PONTOON

```
10 DIMD%(52),P%(2),C%(2),CH%(3):CH%(0)=65:CH%(1)=83:CH%(2)=88:CH%(3)=90
20 A=PEEK(36866)AND128:SC=4*A+64*(PEEK(36869)AND112):CO=37888+4*A
30 D$=" ":W$="                   "
40 REM*SHUFFLE*
50 PRINT" WAIT ONE MOMENT WHILE I SHUFFLE THE CARDS"
60 FORI=1TO52:D%(I)=I:NEXT
70 FORI=1TO52:A=I+INT((53-I)*RND(1)):Z%=D%(A)
80 FORJ=ATOISTEP-1:D%(J)=D%(J-1):NEXTJ
90 D%(I)=Z%:NEXTI:DP=1
100 REM*TWO CARDS EACH*
110 P=1:Z%=DP:PRINT" "
120 PRINTLEFT$(D$,15)SPC(13)"PLAYER":PRINTLEFT$(D$,6)SPC(13)"COMPUTER"
130 FORDP=Z%TOZ%+2 STEP2
140 P%(P)=D%(DP):CD=P%(P):PI=P+3:GOSUB1040:REM PLAYER
150 C%(P)=D%(DP+1):CD=C%(P):PI=P:GOSUB1040:REM COMP
160 P=P+1:NEXTDP
170 PRINTD$:PRINT"    PRESS ANY KEY":GETB$:IFB$=""THEN170
180 REM*PLAYER'S HAND*
190 PRINT" ":V1=0:FORPI=1TO2:CD=P%(PI):GOSUB1040:REM CARD
200 IFV=1THENGOSUB1020:REMI/P ACE
210 V1=V1+V:NEXTPI:GOSUB1000
220 IFV1=21THENGOSUB8000:PRINT" YOU GOT PONTOON!":PW=PW+1:GOTO480
230 REM*PLAYER'S HITS*
240 PRINTD$:PRINT"HIT..(Y/N)?":GETB$:IFB$<>"Y"ANDB$<>"N"THEN240
250 PRINTD$:PRINTW$:IFB$="N"THEN320:REM STICK
260 CD=D%(DP):DP=DP+1:GOSUB1040:PI=PI+1:REM CARD
270 IFV=1THENGOSUB1020:REMI/P ACE
280 V1=V1+V:GOSUB1000
290 IFV1>21THENGOSUB8000:PRINT" YOU'RE BUSTED":CW=CW+1:GOTO480
300 IFV1=21THENGOSUB8000:GOTO320:REM 21
310 GOTO230
320 REM*COMP'S HAND*
330 PRINT" ":V2=0:FORPI=1TO2:CD=C%(PI):GOSUB1040:REM CARD
340 IFV=1ANDV2<11THENV=11
350 V2=V2+V:NEXTPI:GOSUB1010
360 IFV2=21THENGOSUB8000:PRINT" COMPUTER GOT..PONTOON!":CW=CW+1:GOTO480
370 REM*COMP'S HITS*
380 IFV2>V1OR(V2=V1ANDV2>16)THENGOSUB8000:GOTO440:REM STICK
390 CD=D%(DP):DP=DP+1:GOSUB1040:PI=PI+1:REM CARD
400 IFV=1ANDV2<11THENV=11:REM ACE
410 V2=V2+V:GOSUB1010
420 IFV2>21THENGOSUB8000:PRINT" COMPUTER BUST..YOU WON":PW=PW+1:GOTO480
430 GOTO370
440 REM*WHO WON*
450 IFV1>V2THENPRINT" WELL DONE..YOU WON":PW=PW+1
460 IFV1=V2THENPRINT"  STAND OFF"
470 IFV1<V2THENPRINT" TOUGH..COMPUTER WON":CW=CW+1
480 REM*SUMMARY*
490 PRINT" COMPUTER'S WINS..";CW:PRINT" YOUR     WINS..";PW
500 PRINTD$:PRINT" CONT.(Y/N)?":GETB$:IFB$<>"Y"ANDB$<>"N"THEN500
510 IFB$="N"THENPRINT" ":END
```

Listing continues next page

```
520 IFDP<40THEN100:REM DEAL
530 GOTO40
1000 PRINTD$+"YOUR SCORE IS";V1:RETURN
1010 PRINTD$+"COMP SCORE IS";V2:RETURN
1020 PRINTD$:INPUT"ACE=▮▮▮▮▮▮▮▮";B$:V=VAL(B$):IFV<>1ANDV<>11THEN1020
1030 PRINTD$:PRINTW$:RETURN
1040 REM**CARD GOSUB**
1050 S%=INT(CD/13):V=CD-13*S%:IFV=0THENV=13:S%=S%-1:REM SUIT&VAL
1060 RW%=INT((PI-1)/3):CM%=PI-1-3*RW%:DD%=45+6*CM%+198*(RW%AND1):REMFRAME OFFSET
1070 B=SC+DD%:C=CO+DD%
1130 REM*CARD FRAME*
1140 POKEB,85:POKEB+1,64:POKEB+2,64:POKEB+3,64:POKEB+4,73
1145 POKEC,5:POKEC+1,5:POKEC+2,5:POKEC+3,5:POKEC+4,5
1150 POKEB+22,93:POKEB+44,93:POKEB+66,93:POKEB+88,93:POKEB+110,93
1155 POKEC+22,5:POKEC+44,5:POKEC+66,5:POKEC+88,5:POKEC+110,5
1160 POKEB+26,93:POKEB+48,93:POKEB+70,93:POKEB+92,93:POKEB+114,93
1165 POKEC+26,5:POKEC+48,5:POKEC+70,5:POKEC+92,5:POKEC+114,5
1170 POKEB+132,74:POKEB+133,64:POKEB+134,64:POKEB+135,64:POKEB+136,75
1175 POKEC+132,5:POKEC+133,5:POKEC+134,5:POKEC+135,5:POKEC+136,5
1190 IFZ%=DP-2ANDPI=2THEN1400:REM DOWN CARD
1195 REM*PATTERN*
1200 A=CH%(S%):CC=2*(S%AND1):REM CHAR&COL
1210 ONVGOTO1220,1230,1240,1250,1260,1270,1280,1290,1300,1310,1320,1330,1340
1220 GOSUB5000:POKEB+23,1:POKEC+23,0:GOTO1400
1230 GOSUB5010:GOTO1400
1240 GOSUB5010:GOSUB5000:GOTO1400
1250 GOSUB5030:GOTO1400
1260 GOSUB5030:GOSUB5000:GOTO1400
1270 GOSUB5030:GOSUB5050:GOTO1400
1280 GOSUB5030:GOSUB5050:GOSUB5000:GOTO1400
1290 GOSUB5030:GOSUB5060:GOTO1400
1300 GOSUB5030:GOSUB5060:GOSUB5000:GOTO1400
1310 GOSUB5030:GOSUB5060:GOSUB5010:GOTO1400
1320 GOSUB5000:POKEB+23,10:POKEC+23,0:GOTO1400
1330 GOSUB5000:POKEB+23,17:POKEC+23,0:GOTO1400
1340 GOSUB5000:POKEB+23,11:POKEC+23,0:GOTO1400
1400 IFV>10THENV=10
1410 RETURN
5000 POKEB+68,A:POKEC+68,CC:RETURN
5010 POKEB+46,A:POKEB+90,A:POKEC+46,CC:POKEC+90,CC:RETURN
5030 POKEB+23,A:POKEB+25,A:POKEB+111,A:POKEB+113,A
5040 POKEC+23,CC:POKEC+25,CC:POKEC+111,CC:POKEC+113,CC:RETURN
5050 POKEB+67,A:POKEB+69,A:POKEC+67,CC:POKEC+69,CC:RETURN
5060 POKEB+45,A:POKEB+47,A:POKEB+89,A:POKEB+91,A
5070 POKEC+45,CC:POKEC+47,CC:POKEC+89,CC:POKEC+91,CC:RETURN
8000 FORI=0TO2000:NEXT:RETURN
```

2.5 Some special effects

In this section some special effects are given which may be incorporated in other programs. The first uses DATA statements and RESTORE, which resets the pointer for DATA to the first DATA statement in the program. Hence in this case if DATA statements were used in the calling program a certain amount of rearrangement would be necessary.

All three of these routines rely on manipulating the VIC control registers which are discussed in detail in the next chapter.

```
10 REM*PLAY UFO TUNE*
20 FORJ=0TO3
30 U=15/(2↑J):O=2:V=36876
40 GOSUB1000
50 NEXT
60 GOSUB1000
70 U=35:GOSUB1000
80 END
1000 REM**UFO SOUND**
1010 REM* TEMPO U     *
1020 REM*O=1 OR O=2 *
1030 REM*   VOICES   *
1040 REM*V=36875/6IF*
1050 REM*    O=2     *
1060 REM*************
1070 DATA219,223,215
1080 DATA175,201
1090 FORN=1TO5
1100 READA(N):NEXT
1110 DATA1,1,1,1,3.8
1120 FORI=1TO5
1130 READD(I):NEXT
1140 DATA.5,.5,1,1.6,1
1150 FORI=1TO5
1160 READS(I):NEXT
1170 RESTORE
1180 POKE36878,15
1190 FORI=1TO5
1200 POKEV,A(I):T=TI
1210 IFO=2THENPOKEV-2,A(I)
1220 IFTI-T<D(I)*UTHEN1220
1230 POKEV,0:T=TI
1240 IFO=2THENPOKEV-2,0
1250 IFTI-T<S(I)*UTHEN1250
1260 NEXT:RETURN
```

ASDIC

```
10 POKE 36876,227
20 FOR I = 15 TO 0 STEP − .25
30 POKE 36878,I : NEXT : T = TI
40 IF TI − T < 20 THEN 40
50 POKE 36876,240 : POKE 36877,241
60 FOR I = 12 TO 0 STEP −3
70 POKE 36878,I : NEXT
80 POKE 36876,0 : POKE 36877,0
```

CONTROL ROOM HIT

```
 10  FOR L=15 TO 0 STEP −2
 20  POKE 36878,L : POKE 36877,200+L*RND(1)
 30  POKE 36874,129 : POKE 36875,190+L
 40  POKE 36865,38+4*(4*RND(1)−2)
 50  POKE 36864,12+2*(2*RND(1)−2)
 60  IF L=15 THEN POKE 36879,112 : FOR M=0 TO 100 : NEXT
 70  POKE 36879,27
 80  NEXT
 90  POKE 36865,38 : POKE 36864,12 : POKE 36878,0
100  POKE 36874,0  : POKE 36875,0  : POKE 36877,0 .
```

2.6 Hexadecimal representation

In Chapter 1 the idea of the binary representation (base 2) of an integer, as opposed to the decimal representation (base 10), was introduced. With a little practice one is soon able to convert integers in the range 0 to 255 from decimal to binary or vice versa. However, when the number of zeros and ones in the binary representation exceeds 8, rapid conversion is less easy. For this and other good reasons the notion of a *hexadecimal* representation (base 16) is useful in dealing with computers or microcomputers, indeed when working in Assembler or Machine code the hexadecimal representation is indispensable. To begin with let us see how to count to 15 in hexadecimal.

Decimal	Hexadecimal	Binary (4 bits)
0	0	0 0 0 0
1	1	0 0 0 1
2	2	0 0 1 0
3	3	0 0 1 1
4	4	0 1 0 0
5	5	0 1 0 1
6	6	0 1 1 0
7	7	0 1 1 1
8	8	1 0 0 0
9	9	1 0 0 1
10	A	1 0 1 0
11	B	1 0 1 1
12	C	1 1 0 0
13	D	1 1 0 1
14	E	1 1 1 0
15	F	1 1 1 1

When 9 is reached we have run out of conventional *single* digits with which to represent the number. Therefore, for base 16 we need to invent 6 more single-digit symbols, and the first 6 letters of the alphabet are normally used. A number greater than 15 can be expressed in hexadecimal using only the symbols 0, 1, 2, ..., 9, A, B, ..., F.

Example

Decimal 249 = 2*(10↑2)+4*(10↑1)+9   (powers of 10)

Decimal 249 = 1*(2↑7) +1*(2↑6) +1*(2↑5)+1*(2↑4)+
              1*(2↑3) +0*(2↑2) +0*(2↑1)+1   (powers of 2)

Decimal 249 = 15*(16↑1)+9 = F*(16↑1)+9   (powers of 16)

Hence

    249 in binary is   1 1 1 1   1 0 0 1
    249 in hexadecimal is   F   9

Similarly

    250 in hexadecimal is FA
    251 in hexadecimal is FB
    252 in hexadecimal is FC
    253 in hexadecimal is FD
    254 in hexadecimal is FE
    255 in hexadecimal is FF

Notice how easy it is to convert from hexadecimal to binary. Each block of 4 binary bits corresponds to one hexadecimal symbol, this is still true for numbers greater than 255. Thus

                    Binary   1 1 1 1 1 1 1 0
    is the same as Hexadecimal   F   E

                    Binary   1 0 1 0 1 0 0 1 1 0 1 1 0 1 1 1
    is the same as Hexadecimal   A   9   B   7

Viewed in this way hexadecimal representation is no more than a shorthand method of writing binary.

Example

To convert hexadecimal A9B7 to decimal we write

    A9B7 = A*(16↑3) + 9*(16↑2) + B*(16↑1) + 7
         = 10*(16↑3) + 9*(16↑2) + 11*(16↑1) + 7
         = 43447 (decimal).

Now it can happen that a hexadecimal representation looks just like a decimal representation, for example, is 1234 the decimal number 1234 or the hexadecimal number 1234 (= decimal 4660)? To avoid this kind of confusion it is customary to prefix any hexadecimal representation with a $ sign, for example hexadecimal A9B7 is written as $A9B7 and hexadecimal 1234 is written as $1234.

Converting from decimal to hexadecimal is not quite as strightforward as the other way round, although it is not difficult. However, computers are supposed to take the pain out of computation, so here is a little program to do it for you. It will be useful when studying later chapters.

```
10 REM*DECIMAL TO HEX*
20 D$="▒▒▒▒▒▒▒▒▒▒▒▒▒▒▒▒▒▒▒▒▒▒▒▒▒▒▒▒▒":S$="                              "
30 PRINT"⊐"
40 FORI=5TO19
50 PRINT"◄":INPUT"DECIMAL NO.";A$:V=VAL(A$)
60 PRINT"◄":PRINTS$
70 IFV=0THENEND
80 IFV<0ORV>65535THEN50
90 H=INT(V/256):L=V-256*H
100 PRINT:PRINT"  DEC   HI   LO   HEX"
110 PRINTLEFT$(D$,I)+RIGHT$("     "+STR$(V),5)+"   ";
120 PRINTRIGHT$("   "+STR$(H),3)SPC(2)RIGHT$("    "+STR$(L),3);
130 Z=H:GOSUB220:H$=C$
140 Z=L:GOSUB220:L$=C$
150 PRINTSPC(3)"◄"+H$+L$
160 NEXTI
170 PRINTD$:PRINT"CONTINUE?(Y/N)"
180 GETA$:IFA$=""THEN180
190 IFA$="Y"THEN30
200 END
210 REM**BYTE TO HEX**
220 X=INT(Z/16):Y=Z-16*X
230 IFX<10THENX$=RIGHT$(STR$(X),1):GOTO260
240 ONX-9GOSUB310,320,330,340,350,360
250 X$=T$
260 IFY<10THENY$=RIGHT$(STR$(Y),1):GOTO290
270 ONY-9GOSUB310,320,330,340,350,360
280 Y$=T$
290 C$=X$+Y$:RETURN
300 REM*GOSUBS FOR GOSUBS*
310 T$="A":RETURN
320 T$="B":RETURN
330 T$="C":RETURN
340 T$="D":RETURN
350 T$="E":RETURN
360 T$="F":RETURN
```

3
VIC structure

3.1 Introduction

Up to this point we have concentrated on developing BASIC programming without bothering too much about what was actually happening within the VIC. A more detailed knowledge of where in memory different data is stored and how the VIC stores and executes a BASIC program will enable us to do many new things, e.g. to store more than one BASIC program in memory simultaneously.

When a program line is first typed in it is transferred by the operating system from the keyboard to the screen memory. After the RETURN key is depressed the operating system compresses the text of the program line coding it as a sequence of VIC-20 BASIC keyword codes. A table of these codes can be found in Appendix 3, Table A5. The compressed text is then stored in that area of memory allotted as user BASIC program space, building up from the bottom. Before examining this in detail in section 3.4 we should first know in broad terms how the memory of the VIC is divided into blocks each allotted to a specific purpose, that is where in memory different kinds of data are stored.

We recall that a 'bit' is a binary 1 or 0. The 6502 microprocessor has a 16-bit address bus (see Chapter 7) which enables it to access any one of 2^{16} memory locations, numbered from 0 to $2^{16}-1$, i.e. 65535. Thus the *address* of each location is a 16-bit binary number whose decimal value will lie in the range 0 to 65535. The *contents* of each location consists of an 8-bit binary number, a *byte*, whose decimal value will lie in the range 0 to 2^8-1, i.e. 255.

A memory location may be: RAM, random access memory, the contents of which can be changed for example by use of POKE; or ROM, read only memory, the contents of which cannot be changed. Examples of locations on the VIC which are ROM are 32768 to 36863, this 4K block contains the information necessary to print standard upper case, lower case or graphics characters in normal or reversed field and is called the *character matrix;* locations 49152 to 57343 contain the BASIC interpreter which takes the compressed text from the user BASIC program area a line at a time, converts it into a sequence of machine code instructions which the 6502 microprocessor then executes, and then does the same with the next line until the program is ended; and finally locations 57344 to 65535 contain the VIC operating system Kernal routines (see Chapter 7).

Many aspects of the operating system require the use of memory locations whose contents can be varied, that is RAM rather than ROM, and to this end all locations between 0 and 1023 are used by the operating system. A detailed knowledge of what the contents of these locations mean and their effect on the operating system can be of considerable use to the programmer. A list containing a brief explanation of the contents of each of these locations is given in Appendix 3, Table A1.

To interpret this list it is helpful to introduce the concept of a page. Quite simply a *page* consists of a block of 256 consecutive memory locations which contain a total of 256 bytes. Page zero starts at location 0 and ends at location 255. This page is used exclusively by the operating system because it can be accessed more rapidly in 6502 machine code than any other part of memory. Page one starts at 256 and ends at 511, the 6502 microprocessor requires a block of RAM at these addresses as the processor stack area (see Chapter 7). Since there are 2^{16} locations in total this means that altogether there are 256 pages in VIC memory.

Because any address consists of 16 bits it requires the contents of *two* memory locations in order to specify a given address. On the VIC 6502 these are stored in Lo-byte, Hi-byte order.

Example
Suppose the address is 8193 then

$$\text{Hi-byte} = \text{INT} (8193/256) = 32 \qquad \text{(page)}$$
$$\text{Lo-byte} = 8193 - (\text{Hi-byte}) * 256 = 1 \qquad \text{(position)}$$
$$\text{Check} : 8193 = 32 * 256 + 1$$

We may think of the Lo-byte as representing the position of the address in question on its page; and the Hi-byte as the *page number*. Both Hi and Lo bytes can take decimal values in the range 0 to 255.

To see how this works in practice and how useful the memory map of the first 1K block, given in Table A1, can be, we take a specific example in the following section.

3.2 Raising the bottom and lowering the top of memory

According to the Table on p. 164 the pointer to the 'start of user BASIC' is contained in locations 43 and 44. As we have said these will be stored in Lo-byte, Hi-byte order. If you turn on the VIC, without additional RAM, and examine the contents of 43 and 44 using PEEK you will find PEEK(43) = 1, Lo-byte, and PEEK(44) = 16, Hi-byte. This specifies position 1 on page 16 as the start address of user BASIC, that is PEEK(44)*256 + PEEK(43) = 4097. In fact, user BASIC really starts at 4096 but, since the first byte is required always to be 0, it is said to start at 4097.

Because 43 and 44 are RAM locations it is possible for the programmer to change their contents and thereby raise the start address of user BASIC, commonly called the *bottom of memory;* this protects the area between 4096 and the new bottom of memory from being overwritten by the operating system.

To raise the bottom of memory by two pages to 4608 we should RETURN as one line the command

POKE 44, 18 : POKE 4608, 0 : NEW

The first POKE resets the pointer in 44 used by the operating system, the second POKE guarantees that the operating system will find a 0 at the new start location, and NEW is required to initialize the system for the new bottom of memory. ? FRE(0) will now return 3069 instead of 3583, so we have indeed reduced the user BASIC program area by two pages. Any program which was previously completely contained, as compressed text, in pages 16 and 17 is now protected, except from a direct POKE to an address in this area, and cannot be listed or run, since as far as the operating system is concerned this block of memory no longer exists. We can now enter new programs, which may even have the same line numbers as the protected program, edit them, and run them in the normal way. Having done this we can delete these other programs by returning NEW and recover our original program by POKE 44,16, to lower the bottom of memory, and LIST.

Similarly from Table A1 the pointer to the last address of user BASIC, the *top of memory* is contained in locations 55 and 56, again in Lo-byte, Hi-byte order. On a VIC with no additional RAM we find PEEK(55) + 256 * PEEK(56) = 7680, this means the last location available to user BASIC is 7679. In fact the area of memory storing the current screen display, called the *video matrix* or screen RAM, starts at 7680 and uses two pages ending at 8191.

To lower the top of memory by one page to 6426 we simply RETURN the command

POKE 56 , 29 : POKE 52 , 29 : CLR

Note 51 and 52 are the pointers to the start of active space for string storage (which builds down from the top of memory) and CLR is required to set all variables to null.

3.3 Large-scale memory maps

The exact configuration adopted by the VIC when it is turned on varies according to the presence or absence of additional RAM or ROM. On power up the 6502 microprocessor begins execution of a program whose start address is stored in 65532 and 65533, in fact PEEK(65532) + 256*PEEK(65533) = 64802 which is the address in question. You can check this by returning SYS(64802), which will initialize the VIC as if from a cold start. The first function of this program is to check if ROM is present in the 8K block beginning at 40960, it does this by searching for a specific string of five numbers (65, 48, 195, 194, 205) in locations 40964 to 40968. If this test is successful then the program control jumps to whatever address is stored in 40960 and 40961. This is the technique used by commercial ROM-based games. If the test is unsuccessful the normal initialization routine proceeds. With no additional RAM or ROM present this routine will allocate locations 4096 to 7679 as the user BASIC program area, locations 7680 to 8191 for the video matrix, and locations 38400 to 38911 for that area of memory which stores the color of each character in the video matrix, known as the *color matrix*.

Apart from the Super Expander Cartridge, which is dealt with in Chapter 6, standard RAM packs for the VIC are 3K, 8K or 16K. The 3K pack is set to locate between 1024 and 4095. Both the 8K and 16K RAM packs are set to locate from 8192 upwards. Without an Expansion board it is only possible to use one or other of these at a time. If it is desired to use all three RAM packs simultaneously, thereby extending the VIC to its maximum capacity, then it is necessary to alter the links on the 8K RAM pack so that it locates from 24576 upwards (details in Chapter 6). If at most one RAM pack can be used then there are four possible cold start configurations which can result, these are shown in Figure 3.1. These large-scale memory maps will be very useful when we start moving large blocks of memory about.

If it is necessary to protect an area of memory from being overwritten by BASIC, for example one may wish to protect a machine code program, this is usually done by raising the bottom or lowering the top of memory as illustrated in section 3.2. However, one can frequently locate a short machine code program in the cassette buffer (828 to 1020) provided the cassette is not required for SAVE or LOAD. One may be tempted to use the spare block of color RAM, 37888 to 38379 in normal configuration, for the same purpose but there is a snag. Unlike all other RAM, which stores 8 bits (one byte) the color RAM stores only 4 bits (one *nybble*). One can vary the bottom 4 bits but the top 4 bits are fixed and random. Thus numbers in the range 0 to 15 can be stored in the unused portion of color RAM and recovered by PEEK(37888) AND15 for example, but numbers greater than 15 cannot be reliably stored.

Size	LOCATION DEC	HEX	VIC	VIC + 3K	VIC + 8K	VIC + 16K
1K	0 / 1023	0000 / 03FF	MICROSOFT BASIC RAM	MICROSOFT BASIC RAM	MICROSOFT BASIC RAM	MICROSOFT BASIC RAM
3K	1024 / 4095	0400 / 01FF	NON-EXISTENT (3K EXPANSION RAM)	USER BASIC PROGRAM AREA	NON-EXISTENT (3K EXPANSION)	NON-EXISTENT (3K EXPANSION)
3.5K	4096 / 7679	1000 / 1DFF	USER BASIC PROGRAM AREA	PROGRAM AREA	SCREEN RAM 4607 / 4608	SCREEN RAM 4607 / 4608
.5K	7680 / 8191	1E00 / 1FFF	SCREEN RAM (VIDEO MATRIX)	SCREEN RAM (VIDEO MATRIX)	USER BASIC PROGRAM AREA	USER BASIC PROGRAM AREA
8K	8192 / 16383	2000 / 3FFF	NON-EXISTENT (8K EXPANSION ROM/RAM)	NON-EXISTENT		
8K	16384 / 24575	4000 / 5FFF	NON-EXISTENT (8K EXPANSION ROM/RAM)	NON-EXISTENT	NON-EXISTENT	
8K	24576 / 32767	6000 / 7FFF	NON-EXISTENT (8K EXPANSION ROM/RAM)	NON-EXISTENT	NON-EXISTENT	NON-EXISTENT
4K	32768 / 36863	8000 / 8FFF	CHAR ROM (CHARACTER MATRIX)	CHAR ROM (CHARACTER MATRIX)	CHAR ROM	CHAR ROM
	36864 / 36879	9000 / 900F	VIC(6561)CHIP	VIC(6561)CHIP	VIC(6561)CHIP	VIC(6561)CHIP
	36880 / 37135	9010 / 910F	(VIC CHIP?)	?	?	?
	37136 / 37151	9110 / 911F	VIA(6522)CHIPS I/O	VIA(6522)CHIPS I/O	VIA(6522)CHIPS I/O	VIA(6522)CHIPS I/O
	37152 / 37167	9120 / 912F	I/O	I/O	I/O	I/O
1K	37888 / 38399	9400 / 95FF	Free Nybbles	Free Nybbles	COLOR RAM	COLOR RAM
	38400 / 38911	9600 / 97FF	COLOR RAM	COLOR RAM	Free Nybbles	Free Nybbles
2K	38912 / 40595	9800 / 9FFF	EXPANSION? I/O NON-EXISTENT	EXPANSION? I/O NON-EXISTENT	EXPANSION? I/O NON-EXISTENT	EXPANSION? I/O NON-EXISTENT
8K	40960 / 49151	AC00 / BFFF	EXPANSION ROM NON-EXISTENT	EXPANSION ROM NON-EXISTENT	EXPANSION ROM NON-EXISTENT	EXPANSION ROM NON-EXISTENT
8K	49152 / 57343	C000 / DFFF	BASIC ROM	BASIC ROM	BASIC ROM	BASIC ROM
8K	57344 / 65535	E000 / FFFF	KERNAL ROM	KERNAL ROM	KERNAL ROM	KERNAL ROM

Fig. 3.1 — Large scale memory maps.

3.4 Compressed text storage in the user BASIC program area

If we enter a simple program such as

> 10 PRINT " A J J "
>
> 20 END

on a VIC with no additional RAM this will be stored as a sequence of VIC-20 BASIC keyword codes building up from the bottom of memory, normally location 4096. A table of codes is given on p. 173.

We can examine this sequence directly by returning the one line command

> FOR I = 0 TO 19 : PRINT PEEK (4096 + I); : NEXT

(which is not itself a program line). When RETURN is pressed the VIC will respond with

```
0       12          16          10          0          153
    14          65          74          74          34
0       18          16          20          0          128
    0           0           0
```

These numbers are interpreted as follows:

Address	Contents	Interpretation
4096	0	Basic begins with a 0
4097	12	Link address, Lo-byte ⎱ Points to start location of
4098	16	Link address Hi-byte ⎰ next program line (4108)
4099	10	Program line number, Lo-byte
4100	0	Program line number, Hi-byte
4101	153	PRINT
4102	34	"
4103	65	A
4104	74	J
4105	74	J
4106	34	"
4107	0	End of line
4108	18	Link address, Lo-byte ⎱ Points to start location of
4109	16	Link address, Hi-byte ⎰ next program line (4114)
4110	20	Program line number, Lo-byte
4111	0	Program line number, Hi-byte
4112	128	END
4113	0	End of line
4114	0	⎱ Return to
4115	0	⎰ direct mode

Whilst a program is running the line number currently being executed is stored in locations 57 and 58. If the contents of these two locations is zero then a direct mode of operation is indicated. Thus the link address of the last line of the program stored in 4108 and 4109 points not to another link address, as in a normal program line, but to two zero bytes in 4114 and 4115, which indicate a return to direct mode. These zero end bytes mark the end of the program and not the occurrence of the END instruction which may occur anywhere within the program.

Example

A program which rewrites itself the first time it is run.

```
10 PRINT " A J J "
20 POKE 4103,86 : POKE 4104,73 : POKE 4105,67
30 END
```

If you RUN this program and then LIST it, you will obtain

```
10 PRINT "VIC"
20 POKE 4103,86 : POKE4104,73 : POKE4105,67
30 END
```

Of course 86, 73 and 67 are the keyword codes for V, I and C respectively (for characters these are just the CBM ASII codes).

Within a program line any zero is stored in compressed form as a 48, the number zero being reserved as an end of line or program marker.

Example

A program which counts the number of times it has been run.

```
10  REM 0
20  N = PEEK (4103)
30  PRINT N − 47 : N = N + 1
40  N = N AND 255
50  IF N = 0 TNEN N = 48
60  POKE 4103, N
```

The address for the zero after the REM is (provided the space is present) 4103, the zero being stored as 48. Lines 40 and 50 simply ensure that when $N = 256$ its value is wrapped back to 48 so that an illegal quantity error does not occur in 60. Thus this program will count the number of times it has been RUN up to 208, after which it will start counting again from zero. It is a simple exercise to extend the count.

Although the zero end bytes mark the end of a program as far as LIST is concerned they do not directly control the end of file markers used by SAVE or LOAD.

Example

A program which when loaded from tape or disk will not LIST or RUN until it has been 'unlocked'.

We begin by entering

```
10  REM ANY COMMENT
20  FOR I = 0 TO 10
20  PRINT "VIC"
30  NEXT
40  END
```

Before saving the program we determine the correct link address in 4097 and 4098

```
PRINT PEEK(4097), PEEK(4098)
```

which gives

```
19              16.
```

Next

POKE 4097,0: POKE 4098,0 .

The program will now neither LIST nor RUN. Finally SAVE the program to tape or disk.

Upon loading the program will again neither LIST nor RUN, because the zero end bytes have been preserved, but can be 'unlocked' by the command

POKE 4097,19 : POKE 4098,16

When a VIC program is loaded from tape or disk the link addresses are rebuilt.[†] This is obviously necessary, since otherwise a program written and saved with one bottom of memory could not be loaded and RUN with a different bottom of memory, e.g. when a RAM pack is used. Interesting effects can be achieved by changing link addresses to values other than zero end bytes (e.g. try referring a line to itself, then check LIST and RUN) but these will not be preserved after loading because, apart from zeros, the link addresses are rebuilt.

A more useful application is given in the following program which can be used to renumber a program without the Programmer's Aid. It will not renumber GOTOS or GOSUBS although this could be accomplished by a more elaborate routine.

Example

```
10 REM**RENUMBER**
20 REM*S=START OF BASIC*
30 REM*RAISE MEM BEYOND PROGRAM TO BE RENUMBERED*
40 REM* BY POKE44,?:POKE256*?,0:NEW *
50 REM*LOAD AND RUN THIS PROGRAM*
60 REM*LOWER MEM TO RECOVER ORIGINAL PROGRAM*
70 REM*WILL NOT RENUMBER GOTOS GOSUBS ETC.*
80 S=4096:PRINT"J"
90 INPUT"FROM,INTERVAL";X$,Y$
100 X=VAL(X$):Y=VAL(Y$)
110 K=S+1
120 NL=PEEK(K)+256*PEEK(K+1)
130 IFNL=0THENEND
140 LH=INT(X/256):LL=X-256*LH
150 POKEK+2,LL:POKEK+3,LH
160 X=X+Y:K=NL:GOTO120
```

Here

$\quad$ NL = Next link address,
$\quad$ LH = Link address Hi-byte,
$\quad$ LL = Link address Lo-byte,
$\quad$ S = Start of BASIC for program to be renumbered.

When a program is running the operating system has to identify any new variables, arrays or strings which it encounters during execution, and allocate memory locations in which their values may be stored. It does this by building variable or array storage locations *up* from the end of the program, and

†Not true of PETS.

by building string storage locations *down* from the top of memory. The pointer to the end of arrays is contained in locations 49 and 50 (Lo-byte, Hi-byte) and that the bottom of strings in 51 and 52. Storage is therefore allocated dynamically as needed by BASIC and the operating system, an OUT OF MEMORY error occurs if execution of the current command would cause these two pointers to cross. Note that the values of variables, array components, and strings are all stored in the user BASIC program area. Thus a true measure of the amount of space required by a program is not obtained by returning ? FRE(0) after the program has been entered in memory, but only by returning ? FRE(0) immediately after it has been run!

Note that you will *not* get an OUT OF MEMORY error if you try to type in a program which is too long; at the stage at which available memory is exhausted the VIC will simply crash.

3.5 An alternate screen

One of the exciting features of the VIC is that by careful use of the 6561 control registers, which is fairly straightforward once one understands their function, and by manipulating system pointers, a somewhat trickier process, the initial VIC configuration can, within limits, be varied. For example the video matrix can be relocated, to provide an alternate screen. This facility could be used during program execution to provide an 'instantaneous' switch to a previously prepared graphics display.

Normally the video matrix starts on page 30 at 7680. To flip the screen to start at location 7168 on page 28 simply RETURN the command

POKE 36866,22 : POKE 648,28

You can now clear the new screen and start typing. The first POKE is to one of the 6561 control registers and does two things: it moves the start address of the video matrix to 7168 and also shifts the start address of the color matrix from 38400 to 37888, which means we can have a separate set of colors for the characters on the new screen. A detailed explanation of the 6561 control register at address 36866 is given in the next section.

The POKE to 648 (see Table A1) tells the operating system that the screen, which we are seeing, now starts on page 28 rather than page 30. This puts the cursor on the right screen and enables one to use keys like CLR/HOME, which obviously require the operating system to know where the relevant screen is located in memory. To return to the original screen we simply enter

POKE 36866,150 : POKE 648,30

and press RETURN.

It looks simple enough and for many applications during program execution it is quite simple but there are some snags in direct mode. These become apparent if having returned to the original screen we position the cursor on the 'line' POKE36866,22 : POKE649,28, and hit RETURN. We find that things do not work as they did the first time around, the new screen appears as expected but we do not get a cursor. The reason is that although our original screen *looked* the same as it was when we first left it, in fact the operating system did not see it as being the same. Although POKE36866,22:POKE648,28 appears to us as two instructions on one line, when we first jumped to the new screen the link between these two instructions was lost. Consequently the second time around only POKE36866,22 was executed. The result was that the operating system was still under the impression that the screen was located at a start address on page 30 whereas we were actually looking at a display which began on page 28.

Indeed several essential links were broken during the transition from the old screen to the new, but the more important of these can be repaired using the following routines due to Jim Butterfield (see 'Alternate screens', *VIC Computing*, December 1981).

Type the following as a single block without pressing RETURN.

POKE 36866,22 : POKE 648,22 : FOR J=217

TO 228 : POKE J, 156 : NEXT : FOR J=229

TO 240 : POKE J, 157 : NEXT

Proofread carefully, then hit RETURN and flip to the alternate screen. To get back again type, again as a single block,

POKE 36866,150 : POKE 648,28 : FOR J=217

TO 228 : POKE J, 158 : NEXT : FOR J=229

TO 240 : POKE J, 159 : NEXT

Hitting the RETURN key will now recall the original screen. The difference being that this time if the cursor is placed on the original block of instructions and the RETURN key pressed the alternate screen plus cursor will appear; the links in each block of instructions are restored as the corresponding screen appears.

Naturally, if you use an alternate screen in a program, the top of user BASIC should be lowered to protect the additional screen memory.

3.6 The 6561 control registers[†]

It is the task of the 6561 microprocessor to access the data stored in the video matrix, color matrix and character memory and display this information in the correct format on the CRT screen. There are sixteen eight-bit control registers within the 6561 which can be accessed from BASIC, using PEEK or POKE, at addresses 36864 to 36879.

In the previous section we saw an example in which, by manipulating the contents of control register 3 (address 36866), the start address of the video matrix could be relocated. One of the useful features which 6561 control registers gives the programmer is the ability to relocate, within limits, the start addresses of the video matrix and the character matrix.

We next dicuss the function of each control register in some detail.

Control register number 1 (address 36864 : normal contents 12)
In theory bit 7 is supposed to control the interlace mode (0/OFF, 1/ON) which we can activate by POKE 36864, PEEK(36864)OR128. However, with the 6561 chip it would seem that this facility cannot be implemented.

Bits 0 to 6 control the horizontal position of the screen origin (top left-hand corner) on the CRT screen. The effect of varying the contents of this control register can be observed with the following program:

---

†In the United States the corresponding chip is the 6560.

```
10  FOR I = 0 TO 255
20  POKE 36864, I
30  FOR L = 0 TO 500 : NEXT L : REM DELAY
40  NEXT I
50  POKE 36864,12 : END
```

Values of greater than 23 produce garbage on the screen[†] and values greater than 62 move the VIC screen so far to the right it moves off the CRT. Values of I greater than 127 reproduce the response for the range $0 \leqslant I \leqslant 127$ but with bit 7 set to 1.

Control register number 2 (Address 36865: Normal contents 38)
The contents of this register control the vertical position of the screen origin on the CRT screen. The effect of varying the contents can be observed with the following program:

```
10  FOR I = 0 TO 255
20  POKE 36865,I
30  FOR L = 0 TO 500 : NEXT L : REM DELAY
40  NEXT I
50  POKE 36865,38 : END
```

Values of I greater than 150 move the VIC screen so far down it moves off the CRT.

Control register number 3 (Address 36866: Normal contents 150)
Bits 0 to 6 control the number of columns on the VIC screen and are normally set to 22, values other than 22 tend to confuse the screen editor. The effect of varying these bits, whilst keeping bit 7 at 1, can be observed with the following program:

```
10  POKE 36864,7 : REM MOVE SCREEN LEFT
20  FOR I = 128 TO 255
30  POKE 36866,I
40  FOR L = 0 TO 500 : NEXT L : REM DELAY
50  NEXT I
60  POKE 36866,150 : POKE 36864,12 : END
```

Values of greater than 150 (more than 22 columns) produce garbage on the screen, values greater than 165 have no observable effect beyond that produced by 165.

Bit 7 is important. It is bit 9 of the binary number which specifies the start address (base location) of the video matrix. Changing this bit moves the screen 2 pages in memory ($2 \uparrow 9 = 512$) as in the alternate screen routine of 3.5. This is best discussed in conjunction with control register number 6 (36869).

Bit 7 of address 36866 also controls which block of color RAM is used.

Bit 7 = 1 — color matrix starts at 38400

Bit 7 = 0 — color matrix starts at 37888

Hence we find the start of the color matrix with the formula

CO = 37888 + 4 * ((PEEK(36866) AND 128))

---

† Because more screen memory is needed.

Control register number 4 (Address 36867: Normal contents variable 46/174)
Bit 0 is used to select the pixel dot format of a character cell, either 8×8 (bit 0=0) or 16×8 (bit 0 = 1). If *full* screen Hi-Res graphics are required it is necessary to set bit 0 to 1, this is explained fully in Chapter 4.

Bits 1 to 6 control the number of rows on the VIC screen. The total value of these bits can be read by PEEK(36867) AND 126 and is normally 46, viz. twice the number of rows. The effect of varying these bits whilst leaving bit 0=0 and bit 7 uninfluenced can be observed with the following program

```
10  POKE 36865,20 : REM MOVE SCREEN UP
20  FOR I = 0 TO 63
30  POKE 36867, (PEEK(36867) AND 128) OR (2 * I)
40  FOR L = 0 TO 100 : NEXT : REM DELAY
50  NEXT I
60  POKE 36867,46 : POKE 36865,38 : END
```

Values of I greater than 23 (more than 23 rows) produce garbage on the screen.

Bit 7 is the least significant bit of current raster line number, that is the number of the line currently being scanned by the CRT raster beam.

Control register number 5 (Address 36868: Normal contents variable)
This register contains bits 1 to 8 of the current raster line number.

Control register number 6 (Address 36869: Normal contents 240)
This is the single most important 6561 control register and usually the one which causes most confusion. The full *uses* of this register are explained in Chapter 4, but the details of what it actually *does* are given here. Briefly

Bits 0 to 3 control the start address of the character matrix.

Bits 4 to 6 in conjunction with bit 7 of 36866 control the start address of the video matrix.

Bit 7 must be 1.

Now for the details. Let us begin with the screen start address and let

$$B_v^r = \begin{cases} \text{the } r\text{th bit of the base location of} \\ \text{the video matrix.} \end{cases}$$

Then the decimal of the start of the screen in memory is

$$(2\uparrow12)* B_v^{12} + (2\uparrow11)*B_v^{11} + (2\uparrow10)*B_v^{10} + (2\uparrow9)*B_v^9$$

B_v^0 to B_v^8 are not within our control and are set to 0. Between registers 36866 and 36869 the distribution of those B_v^r which are within our control is

36866 Bit 7 = B_v^9

36869 Bit 6 = B_v^{12}, Bit 5 = B_v^{11}, Bit 4 = B_v^{10}

This leads to the following possible screen start addresses:

B_v^{12}	B_v^{11}	B_v^{10}	B_v^9	Screen start
1	0	0	0	4096
1	0	0	1	4608
1	0	1	0	5120
1	0	1	1	5632
1	1	0	0	6144
1	1	0	1	6656
1	1	1	0	7168
1	1	1	1	7680

Assuming the character matrix start address (which depends on bits 0 to 3 of the contents of 36869) *remains fixed at* 32768, these screen start addresses can be accomplished by POKEing the following numbers into 36866, 36869 and 648 (if you want the operating system to know where the screen is) respectively:

				7	6 B_v^{12}	5 B_v^{11}	4 B_v^{10}	3	2	1	0	Bit
screen start	36866	36869	648				←	CM bits			→	
4096	22	192	16	1	1	0	0	0	0	0	0	
4608	150	192	18	1	1	0	0	0	0	0	0	
5120	22	208	20	1	1	0	1	0	0	0	0	
5632	150	208	22	1	1	0	1	0	0	0	0	
6144	22	224	24	1	1	1	0	0	0	0	0	
6656	150	224	26	1	1	1	0	0	0	0	0	
7168	22	240	28	1	1	1	1	0	0	0	0	
7680	150	240	30	1	1	1	1	0	0	0	0	

|← —————————— 36869 ——— —————→|

|←——————— · ·→|
CM at 32768

Example

A 30 × 30 low resolution screen for the VIC. This example uses several of the control registers discussed above to create a larger screen than usual. Because the operating system is written for a 23 × 22 screen the large screen cannot be PRINTed to, *but it can be written to using* POKE. It is essential to move the pointer to color RAM to point to 37888 since 900 color nybbles are needed for the large screen. The following commands used in a program will set up a 30 × 30 screen with base location SC = 6144 (don't forget to lower the top of memory).

```
POKE 36867, (PEEK(36867) AND 128) OR (2 * 30) : REM 30 ROWS
POKE 36866, 30 : REM 30 COLS AND SC (COL TO 37888)
POKE 36869, 224 : REM SET SC TO 6144
POKE 36864, 7 : POKE 36865, 20 : REM ORIGIN TO TOP LEFT
```

To restore the usual screen set-up at the end of the program just POKE the normal values back into all these registers.

We next examine the character matrix. In order to display a character on the screen the following sequence of events takes place.

Firstly the screen code of the required character is obtained from the corresponding part of the video matrix. If 8 × 8 pixel dot characters are being used this value is then multiplied by 8 (since each character will require 8 bytes of memory) and the number so obtained is used as an offset from the base location of the character matrix, i.e.

Let the screen code be X ($0 \leqslant X \leqslant 255$) then number computed is 8 * X + (Base location of CM).

This number represents the address of the first of 8 bytes in the character matrix which describe the character with screen code X. In this way the correct 8 bytes required to describe the given character are located by the operating system and transferred to the screen.

Normally the base location of the character matrix is 32768. From this address upwards the subsequent 4K of ROM is divided into blocks of 8 bytes, each block specifying a standard character. If, however, we wish to define non-standard characters then the base location of the character matrix must be moved into RAM, which is accomplished by changing bits 0 to 3 of 36869.

Let

$$B_c^r = \begin{cases} \text{the } r\textit{th} \text{ bit of the base location of} \\ \text{the character matrix.} \end{cases}$$

Bits 0 to 3 of 36869 have the following function

$$36869 \text{ bit } 3 = \begin{cases} 0, \text{ if character matrix is in ROM} \\ \\ 1, \text{ if character matrix is in RAM} \end{cases}$$

$$\text{bit } 2 = B_c^{12}, \text{ bit } 1 = B_c^{11}, \text{ bit } 0 = B_c^{10}$$

Thus if bit 3 = 1 the decimal value of the start of the character matrix in RAM is

$$(2\uparrow 12)*B_c^{12} + (2\uparrow 11)*B_c^{11} + (2\uparrow 10)*B_c^{10}$$

In fact the following are possible character matrix start addresses

36869 Bit	3	2	1	0	
	ROM/RAM	B_c^{12}	B_c^{11}	B_c^{10}	C M start
↑	0	0	0	0	32768
Available ROM	0	0	0	1	33792
locations	0	0	1	0	34816
↓	0	0	1	1	36864
↑					
Available RAM	1	1	0	0	4096
locations	1	1	0	1	5120
	1	1	1	0	6144
↓	1	1	1	1	7168

Assuming the screen start address (which depends on bits 4 to 6 of the contents of 36869) remains fixed at 7680, the different CM start addresses in RAM can be accomplished by POKEing the following numbers into 36869

CM start	36869	7 FIXED	6 B_v^{12}	5 B_v^{11}	4 B_v^{10}	3 ROM/RAM	2 B_c^{12}	1 B_c^{11}	0 B_c^{10}	Bit
4096	252	1	1	1	1	1	1	0	0	
5120	253	1	1	1	1	1	1	0	1	
6144	254	1	1	1	1	1	1	1	0	
7168	255	1	1	1	1	1	1	1	1	

Screen at 7680

←————————————→

We now know how to vary the screen start or character matrix start address, leaving the other fixed. To vary both simultaneously is just a matter of assembling the right combination of bits for 36869 and possibly 36866 as well.

Example
To locate the screen at 4608 and the character matrix at 5120 we need the following bit pattern in 36869

Bit	7	6	5	4	3	2	0	1	
	FIXED	B_v^{12}	B_v^{11}	B_v^{10}	RAM	B_c^{12}	B_c^{11}	B_c^{10}	
	1	1	0	0	1	1	0	1	= Decimal 205

We also need $B_v^9 = 1$ (Bit 7 of 36866). Hence the corresponding instructions are

    POKE 36866,150 : POKE 36869,205

Remarks
With no additional RAM this leaves just 512 bytes for the program (!) with a 3K RAM pack it gives 3.5K for user BASIC. The character matrix in this example can go from 5120 up to 8192 i.e. about 3K (not quite sufficient for full screen high resolution graphics). If we were to use this configuration in practice we should also protect the screen and character matrix by lowering the top memory to 4608 i.e.

    POKE 56,18 : POKE 52,18 : CLR

For examples of programs which employ user-defined graphics the reader is referred to Chapter 4.
Finally in this connection we observe the start of the screen memory SC and of the character matrix CM can be determined by the formulae

    SC = 4* (PEEK(36866)AND128) + 64*(PEEK(36869)AND112)

    CM = 32768*(1 − (PEEK(36869)AND8)/8) + (2↑10)*(PEEK(36869)AND7)

[However, it would not be possible to read the value of CM, if the character matrix is in RAM, without first copying some standard characters from ROM with a routine such as

FOR I = 0 TO 512 : POKE CM + I, PEEK (32768 + I) : NEXT

!]

Control registers 7 and 8 (Addresses 36870 and 36871: Normal contents 0)
These registers contain respectively the latched horizontal and vertical position of a light pen, when in use. An example of a program which uses these registers to plot a character to the screen under the direction of a light pen is given in Chapter 6.

Control registers 9 and 10 (Addresses 36872 and 36873: Normal contents 255)
These registers contain respectively the digitized value of input for the horizontal and vertical axis of a potentiometer joystick, when in use. Top left is (255,255), bottom right is (0,0). As the coordinates can be read directly from these two registers a potentiometer joystick is somewhat easier to program for than the switch joystick discussed in Chapter 6. A potentiometer joystick also gives greater precision of control since each coordinate can take values in the range 0 to 255.

Control registers 11, 12, 13 and 14 (Normal contents 0)
These control the audio oscillators

        11. Address 36874 — Low voice
        12. Address 36875 — Mid voice
        13. Address 36876 — High voice
        14. Address 36877 — White noise

In each case bits 0 to 6 set the frequency of oscillator and bit 7 turns it on (bit 7 = 0). A program illustrating the use of the audio oscillators is given in Chapter 1.

Control registers 15 (Address 36878: Normal contents 0)
This register has two functions:

Bits 0 to 3 set the volume (0 = off, 15 = max) of the composite signal generated by any audio oscillators that are on.
Bits 4 to 7 define the auxiliary color used in Multicolor mode (see Chapter 4).

Control register 16 (Address 36879: Normal contents 27)
This is a color control register.

Bits 0 to 2 select one of 8 colors for the exterior border area of the screen, i.e. the area on the CRT outside the VIC screen. In Multicolor mode this color is one of the four possible 1 X 2 pixel dot colors which can occur within a character cell.
Bits 4 to 7 select one of 16 colors for the background common to all characters on the screen.
Bit 3 determines whether the video matrix is displayed as different colored characters in a common background (bit 3 =1), or inverted (bit 3 = 0) so that all characters are the same color (i.e. the background color determined by bits 4 to 7) whilst each character cell background will be a color determined by the associated color nybble. Note that bit 3 has no effect if the associated color nybble indicates Multicolor mode for the character cell in question.

4

Graphics

4.1 The construction of characters

To create user-defined graphics characters or to plot an individual pixel dot to a specified point on the screen, it is first necessary to understand how the standard characters are displayed on the screen.

As we know there are two distinct ways to put a character on the screen, we can use PRINT or, simply POKE the appropriate screen code into the required address in the video matrix (screen memory). In either case the sequence of events which then takes place is the same, it was sketched briefly in Chapter 3. The screen code is read from the video matrix, multiplied by 8 (or 16 if bit 0 of 36867 is set to 1) and the resulting number is used as an offset, from the base location of the character matrix, to find the start address of the 8 (or 16) bytes which describe the character in question.

Normally the base location of the character matrix is at 32768 in ROM. If we PEEK the first 16 locations we can see how the first two characters are constructed, as in Table 4.1.

Screen codes take values in the range 0 to 255, therefore the total number of bytes for a single block of immediately accessible character matrix is 256*8, i.e. 2K. Unfortunately 256 characters are not enough to give all combinations of upper case, lower case, graphics and reversed characters. To overcome this limitation and use the remaining 2K of character ROM we must move the base location of the character matrix to 34816, but then of course *every* character on the screen will change. This is what happens when you use the SHIFT+CBM combination of keys or alternatively POKE 36869, 242. The layout of the character matrix in ROM is given in Table 4.2.

If you study the bit patterns in Table 4.1 you will see exactly how an individual character is constructed. Each bit represents one of 64 pixel dots, if the bit is zero that pixel dot is not lit on the screen, if the bit is set to 1 then the pixel dot will be lit provided the color nybble associated with the character cell indicates a color distinct from the screen background color.

Table 4.1

Screen code	Decimal address	Decimal contents	7	6	5	4	3	2	1	0	Character row
0	32768	28				1	1	1			0
	32769	34			1				1		1
CHAR	32770	74		1			1		1		2
@	32771	86		1		1		1	1		3
	32772	76		1			1	1			4
	32773	32			1						5
	32774	30				1	1	1	1		6
	32775	0									7
1	32776	24				1	1				0
	32777	36			1			1			1
CHAR	32778	66		1					1		2
A	32779	126		1	1	1	1	1	1		3
	32780	66		1					1		4
	32781	66		1					1		5
	32782	66		1					1		6
	32783	0									7

Table 4.2 — ROM character matrix layout.

	Decimal start address	Contents of CM		Screen codes	Keyboard entry
'Normal' mode 2K block POKE 36869,240	32768	Upper case + Misc. Graphics/Graphics		0–63 64–127	No SHIFT SHIFT/CBM
	33792	Upper case + Misc. Graphics/Graphics	Reverse field	128–191 192–255	No SHIFT SHIFT/CBM
'Text' mode 2K block POKE 36869,242	34816	Lower case + Misc. Upper case/Graphics		0–63 64–127	No SHIFT SHIFT/CBM
	35840	Lower case + Misc. Upper case/Graphics	Reverse field	128–191 192–255	No SHIFT SHIFT/CBM

In 16 X 8 mode (bit 0 of 36867 set to 1) each character cell is composed of 128 pixel dots and each such double-sized character cell is accessed by a single screen code. This can be illustrated by entering the command

> POKE 36867, PEEK (36867) OR 1 : PRINT CHR$(147)"@"

When RETURN is pressed the effects are quite dramatic. The first thing we notice is that the bottom of the VIC screen has moved below the bottom of the CRT. This is because our first command, which sets bit 0 of 36867 to 1, has doubled the vertical height of each character cell. The number of rows is still 23 but each row takes twice the room it did previously. The next command is to print CLR/HOME (CHR$(147)) and then @. In the top left of the screen you should see

> @
>
> A

In 16 X 8 mode the instruction which says essentially 'print the character with screen code 0' causes the first 16 bytes of the character matrix to be taken as the 16 rows of the character to be displayed. The same effect could have been achieved by

> POKE 36867, PEEK(36867) OR1 : PRINT CHR$(147) : POKE 7680,0 : POKE 38400,6

In general, in 16 X 8 mode, if the screen code is X then the 16 bytes of the character matrix which start at

> $16*X + $ (Base location of CM)

will be taken to represent the 16 rows of the character to be displayed.

It is apparent that in 16 X 8 mode, 256 screen codes gives the total number of bytes for a single block of immediately accessible character matrix as 256 X 16, i.e. 4K. In the final analysis this factor determines the maximum possible size of a hi-resolution screen. However, if only a 3K RAM pack is available then useful RAM ends at 8191. In this case you cannot actually have a character matrix quite as large as 4K because the 6561 chip requires both the video matrix (about ½K) *and* the character matrix to start between 4096 and 8191. If you fill the 4K with character matrix then there would be nowhere left for the video matrix! If an 8K or 16K RAM pack is used then the bottom of memory should be raised above the top of the character matrix *before* loading any BASIC program. Under these circumstances a 4K character matrix *can* be used.

4.2 User-defined graphics characters in 8 X 8 mode

Suppose that on a VIC with no additional RAM we want the letters of the alphabet and the numbers 0 to 9, preferably called with the usual PRINT or POKE, plus a reasonable selection of our own graphics characters and room for a sensible BASIC program. The screen codes for the alphabet, miscellaneous symbols, and the numbers 0 to 9 run from 0 to 57 and therefore these characters will occupy $58*8 = 464$ bytes of our character matrix.

If we put the character matrix base location at 7168 there will be just $7680 - 7168 = 512$ bytes of RAM for the character matrix, remember the screen starts at 7680. We have already used 464 bytes so there are just $512 - 464 = 48$ bytes left for our own graphics characters. This gives just 6 characters for us to design, enough for many purposes, which we can assign to screen codes 58 to 63. We have to promise ourselves not to POKE any number greater than 63 to a screen memory address, or to issue a PRINT command for a character whose screen code is greater than 63, for otherwise we should send the operating system to the screen memory, or no memory (> 8191), to collect character matrix data! We can lower the top of memory to 7168 to protect our baby character matrix, with POKE 56,28 : POKE 52,28 : CLR, and have the area between 4096 and 7168, i.e. 3K, for the BASIC program.

Alternatively we can put the base of the character matrix at 6144 giving 7680−6144 = 1536 bytes for the character matrix. Using 464 bytes for standard characters this gives 1536−464 = 1072 bytes, enough for 134 of our own characters which we can assign screen codes 58 to 191; we avoid screen codes greater than 191 in our program. However, the top of memory must now be lowered to 6144, i.e. page 24, with POKE 56,24 : POKE 52,24 : CLR, giving just 6144−4096 = 2048 bytes, i.e. 2K, for the BASIC program − which is not much. However, not many programs are likely to need 134 idiosyncratic graphics characters.

A useful number between 6 and 134 would be 22, since we could then plot the graph of many single-valued functions across the entire VIC screen in single pixel dots (moving the 22 character cells vertically up and down as required by the function). We could do this provided the slope of the function plotted had absolute value between −1 and +1 at all points. However, because we have only limited control over the start address of the character matrix, any compromise between 6 and 134 user-defined characters is not possible.

Example

In this example we adopt the first of the two possibilities mentioned above and put the start of the character matrix at 7168. We define our 6 user graphics characters to be upside-down copies of 0, 1 ..., 5 corresponding to screen codes 58 to 63.

```
10 REM 6 8*8 USER DEFINED CHARS AND 3K FOR PROGRAM
20 POKE36869,255:REM CM TO 7168
30 POKE56,28:POKE52,28:CLR:REM LOWER MEMTOP
40 PRINT"J"
50 REM NOW COPY FIRST 58 CHARS FROM ROM TO RAM
60 FORI=0TO57*8+7
70 POKE7168+I,PEEK(32768+I)
80 NEXT
90 REM NEXT COPY FIRST 6 NUMBER CHARS UPSIDE DOWN
100 Z=58*8:W=48*8
110 FORJ=0TO5
120 FORI=0TO7
130 POKE7168+Z+8*J+I,PEEK(32768+W+8*J+7-I)
140 NEXT:NEXT
150 REM NOW DISPLAY ALL 64 CHARS ON SCREEN WITH POKE
160 FORI=0TO63
170 POKE7680+I,I:POKE38400+I,2
180 NEXT
190 REM NOW DISPLAY OWN CHARS WITH PRINT
200 PRINT"    "
210 PRINT":;<=>?"
220 GETA$:IFA$=""THEN220
230 POKE36869,240:PRINT"J":END
```

For more interesting characters than upside-down numerals the procedure is first to design them, i.e. specify the decimal number for each row, as in Table 4.1. Having designed the characters, the decimal numbers can be listed in DATA statements and then POKEd into the correct locations in the character matrix.

The use of user-defined characters becomes more exciting if they are displayed in Multicolor mode.

4.3 Multicolor mode

In Multicolor mode it becomes possible to have four colors within a single character cell as opposed to two. There is a price to be paid, in that horizontal resolution is now in pairs of pixel dots rather than single pixel dots.

Let us first design a character:

Row	Decimal value	Bit							
		7	6	5	4	3	2	1	0
0	0	0	0	0	0	0	0	0	0
1	60	0	0	1	1	1	1	0	0
2	125	0	1	1	1	1	1	0	1
3	60	0	0	1	1	1	1	0	0
4	60	0	0	1	1	1	1	0	0
5	130	1	0	0	0	0	0	1	0
6	40	0	0	1	0	1	0	0	0
7	0	0	0	0	0	0	0	0	0

Each pair of pixel dots now becomes a single long dot whose color is defined as follows:

Bit pattern	Color	Value	Determined by
0 0	Background	BC	Bits 4–7 of 36879
0 1	Exterior border	EC	Bits 0–2 of 36879
1 0	Foreground	FC	Associated color nybble
1 1	Auxiliary	AC	Bits 4–7 of 36878

To display a character in Multicolor mode add 8 to the associated color nybble. When displaying characters with a POKE to the screen this is no problem since we can just OR the associated foreground color code with 8 when we POKE the color nybble into the color matrix. There is a neat way to set PRINT to Multicolor mode. This is to use the address 646 which contains the active color nybble. Thus

POKE 646,6OR8 : PRINT "A" : POKE 646,6

will result in a blue A being printed in Multicolor mode.

Note that one can only change the foreground color of a Multicolor character without changing the color of all Multicolor characters on the screen.

The values BC, EC, FC and AC are selected from Table 4.3.

Table 4.3 – Color codes.

Value	Background (BC) Auxiliary (AC)	Exterior border (EC) Foreground (FC)
0	Black	Black
1	White	White
2	Red	Red
3	Cyan	Cyan
4	Magenta	Magenta
5	Green	Green
6	Blue	Blue
7	Yellow	Yellow
8	Orange	
9	Light orange	
10	Pink	Not applicable
11	Light cyan	
12	Light magenta	
13	Light green	
14	Light blue	
15	Light yellow	

To set background and exterior border colors and leave bit 3 of 36879 unchanged:

POKE 36879, (16 * BC)OR EC OR(PEEK(36879)AND 8)

To set the auxiliary color, whilst leaving the volume of any sound unchanged:

POKE 36878, (16 * AC)OR(PEEK(36878)AND15)

Example
Taking the character we designed earlier let us choose the following colors

```
0   0  Background   = Pink   : BC =  10
0   1  Exterior     = Blue   : EC =   6
1   0  Foreground   = Red    : FC =   2
1   1  Auxiliary    = Orange : AC =   8
```

```
10 REM**GRAPHICS DEMO**
20 REM 6 8*8 USER DEFINED CHARS AND 3K FOR PROGRAM
30 POKE36869,255:REM CM TO 7168
40 POKE56,28:POKE52,28:CLR:REM LOWER MEMTOP
50 PRINT"J"
60 REM NOW COPY FIRST 58 CHARS FROM ROM TO RAM
70 FORI=0TO57*8+7
80 POKE7168+I,PEEK(32768+I)
90 NEXT
100 REM NEXT COPY CHAR FROM DATA GIVE SCREEN CODE 58
110 DATA0,60,125,60,60,130,40,0
120 FORI=1TO7
130 READX
140 POKE7168+58*8+I,X
150 NEXT
160 REM NOW DISPLAY ALL 59 CHARS ON SCREEN WITH POKE
170 FORI=0TO58
180 POKE7680+I,I:POKE38400+I,2
190 NEXT
200 REM NEXT SET COLS
210 POKE36879,(16*10)OR6OR(PEEK(36879)AND8):REM BC AND EC
220 POKE36878,(16*8)OR(PEEK(36878)AND15):REM AC
230 REM NOW DISPLAY CHAR 58 IN MULTICOL USING POKE
240 POKE7680+60,58:POKE38400+60,2OR8:REM FC
250 REM NOW DISPLAY CHAR 58 IN MULTICOL USING PRINT
260 PRINT"XXXXXX"
270 POKE646,2OR8:PRINT":":POKE646,6
280 GETA$:IFA$=""THEN280
290 POKE36869,240:POKE36879,27:POKE36878,0
300 REM RESTORE
310 END
```

4.4 Hi-resolution graphics in 8 X 8 mode

In Hi-resolution graphics the object is to have a fixed area on the screen within which every pixel dot may be addressed independently. This area is usually chosen to be as large as possible.

With user-defined graphics the characters are initially written into the character matrix and subsequently moved about the screen as if they were normal characters. After the character matrix is generated it is normally left severely alone [although of course if you had a machine code routine to make a 'little man' character appear to be running ...].

With Hi-resolution graphics exactly the reverse procedure is employed. The *position* of each character on the screen is left fixed; this is known as *bit-mapping* the screen. Pixel dots are then moved about the screen by directly addressing the corresponding bit in the character matrix. Hence in Hi-resolution graphics it is the contents of the character matrix memory which varies.

To bit-map the screen we POKE the character with screen code N into the N*th* character cell with the routine

```
1000 REM BIT – MAP SCREEN
1010 PRINT CHR$(147)
1020 FOR I = 0 TO 255
1030 POKE 7680 + I, I
1040 POKE 38400 + I,6 : REM PIXEL DOT COLOR BLUE
1050 NEXT
```

Table 4.4 shows at a glance that, with 256 available screen codes, just over half the VIC screen can be bit-mapped. In fact we can bit-map the first 11 rows and have 14 characters to spare. With 8 × 8 character cells this will require 8 *256 = 2048 bytes, i.e. 2K, will fill half the screen, and will leave just 1176 bytes for user BASIC because the character matrix must start at 5120. There is nothing to be done about the wasted RAM from 7168 to 7680 because user BASIC demands an unbroken block of memory.

Having bit-mapped the screen the next problem is: given the screen coordinates of a pixel dot how can we set the corresponding bit in the character matrix to 1 and thereby plot the dot on the screen?

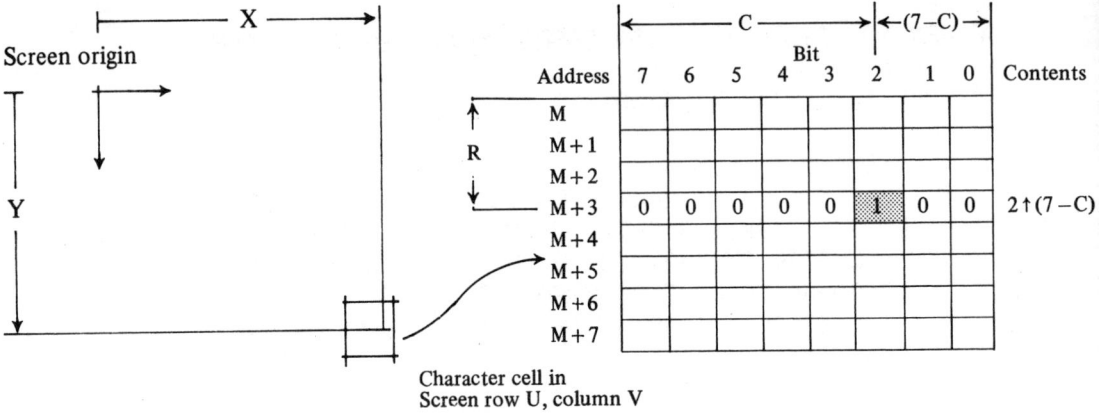

Character cell in
Screen row U, column V

X,Y – pixel dot coordinates   U,V character cell row, column
$0 \leqslant X \leqslant 22 * 8 - 1 = 175$,   R,C pixel dot row, column
$0 \leqslant Y \leqslant 11 * 8 - 1 = 87$ within character cell.

U = INT $(Y/8)$: V = INT $(X/8)$
CM = character matrix start address
M = CM + $(22 * U + V)*8$: ADDRESS OF FIRST BYTE OF CHAR IN CHAR MATRIX
R = Y AND 7 : REM REMAINDER AFTER DIVISION BY 8
C = Y AND 7 : REM REMAINDER AFTER DIVISION BY 8
Address of byte is M + R

To set the correct bit of this byte without disturbing any other bit

$$\text{POKE } M + R, (2\uparrow(7-C)) \text{ OR PEEK}(M + R)$$

Figure 4.1 – Which bit is the pixel dot?

The solution to this problem is summarized in Figure 4.1; $2\uparrow(7-C)$ has been used for clarity, in practice one would create an array of the first 8 powers of 2 and use it as a look up table to speed the PLOTSUB. Both bit-mapping and individual pixel-dot addressing are used in the next example which can be run on a VIC with no additional RAM.

Table 4.4 — Bit-mapping the VIC screen.

Row (U) \ Column (V)	0	1	2	3	4	5	6	7	8	9	10	11	12	13	14	15	16	17	18	19	20	21
0	0	1	2	3	4	5	6	7	8	9	10	11	12	13	14	15	16	17	18	19	20	21
1	22	23	24	25	26	27	28	29	30	31	32	33	34	35	36	37	38	39	40	41	42	43
2	44	45	46	47	48	49	50	51	52	53	54	55	56	57	58	59	60	61	62	63	64	65
3	66	67	68	69	70	71	72	73	74	75	76	77	78	79	80	81	82	83	84	85	86	87
4	88	89	90	91	92	93	94	95	96	97	98	99	100	101	102	103	104	105	106	107	108	109
5	110	111	112	113	114	115	116	117	118	119	120	121	122	123	124	125	126	127	128	129	130	131
6	132	133	134	135	136	137	138	139	140	141	142	143	144	145	146	147	148	149	150	151	152	153
7	154	155	156	157	158	159	160	161	162	163	164	165	166	167	168	169	170	171	172	173	174	175
8	176	177	178	179	180	181	182	183	184	185	186	187	188	189	190	191	192	193	194	195	196	197
9	198	199	200	201	202	203	204	205	206	207	208	209	210	211	212	213	214	215	216	217	218	219
10	220	221	222	223	224	225	226	227	228	229	230	231	232	233	234	235	236	237	238	239	240	241
11	242	243	244	245	246	247	248	249	250	251	252	253	254	255								
12																						
13																						
14																						
15																						
16																						
17																						
18																						
19																						
20																						
21																						
22																						

Example
Plot a sine curve using 8 × 8 Hi-resolution graphics.
This example could be used as the basis of a simple graph-plotting program.

```
10 REM**SINE CURVES**
20 POKE36869,253:REM CM TO 5120
30 POKE56,20:POKE52,20:CLR:REM LOWER MEMTOP
40 GOSUB1000:REM BITMAP
50 GOSUB2000:REM CLR CM
60 REM NOW PLOT SINE CURVE
70 FORX=0TO175
80 Y=43-INT(42*SIN(8*π*X/176))
90 GOSUB3000:REM ERROR CHECK
100 GOSUB4000:REM PLOTSUB
110 NEXT
120 GETA$:IFA$=""THEN120
130 POKE36869,240:POKE56,30:POKE52,30:CLR:PRINT"J":END
1000 REM*BIT-MAP SCREEN*
1010 PRINTCHR$(147)
1020 FORI=0TO241:REM 11 ROWS
1030 POKE7680+I,I
1040 POKE38400+I,6:REM PIXEL DOT COLOUR BLUE
1050 NEXT:RETURN
2000 REM*CLR CM*
2010 FORI=0TO241*8+7
2020 POKE5120+I,0
2030 NEXT:RETURN
3000 REM*CHECK X,Y IN RANGE*
3010 IFX<0ORX>175THEN3040
3020 IFY<0ORY>87THEN3040
3030 RETURN
3040 POKE36869,240:PRINT"J"
3050 PRINT"ERROR"X,Y:END
4000 REM*PLOTSUB*
4010 U=INT(Y/8):V=INT(X/8)
4020 M=5120+(22*U+V)*8
4030 R=YAND7:C=XAND7
4040 POKEM+R,(2↑(7-C))ORPEEK(M+R)
4050 RETURN
```

4.5 Hi-resolution graphics in 16 × 8 mode

In the following example exactly the same principles used in the previous program are applied to obtain a full screen Hi-resolution curve plot. The first 10 rows are bit-mapped, but bit 0 of 36867 is set to 1 so that 16 × 8 character cell format is used. Control register 36867 is also adjusted so that the number of (double height) rows displayed is 10. The character matrix is relocated to 4096 and contains 16 * 220 = 3520 bytes, because each of the 220 character cells now uses 16 bytes. Plainly, a 3K RAM pack will be needed.

The important part of the character matrix ends at 7616 and we have used 220 screen codes in the bit-mapping. Between 7616 and 7680 (the screen) there are just 64 bytes, enough for four characters in 16 X 8 mode, these could be assigned screen codes 220 to 224.

Note the changes in the PLOTSUB. The characters are 16 pixel dot rows high so R = Y AND 7 is replaced by R = Y AND 15 (the remainder after Y is divided by 16), also an array C%( ) has been created to avoid executing $2 \uparrow (7-C)$ every time PLOTSUB is called. The function $X \uparrow Y$ is rather slow and the gain in speed is quite noticeable.

Parametric plotting is illustrated by the final graph, that of an equiangular spiral, a curve which has several remarkable properties and was first examined by Descartes in 1638.

Example

Plot curves using 16 X 8 Hi-resolution graphics.

```
10 REM 16*8HI-RES CURVE PLOT
20 REM 22 COLUMNS 10 ROWS
30 PRINT"JTHIS PROGRAM NEEDS A      3K RAM PACK":PRINT
40 PRINT" HIT    RETURN TO END "
50 FORL=0TO600:NEXT:REM DELAY
60 PRINT"J"
70 POKE36869,252:REM CM TO4096
80 POKE56,16:POKE52,16:CLR:REM LOWER MEMTOP
90 POKE36867,149:REM 16*8 AND 10ROWS
100 POKE36879,126:REM COLOUR
110 GOSUB540:REM CLEAR CM
120 FORI=0TO7
130 C%(I)=2↑(7-I)
140 NEXT
150 REM**BIT-MAP SCREEN
160 FORS=0TO219:REM 10 ROWS
170 POKE7680+S,S
180 POKE38400+S,0:REM PIXEL DOT COLOUR BLACK
190 NEXTS
200 REM**AXES**
210 X0=87:Y0=80:GOSUB580
220 REM**DRAW 3 SINE CURVES**
230 FORK=0TO2
240 D=175*K/80
250 FORX=0TO175
260 Y=80-INT(75*SIN(8*π*X/175-D))
270 GOSUB640
280 NEXTX
290 NEXTK
300 GETA$:IFA$=CHR$(13)THEN510
310 GOSUB540
320 POKE36879,238:REM COLOUR
330 REM**AXES**
340 X0=0:Y0=80:GOSUB580
```

Listing continues next page

```
350 REM**DRAW DAMPED SINE CURVE**
360 FORX=0TO175
370 Y=80-INT(90*EXP(-X/40)*SIN(8*π*X/175))
380 GOSUB640:NEXTX
390 GETA$:IFA$=CHR$(13)THEN510
400 GOSUB540
410 POKE36879,233
420 REM**AXES**
430 X0=87:Y0=80:GOSUB580
440 REM**DRAW SPIRAL**
450 FORA=0TO10*πSTEPπ/60
460 X=87+INT(80*EXP(-A/10)*COS(A+π/2))
470 Y=80-INT(80*EXP(-A/10)*SIN(A+π/2))
480 GOSUB640:NEXT
490 GETA$:IFA$=""THEN490
500 IFA$=CHR$(13)THEN510
510 PRINT"⊐":POKE56,30:POKE52,30:CLR
520 POKE36867,174:POKE36869,240:POKE36879,27:END
530 REM**CLEAR CM**
540 FORI=0TO3523:POKE4096+I,0:NEXT
550 RETURN
560 REM**DRAW AXES**
570 REM*ORIGIN X0,Y0*
580 FORX=0TO175:Y=Y0
590 GOSUB640:NEXT
600 FORY=0TO159:X=X0
610 GOSUB640:NEXT
620 RETURN
630 REM**PLOTSUB**
640 U=INT(Y/16):V=INT(X/8)
650 S=22*U+V
660 IFS>219THEN700
670 R=YAND15:C=XAND7
680 M=4096+16*S
690 POKEM+R,C%(C)ORPEEK(M+R)
700 RETURN
710 REM X=0TO175
720 REM Y=159TO0
```

Having plotted a picture or curve into the character matrix the next step is to save the entire character matrix to tape or disk. Machine code programs for this procedure are given in later chapters. Having saved the character matrix, the final step is to run another program which loads the character matrix back into its original location and then outputs it in Hi-resolution graphics to the VIC printer. A listing of this final program is given in Appendix 2; it requires a machine code subroutine for LOAD (again given later) and takes about 15 minutes to output a Hi-resolution screen. The results for the three graphs plotted in the last example are given in Figure 4.2.

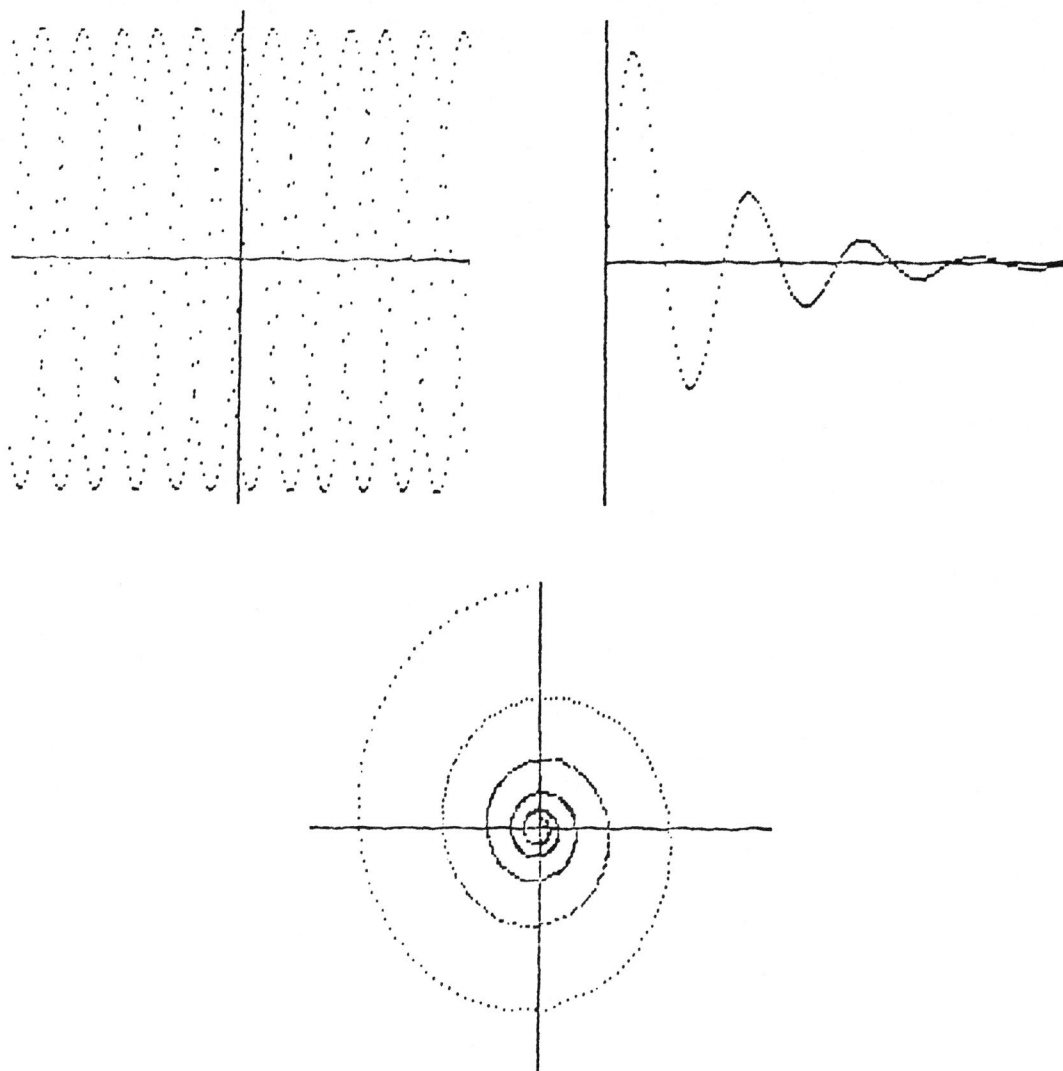

Figure 4.2 – Hi-resolution output to printer.

5

Peripheral devices

5.1 Device numbers

In this chapter we look at the way the VIC-20 operating system organizes the flow of information to and from external input/output devices, usually termed peripheral devices, such as cassette, disk drive and printer.

There are three different types of peripheral device' those that input data to the operating system ('talk'), those that receive data ('listen') and those that do both.

All input/output communication is controlled by the operating system by means of the two VIA 6522 chips (see Chapters 6 and 7). Each device, including the screen and keyboard, is assigned a unique *device number* (a *primary* or *first* address), which serves to identify it. Device numbers take values in the range 0 to 255. The present allocation of device numbers is given in Table 5.1. The operating system stores the device number of the device currently being accessed in address 186.

Table 5.1 − Device numbers.

Device	Device number	Functions
Keyboard	0	Talk
Cassette unit	1	Talk and Listen
RS232 device	2	−
Screen	3	Listen
Printer (Serial IEEE) {	4	Listen
or {	5	Listen
Other Serial IEEE {	6	−
devices {	7	−
Disk drive (Serial IEEE)	8	Talk and Listen
Other Serial IEEE {	9	−
devices {	to 255	−

5.2 The keyboard

From the first appearance of the flashing cursor after the VIC-20 is switched on, the operating system scans the matrix of keyboard switches every 1/60 second. This is part of the periodic service routine triggered by an 1RQ interrupt generated by one of the VIA 6522s. When a key is pressed, a number derived from the key's position in the keyboard matrix is stored in address 197. The contents of 197 are used as a pointer to the address in a keyboard character table where the ASCII code corresponding to the key pressed is stored. The final ASCII code is then transferred to a 10-byte keyboard buffer at addresses 631 to 640. For a key pressed in conjunction with SHIFT, CBM, SHIFT + CBM or CTRL, alternate tables are consulted for the ASCII codes.

Distinct from all other keys are RUN/STOP and RESTORE. If RUN/STOP is pressed the number 254 ($FE) is placed in address 145($91). When RESTORE is pressed in conjunction with RUN/STOP a system reset or warm start is initiated.

When a new character code is stored in the keyboard buffer the buffer counter, contained in address 198, is incremented by 1. This directs the next keyboard input to the next available buffer location.

Character codes are extracted from the keyboard buffer one at a time, in the order in which they are stored, by the screen handling routines. As each character is removed, the keyboard buffer counter is decremented by 1 and the buffer closed up. In practice character codes are removed from the keyboard buffer as they are stored, unless a program is running. If a program is running, character codes are queued in the keyboard buffer until the program performs a GET or INPUT from the keyboard. If no GET statements are executed any characters input during program execution will be displayed on the screen upon a return to direct mode. If the keyboard buffer is full, further keypresses are lost. The contents of address 649, normally 10, are used to determine the maximum number of characters permitted in the keyboard buffer. If this number is changed to a value greater than 10 the keyboard and screen handling routines tend to get confused, but it is sometimes useful to use a smaller value.

Address 650 holds the keyboard repeat flag which is normally 0 for cursor control repeats only. The following two commands are sometimes useful

POKE 650,64   Disables all repeats.
POKE 650,128   Enables all keys to repeat.

The following program prints the keyboard matrix number and the ASCII code of the last key pressed.

```
10 PRINT"⌂"
20 GETA$:IFA$=""THEN20
30 PRINT"MATRIX NO="PEEK(197)
40 PRINT"SHIFT FLAG="PEEK(653)
50 PRINT"ASCII CODE="ASC(A$)
60 PRINT"CHAR="A$
70 PRINT:GOTO20
```

In normal use it is unnecessary to specify a device number for the keyboard and the screen as the contents of addresses 153 (current input device) and 154 (current output device) are automatically set to 0 (keyboard) and 3 (screen) respectively. Normally the operating system will change the contents of these addresses as required. However, it is possible, if you are *very* cunning, to manipulate the choice of input and output device directly. In this context see the article 'Magic Merge', *VIC Computing*, by Jim Butterfield (patron saint of PET and VIC users). Here he gives a sequence of commands, one of which changes the contents of 153 from 0 to 1, which loads *as a program* a previously saved ASCII data file listing of the program! The procedure whereby such a strange data file is created is explained in connection with CMD in section 5.6.

5.3 Logical files and secondary addresses

The command OPEN prepares a VIA 6522 input/output channel (logical file). The full syntax of OPEN is

OPEN Logical file no, Device no, secondary address, "FILENAME"

The concept of a *logical file* is rather subtle, it is a quite separate thing from the actual physical record referred to as "FILENAME". A logical file is best viewed as a channel through which information or instructions[†] can be sent and information received by the operating system. Every such channel should be OPENed to a specific device and many channels may be open simultaneously. To distinguish between them each is given a unique number, chosen by the programmer, in the range 1 to 255. The number is known as a logical file number. Up to 10 logical files may be open at any one time with at most 5 of these open to Serial IEEE devices. The logical file number in current use is stored by the operating system at location 184.

A *secondary address* determines the manner in which the selected device will behave. Table 5.2 lists the most frequently used secondary adresses. The secondary address in current use is stored by the operating system at location 185.

Table 5.2 – Secondary addresses.

Peripheral	Secondary address	Function
Cassette unit {	0	Read file to tape
	1	Write file to tape
	2	Write file to tape with 'end of tape' marker
Printer {	0(?)	Set character set to UPPER CASE/GRAPHICS
	7	Set character set to UPPER CASE/LOWER CASE
Disk drive	15	Access the command channel

We shall see how to use the command OPEN in conjunction with the cassette unit, disk drive and printer in the following sections. The way that input/output operations are controlled by the user may at first seem complicated. We can picture the organization more easily if we imagine the VIA chips as banks of railway points controlled by a skilled signalman, the operating system, under the command of the railway manager, you!

5.4 The VIC C2N cassette unit

The VIC-20 operating system communicates with the cassette unit via four lines connected to the VIA 6522s: Read, Write, Sense and Motor. A separate power supply of +5 volts and Ground are also used.

---

†See section 5.7.

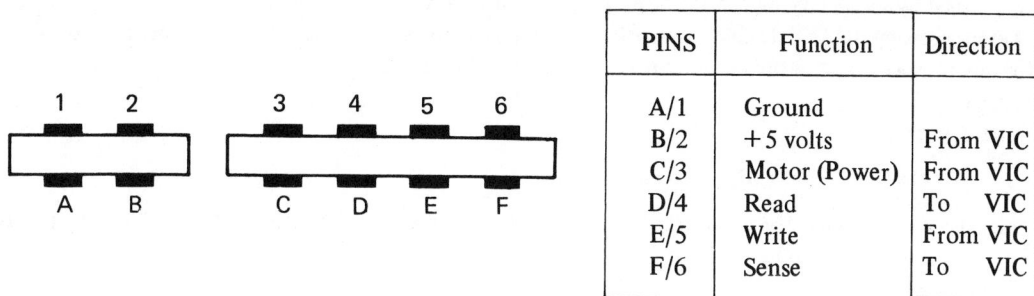

PINS	Function	Direction
A/1	Ground	
B/2	+5 volts	From VIC
C/3	Motor (Power)	From VIC
D/4	Read	To VIC
E/5	Write	From VIC
F/6	Sense	To VIC

Figure 5.1 – Cassette unit connections.

Figure 5.1 gives the VIC-20 PCB edge connections for the cassette unit. The separate power lines through pins A and B are not used by the cassette motor, but are instead used to supply signal amplification and pulse shaping circuitry within the cassette. The Motor line supplies +9 volts at 500 mA to the cassette motor. The Sense line is used to detect that PLAY has been pressed, often in response to the screen prompt PRESS PLAY ON TAPE or PRESS RECORD AND PLAY ON TAPE. It is worth remarking that the pressing of FAST FORWARD or REWIND are also sensed as a depression of PLAY. Similarly, if when attempting to SAVE to cassette PLAY is pressed but not RECORD, the operating system cannot sense that RECORD has not been pressed and will continue a fruitless effort to write to tape until RUN/STOP is pressed.

The cassette unit is allocated a 192-byte buffer at addresses 828 to 1019, through which all data to be written to or read from tape normally passes. The contents of 178 and 179 point to the start address of the cassette buffer. When writing to tape the operating system waits until the buffer is full before turning on the cassette motor, thus tape files are saved in 192 byte blocks.

5.5 File handling to cassette

It is possible to write two kinds of file to the cassette: program files (PRG) and data files (SEQ). This terminology can be confusing since data may be stored as a program (PRG) file, and programs can be stored as a data (SEQ) file, although they very rarely are.

Program files (PRG) are normally SAVEd as a RAM dump from the bottom of user BASIC to the end of the BASIC program in RAM. A program file (PRG) is therefore normally a copy of the bytes which describe the compressed text of a user BASIC program. However, if the PRG file were created by a machine code routine which saved a specified block of RAM to tape, as in HI–DRAW of Appendix 1, then the PRG file could represent any data, not necessarily a BASIC program. *Data files* (SEQ), often called ASCII files, are sequential files created by the programmer using a combination of BASIC commands such as OPEN, PRINT# etc.

We first discuss the creation of program files. The command

SAVE "FILENAME"

saves the current BASIC program to tape. The SAVE command places a pointer to the start address of the RAM to be SAVEd in locations 172 and 173. For an unexpanded VIC-20 the numbers 1 and 4 would be placed in 172 and 173 respectively, since these are the Lo and Hi bytes of the start address of user BASIC (see Chapter 3). Similarly SAVE places the Lo and Hi bytes of the address at which the program ends in 174 and 175 respectively.

The file is saved to tape with a 192-byte PRG header consisting of a file name of up to 16 characters (bytes) plus 4 bytes specifying the Lo-byte, Hi-byte RAM pointers stored in 172 to 174.

Upon pressing RECORD and then PLAY the operating system first takes 10 seconds to run the motor up to speed and write a synchronizing leader, it then writes the header block followed by the RAM save.

The command

LOAD "FILENAME"

searches the cassette tape for a file header containing the specified filename, and upon locating it loads the file into RAM from the bottom of memory upwards.[†]

The command

VERIFY "FILENAME"

operates in a similar manner to LOAD except that when the file is found its contents are compared with the BASIC program currently stored (as compressed text) in RAM. This provides a positive check on the accuracy of the SAVE.

A PRG file can be loaded back into the RAM from which it was originally saved by the command

LOAD "FILENAME",1,1

Here the first 1 is the device number (cassette) whereas the 'secondary address', consisting of the second 1, tells the operating system to pay attention to the 4 bytes of RAM pointers in the file header block. This is particularly useful when loading a previously saved machine code program from BASIC.

In order to create a *data file* (SEQ) on tape, the command

OPEN 1, 1, 1, "FILENAME"

can be used. This opens logical file 1 to device 1 (cassette) with secondary address 1 (write) as discussed in sections 5.1 and 5.4.

The file handing commands INPUT#, GET#, PRINT# or CMD, which take a logical file number as a parameter, are used to get information from or pass information to a previously OPENed logical file. Thus the usual format to write a data file (SEQ) to cassette is

OPEN 1, 1, 1, or 2, "FILENAME"
PRINT# 1, N or A$
CLOSE 1

where N or A$ is the variable or string to be entered on the file. The data file is written to tape with a 192-byte SEQ header block similar to the PRG header created by SAVE. For a data file the Lo-byte, Hi-byte RAM pointers refer to the beginning and end of the cassette buffer, rather than to a block of RAM saved.

Items are separated on a data file by two *delimiters,* a comma or a carriage return. The command

PRINT# 1,N

where N is a numeric variable, will automatically write a carriage return following the variable N.

The effect of using commas or semicolons is just as if PRINTing to the screen. If commas are used as in PRINT#1, A$, B$, C$ then extra spaces will appear, a semicolon will leave no space. The command

PRINT#1, A$; CHR$(13); N; CHR$(13); B$

---

†Wherever that happens to be.

will result in each data item being written to tape separated by a carriage return.

The usual format to read a data file from tape is

```
OPEN     1, 1, 0, "FILENAME"
GET#     1, N or A$
or INPUT# 1, N or A$
CLOSE 1
```

The command GET# reads one character at a time from the file; it is similar to GET which obtains one character at a time from the keyboard. GET# reads characters, file delimiters, such as commas or carriage returns, and anything else on the tape. This can be particularly useful to access data on a byte by byte basis. Thus

```
10 GET# 1, A$ : IF A$ = " " THEN 10
20 X = ASC(A$)
```

will read one byte from tape, screening out null characters, and give the numerical value as X

The INPUT# statement will read numeric or string variables. Thus

```
INPUT# 1, N,M
```

will attempt to read the next two data items as numbers. As with INPUT, problems will arise if the data is a string and not a number. When reading strings each INPUT# will read all string variables up to the next carriage return delimiter. Therefore, you can only use commas to separate string variables that will always be read back as a group, as in

```
INPUT# 1, A$, B$, C$
```

When the write operations are concluded the file must be CLOSEd. This will ensure that the contents of the cassette buffer, whether or not the buffer is full, will be written to tape followed by an end-of-file marker (64), or an end of tape marker (−128) if the file was OPENed with a secondary address of 2.

Example

The following program illustrates the procedures for creating, reading and, if required, outputting a data file to the VIC 1515 printer. If the printer is not required lines 250,260, 370,380 and 400 to 530 can be omitted.

```
10 REM**DATA  FILES**
20 REM**ON  TAPE **
30 PRINT"J"
40 PRINTTAB(5)"****MENU****":PRINT:PRINT
50 PRINT"CREATE DATA FILE    )C)"
60 PRINT"READ EXISTING FILE  )R)"
70 PRINT"TO QUIT PROGRAM     )Q)"
80 GETA$:IFA$=""THEN80
90 IFA$="C"THEN120
100 IFA$="R"THEN280
```

Listing continues next page

```
110 IFA$="Q"THENEND
120 REM**CREATE FILE**
130 PRINT"......WRITING FILE":PRINT
140 PRINT"INPUT     TO END":PRINT
150 INPUT"FILE NAME";B$
160 REM**WRITE**
170 OPEN1,1,1,B$
180 PRINT"   INPUT LINES OF TEXT..."
190 INPUTA$
200 IFA$="@"THEN230
210 PRINT#1,A$
220 GOTO190
230 PRINT"*****FILE  CLOSE*****"
240 PRINT#1,"END":CLOSE1
250 INPUT"PRINTER(Y/N)";C$
260 IFC$="Y"THEN400
270 GOTO30
280 REM**READ EXISTING FILE**
290 PRINT"   FILE READ..."
300 INPUT"FILE NAME";B$
310 PRINT"  READING "+B$
320 OPEN1,1,0,B$
330 INPUT#1,A$
340 PRINTTAB(3)A$
350 IFST=0THEN330
360 CLOSE1
370 INPUT"PRINTER(Y/N)";C$
380 IFC$="Y"THEN400
390 GOTO30
400 REM**OUTPUT TO PRINTER**
410 PRINT"  PLEASE REWIND TAPE -    THEN HIT ANY KEY."
420 GETZZ$:IFZZ$=""THEN420
430 OPEN1,1,0,B$
440 OPEN4,4
450 PRINT#4,CHR$(14)
460 PRINT#4,CHR$(16)CHR$(51)CHR$(50)B$
470 PRINT#4,CHR$(15)
480 INPUT#1,A$
490 ZZ=ST
500 PRINT#4,CHR$(16)CHR$(48)CHR$(53)A$
510 IFZZ=0THEN480
520 CLOSE1:CLOSE4
530 GOTO30
```

Note the use of the error status byte ST in lines 350 and 490. This serves either to detect the end-of-file marker or to ensure automatic closure of the file if a read error is detected.

The command

      CMD Logical file no.

used in conjunction with the OPEN statement, changes the current output device from the screen to the specified device. Thus

      OPEN 3, 4 : CMD 3

will direct output to the printer, and

      OPEN 3, 4 : CMD 3 : LIST

will output an untokenized ASCII listing of a BASIC program in RAM to the printer. To reset the output device back to the screen the format

      PRINT# 3 : CLOSE 3

can be used.

Similarly

      OPEN 1,1,1, "PROGNAME"
      CMD 1 : LIST

writes an ASCII data file (SEQ), consisting of an untokenized BASIC program, to tape under the file name PROGNAME. Note that the READY, normally printed on the screen after execution of LIST, will also be written to tape. The output device can be reset to the screen by

      PRINT# 1 : CLOSE 1

Of course it is not possible to simply load such a data file, as if it were a program file, using LOAD. All this could succeed in doing would be to dump an ASCII listing in completely untokenized form into the area reserved for a tokenized BASIC PROGRAM. The Interpreter (see Chapter 7) would not like that at all!

5.6 Error checking and ST

Regardless of which type of file is to be stored the method of storing an individual byte is the same. Each character is stored on tape using 10 bits: 8 bits for the data-byte, a parity bit used in error checking, and a special 'word marker' pulse to separate one data-byte from the next. The parity bit is computed prior to writing the data-byte and indicates whether the number of '1's is odd or even. A '1' is encoded as a long pulse followed by a short pulse and a '0' as a short pulse followed by a long pulse.

A program (PRG) file is saved in one continuous block and then saved again. This results in an effective data rate transfer of around 300 bits per second.

When the tape file is read back the parity bit of each byte is recomputed. If the byte is bad an error count is incremented and the location where the error occurred is stored. The operating system then picks the best data from each pass. In the event of there being more errors than the system can handle an *unrecoverable read error* is indicated by an ST value of 16 and a LOAD ERROR message is generated.

Data (SEQ) files differ from program (PRG) files in that the user can terminate the write to tape at any time. Hence the entire file cannot be saved twice as is a PRG file. Instead each block of 191 bytes is recorded twice, together with a checksum for each block. If on reading the file back the recomputed checksum differs from the recorded checksum a *checksum error* is indicated by an ST value of 32.

A value of ST is returned after every input/output operation and stored in address 144. Table 5.3 gives the meaning of the various CBM ST codes.

Table 5.3 – ST values for I/O devices.

Bit position	ST value	Cassette read	Cassette LOAD/VERIFY	Serial IEEE devices Read/Write
0	1	–	–	Time out write
1	2	–	–	Time out read
2	4	Short block	Short block	–
3	8	Long block	Long block	–
4	16	Unrec. read error	Any mismatch	–
5	32	Checksum error	Checksum error	–
6	64	End of file	–	EOI
7	−128	End of tape	End of tape	Device not present

Because of the elaborate error checking procedures used for tape encoding the VIC C2N cassette unit is very reliable, but to ensure consistently accurate read/write operation the read/write and erase heads should be periodically cleaned using a cotton tipped stick slightly moistened with a proprietary brand of head-cleaning fluid. Particles of tape can adhere to the heads and dramatically affect the efficiency of the unit. The unit itself, and cassette tapes, should be kept away from strong magnetic fields. Read/write errors appear to be more frequent if the cassette unit is less than 2 feet from the television.

5.7 The VIC 1540 floppy disk drive

The addition of the VIC 1540 5¼-inch floppy disk drive dramatically increases the power and flexibility of the VIC-20 system. Program and data files can be accessed directly and files can be written to or read from disk far faster than with the cassette unit. Both the VIC 1515 printer and the disk drive communicate with the microprocessor via the serial IEEE-488 interface (see Chapter 7). Up to five serial IEEE devices may be 'daisychained' in this way.

A disk drive can also be used to create Random Access files, in which a specified part of a file can be processed without having to needlessly access the preceding data. Such files are not possible on cassette since tape data access is sequential. Random Access files use advanced disk handling commands not covered in this section but an example of random access file handling is given on the TEST/DEMO disk supplied with the floppy disk drive.

Unlike many microcomputer disk drives the VIC 1540 is an intelligent peripheral controlled by its own 6502 microprocessor, two 6522 chips, 2K of RAM and 8K of ROM. The ROM contains the Disk Operating System (DOS) which performs all disk management routines. This enables many powerful new commands and error messages to be accessed directly from BASIC without using large amounts of precious VIC-20 RAM. In what follows it is assumed that the reader is familiar with the file handling procedures outlined in sections 5.3 and 5.5 in connection with the cassette unit.

Storage of data on a diskette is in *blocks* of 254 bytes, an additional 2 bytes are used to point to the next linked block (if any). A data (SEQ) or program (PRG) file therefore consists of a sequence of linked blocks.

Physically the blocks are distributed within *tracks* and *sectors*. There are 35 tracks each consisting of an area of diskette between two concentric circles (an annulus). A sector is an arc of a track which, in addition to one data block with its two-byte pointer, also contains information relating to timing, self-identification and checksums.

To determine which block is where, in terms of track and sector, is the job of the DOS. To perform this task the DOS creates a Block Availability Map (BAM) and a disk *Directory*. The BAM consists of 144 bytes, contained in track 18, sector 0, recording which blocks are in use and which are free to accept data. The Directory, which begins on track 18, sector 1, is a list of data or program files which have already been stored on the disk. Both the BAM and the directory are continually updated as disk write operations are performed. When a data or program file is named for loading into the VIC-20, the DOS looks up the track and sector of the first block and begins loading linked blocks.

A useful feature of Commodore DOS is that the disk directory may be loaded into the microcomputer as a BASIC program. Of course as a *program* the directory is meaningless and will not RUN, but as a list of all files on the disk the directory is invaluable. The directory is loaded by entering the command

LOAD " $ ", 8

When LOADed the directory can be LISTed in the same manner as a BASIC program.

A BASIC program file listed in the directory can be loaded by first RETURNing NEW, to delete the directory as a program in RAM, and then entering the command

LOAD " FILENAME ", 8

A PRG file, essentially a RAM save, can be loaded back into the memory locations from which it was originally SAVEd by

LOAD " FILENAME ", 8,1

This is especially useful when loading machine code programs from BASIC.

The first step in preparing a new disk, which can be any good quality soft-sectored, 5¼ inch diskette, is to *format* it. Until it is formatted a disk has no BAM, no directory and no timing workers. Formatting is accomplished by the commands

OPEN 15,8,15
PRINT# 15, "N : DISKTITLE, DI"
CLOSE 15

IMPORTANT NOTE. If a previously used disk is reformatted all data contained on the disk is lost.

Here 'N' (New) is the *disk maintenance command* and DI is a two-character disk identifier assigned by the user. It is good practice to arrange that no two of your disks have the same identifier; otherwise a change of disk may go unnoticed by DOS, which will probably cause a mess, including loss of data. Formatting takes about 85 seconds.

On the front panel of the VIC 1540 disk drive there are two LEDs. The green LED merely indicates whether the unit is on or off. The red LED is more useful:

Red on	:	reading or writing to disk
Red off	:	awaiting command
Red flashing	:	DOS has detected an error

If the red LED is flashing at the end of formatting it is possible that the disk is faulty. Occasionally more than one attempt to format is necessary but a suspect disk can be tested using the CHECK DISK program on the TEST/DEMO disk. However, be warned that CHECK DISK takes about 3 hours to run!

The DOS error channel may be read with the following BASIC program.

```
10  REM ERROR CHECK
20  OPEN 15,8,15
30  INPUT# 15, EN, EM$, ET, ES
40  PRINT CHR$(147)
50  PRINT "ERROR NO" EN
60  PRINT EM$
70  PRINT "TRACK" ET
80  PRINT "SECTOR" ES
90  CLOSE 15: END
```

A list of Error codes and their meanings is contained in the VIC 1540 User's Manual. Upon execution of this program the red LED should go out as the error status is returned to normal automatically following a read of the error channel.

In this program, and in the previously given command sequence, the secondary address of '15' in OPEN 15,8,15 has special significance for the disk drive. Here '15' refers to the *command channel* on which information supplied by the DOS may be read after every I/O operation, and through which the user transmits disk maintenance commands such as 'N'.

It is good programming practice to include the error checking routine after every BASIC read or write to disk. There is one slight problem in that CLOSEing the command channel will also close *all* other logical files OPENed to the disk drive! Hence

IMPORTANT NOTE: The command channel should be OPENed early in a disk handling program and CLOSEd after the last disk read or write.

The maximum length of a disk maintenance command string is 40 characters. The syntax of the disk maintenance commands is

New	OPEN 15,8,15, "N: DISKTITLE, DI"
	or
	OPEN 15,8,15
	PRINT#15, "N: DISKTITLE,DI"
Initialize	OPEN 15,8,15, "I"
	or
	OPEN 15,8,15
	PRINT#15, "I"
Validate	OPEN 15,8,15, "V"
	or
	OPEN 15,8,15
	PRINT#15, "V"
Rename	OPEN 15,8,15, "R: NEWNAME 1, FILENAME 2, ..."
	or
	OPEN 15,8,15
	PRINT#15, "R: NEWNAME = OLDNAME"

Scratch   OPEN 15,8,15, "S: FILENAME 1, FILENAME 2, . . ."
or
OPEN 15.8.15
PRINT#15, "S: FILENAME1, FILENAME2, . . ."

Copy (i) To make multiple copies of the same file on the same disk

OPEN 15,8,15
PRINT#15, "C : DUPFILENAME = ORIGFILENAME"

(ii) To concatenate SEQ files on the same disk into a single SEQ file, also on the same disk

OPEN 15,8,15
PRINT#15, "C : CONFILENAME = FIRSTNAME, SECONDNAME, . . ."

Ideally every disk should be *Initialized* when inserted into the disk drive, this is certainly the case if it is intended to write to disk. Initialization ensures that the BAM held in the disk drive RAM corresponds to the BAM recorded on the disk. Failure to initialize can result in a DISK ID MISMATCH ERROR and/or loss data. However, it is *not* necessary for the user to initialize disks if every disk used has a distinct two-character disk identifier.

Validate is a powerful disk maintenance command which in common with *Scratch* should be used with extreme care. Execution of Validate causes the DOS to trace through each block contained in all files on the disk. If this trace is successful a new BAM is written on the disk. Any blocks which have been allocated by more advanced commands (such as BLOCK-ALLOCATE) and which are not associated with an explicit directory entry will be freed for use. In addition to constructing a new BAM, Validate also deletes files on the directory which were not properly closed after they were written. If the block trace is unsuccessful a Validate error will be generated and the disk left in its original state.

Rename changes the directory listing of the specified file and *Scratch* removes the specified files from the disk.

The final disk maintenance command *Copy*, when used on the VIC 1540 single disk drive, can make multiple copies of the same file or concatenate SEQ data files.

In addition to the disk maintenance commands the familiar BASIC commands LOAD, SAVE and VERIFY are used with device number 8 to handle BASIC programs on disk, as in

VERIFY "FILENAME", 8

The logical file handling commands OPEN, CLOSE, PRINT#, INPUT#, and GET# are used, as with the cassette unit, to read and write data for a SEQ data file.

Example
The use of INPUT# is illustrated on the following program which can be used to create and read an SEQ file on disk. If required the program will also output the file to the VIC 1515 printer.

It should be noted that the maximum length of a character string which can be read by INPUT# is 88, moreover the string should not contain a ',' since this acts as a delimiter. The program determines the end of the file by use of the status bit ST and includes the DOS error checking routine in lines 670 to 720.

```
10 REM**SEQ FILES**
20 PRINT"J"
30 PRINTTAB(5)"****MENU****":PRINT:PRINT
40 PRINT"CREATE SEQ FILE      C"
50 PRINT"READ EXISTING FILE   R"
60 PRINT"TO QUIT PROGRAM      Q"
70 GETA$:IFA$=""THEN70
80 IFA$="C"THEN110
90 IFA$="R"THEN310
100 IFA$="Q"THENEND
110 REM**CREATE FILE**
120 GOSUB610
130 PRINT"....WRITING FILE":PRINT
140 GOSUB670
150 PRINT"INPUT @ TO END":PRINT
160 INPUT"FILE NAME":B$
170 REM**WRITE**
180 OPEN2,8,2,B$+",S,W"
190 GOSUB670
200 PRINT"INPUT LINES OF TEXT..."
210 INPUTA$
220 IFA$="@"THEN260
230 PRINT#2,A$
240 GOSUB670
250 GOTO210
260 PRINT"*****FILE  CLOSED*****"
270 PRINT#2,"END":CLOSE2
280 INPUT"PRINTER(Y/N)":C$
290 IFC$="Y"THEN480
300 CLOSE15:GOTO20
310 REM**READ EXISTING FILE**
320 GOSUB610
330 PRINT"FILE READ..."
340 INPUT"FILE NAME":B$
350 PRINT"READING "+B$
360 OPEN2,8,2,B$+",S,R"
370 GOSUB670
380 INPUT#2,A$
390 ZZ=ST
400 GOSUB670
410 PRINTTAB(3)A$
420 IFZZ=64THEN440
430 GOTO380
440 CLOSE2
450 INPUT"PRINTER(Y/N)";C$
460 IFC$="Y"THEN480
470 CLOSE15:GOTO20
```

Listing continues next page

```
480 REM**OUTPUT TO PRINTER**
490 OPEN2,8,2,R$+",S,R"
500 OPEN3,4
510 PRINT#3,CHR$(14)
520 PRINT#3,CHR$(16)CHR$(51)CHR$(50)R$
530 PRINT#3,CHR$(15)
540 INPUT#2,A$
550 ZZ=ST
560 GOSUB670
570 PRINT#3,CHR$(16)CHR$(48)CHR$(53)A$
580 IFZZ<>64THEN540
590 CLOSE2:CLOSE3:CLOSE15
600 GOTO20
610 REM**CMD CHANNEL/INIT**
620 PRINT"    INSERT FORMATTED DISK-":PRINT
630 PRINTTAB(9)"PRESS"
640 PRINT"  RETURN  TO CONTINUE"
650 GETC$:IFC$=""THEN650
660 OPEN15,8,15,"I":RETURN
670 REM**READ ERROR CHANNEL**
680 INPUT#15,EN,EM$,ET,ES
690 IFEN=0THENRETURN
700 PRINT"J"
710 PRINT"ERROR#"EN:PRINTEM$:PRINT"TRACK"ET:PRINT"SECTOR"ES:PRINT""
720 CLOSE2:CLOSE15:END
```

Finally we should mention the advanced disk handling commands BLOCK-READ/WRITE/EXE-CUTE, BLOCK-ALLOCATE, BLOCK-FREE, BUFFER POINTER, MEM-READ/WRITE/EXECUTE and USER used in Random Access file handling and machine code routines. A detailed explanation of these commands is unfortunately beyond the scope of this book.

The TEST/DEMO disk supplied with the VIC 1540 disk drive contains several useful programs. VIEW BAM provides a display of the BAM showing which tracks and sectors currently contain data, that is have been allocated by DOS. DISPLAY T&S, which as written requires additional RAM to run success-fully, shows the contents of any specified track and sector.

Floppy disks should always be handled with great care: the disk surface should *never* be touched and the disk should always be replaced in its sleeve after removal from the disk drive. The read/write head moves over the disk in contact with the surface, therefore any small particle on the disk surface creates the possibility of a read/write error. The disk drive should not be switched on or off with a disk already in place.

Compared to the other components of the VIC-20 system the disk drive is delicate and should be treated accordingly. It represents an example of precision engineering comparable to a traditional Swiss watch and will not take kindly to rough treatment. On the other hand, if treated well, it will function perfectly for hundreds of hours. The proprietary disk manufacturers supply specially impreg-nated cleaning diskettes which can be used to clean the read/write head after approximately 10 hours' use, although this practice is not approved by the manufacturer.

5.8 The VIC 1515 printer

The VIC 1515 printer is based on the Seikosha GP 80 printer with the addition of a modified printed circuit board containing an INTEL 8041 microprocessor. Contained within the 8041 is 1K ROM and 64 bytes of RAM as a printer buffer. Input to the printer is controlled via the serial IEEE-488 bus described in Chapter 7.

Printing is achieved by the movement of the print head across the paper in exact time with the action of a highly accurate 'hammer' hitting the ink ribbon against the paper. This is carried out under the control of the 8041 microprocessor in accordance with the instructions and data sent to the printer. An electric motor pulls the print head past the paper by means of a wire under tension. On completion of one line a carriage return is achieved by the action of a solenoid turning the platen and allowing the the print head return spring to pull the print head back to the far left start position.

The ribbon cartridge contains a continuous loop of ribbon that is inked, via the action of a roller within the cartridge, as the ribbon is pulled around. The ribbon is moved with the print head by the ribbon cam trapping it against the ribbon feed board during a line print (Figure 5.2).

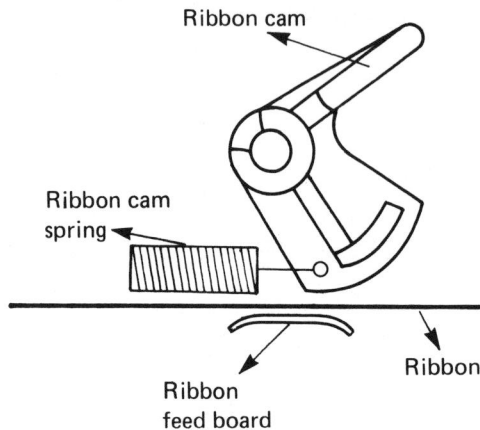

Figure 5.2 – Ribbon feed mechanism.

During a carriage return the operation of the ribbon cam causes the ribbon to slip between the cam and the ribbon feed board, allowing the ribbon to remain in place. The angle of the ribbon feed board in relation to the cam is critical for correct ribbon movement.

When the printer is switched on the print head is moved partway along an empty print line and then returned to the start position as part of the printer initialization procedure.

In normal operation characters are printed by the print hammer as a 7×5 matrix of dots, corresponding to the appropriate CBM ASCII code, as illustrated in Figure 5.2.

A sixth column is addressed by the printer in normal mode but is always empty to provide a space between characters. To enable high resolution printing in 'graphic' mode each column of 7 dots is bit addressable in a maximum 480-column print line. The printer also has the capability to print double-width characters giving a bold 7×10 dot matrix character.

Data is input to the printer and stored in the 64-byte printer buffer until the buffer is full. In normal operation characters are transferred by the 8041 microprocessor to the print head sequentially, one character at a time, in the order stored. In graphic mode the contents of the buffer are printed as a block followed by the return of the print head to the start position to await the next buffer block.

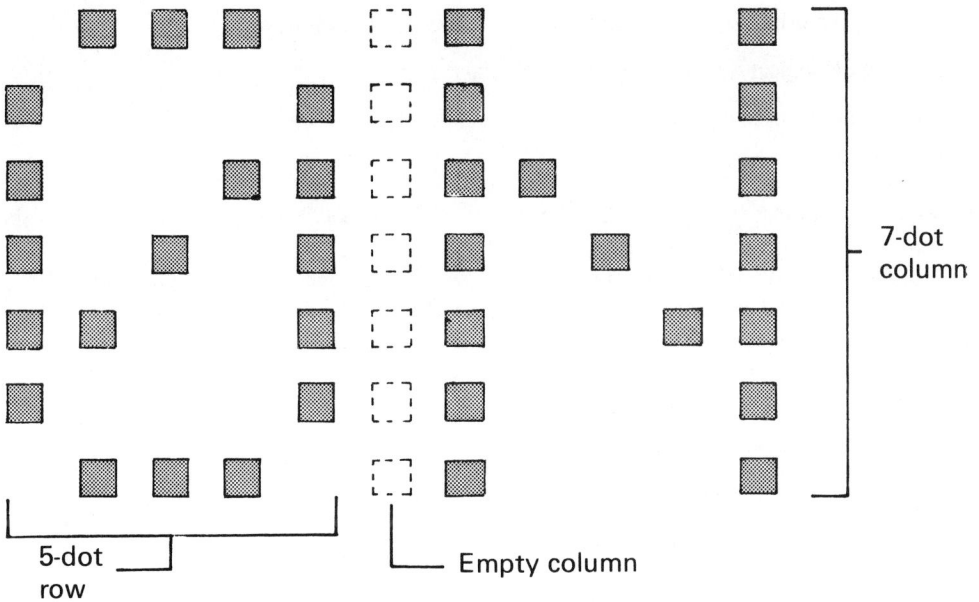

Figure 5.3 – Character construction.

The VIC 1515 printer is fitted with a switch at the rear of its case that enables the user to change the printer device number from a factory set 4 to 5. This allows the use of two VIC 1515 printers on the same serial bus. The switch also has a test position 'T' which, if selected prior to initialization, will print the full printer character set.

As a serial IEEE-488 device the printer is subject to the same general output commands as discussed in relation to the floppy disk drive. In addition, the printer can be commanded by the use of special control CBM ASCII codes as in Table 5.4.

Table 5.4 – CBM ASCII printer control codes.

Control Code	Function
CHR$ (8)	SET GRAPHIC MODE
CHR$ (10)	LINE FEED (do not use)
CHR$ (13)	CARRIAGE RETURN
CHR$ (14)	SET DOUBLE-WIDTH CHARACTERS
CHR$ (15)	SET STANDARD-WIDTH CHARACTERS
CHR$ (16)	SET PRINT START POSITION
CHR$ (26)	SET GRAPHIC DATA REPEAT
CHR$ (27)	SET DOT ADDRESS START POSITION IN GRAPHIC MODE
CHR$(145)	CURSOR UP MODE (UPPER CASE/GRAPHIC)
CHR$ (17)	CURSOR DOWN MODE (LOWER CASE/UPPER CASE)
CHR$ (18)	SET REVERSE FIELD ON
CHR$(146)	SET REVERSE FIELD OFF

(*Note.* A full list of CBM ASCII codes is given in Appendix 3, Table A2.)

To address the printer it is necessary to OPEN a logical file as follows

OPEN logical file no, device no, secondary address

In normal use the format would be

OPEN 4, 4, 0 or 7

where secondary address 0 or 7 set CURSOR UP or CURSOR DOWN modes, respectively. If the secondary address is omitted the command defaults to 0.

CURSOR UP mode selects the character set containing upper case characters and CBM graphics characters. CURSOR DOWN mode selects lower case characters and upper case characters. It is usually unnecessary to specify a secondary address as control codes CHR$(145) and CHR$(17) perform the same function within a program or command sequence.

All instructions to the printer must be preceded by the command

PRINT # logical file number, variable

apart from the command channel initialization instruction

CMD logical file number

which sets the stated logical file as the current normal output channel instead of the screen, as illustrated by the following program. When the program is RUN this exact printout is obtained.

```
PROGRAM PRINTOUT


10 OPEN4,4
20 PRINT#4,"PROGRAM PRINTOUT"
30 CMD4:LIST
40 PRINT#4:CLOSE4

READY.
```

In this example PRINT#4 is used in the same manner as PRINT when displaying characters on the screen. CMD 4 sets the logical file 4 as the current normal output channel and the BASIC command LIST prints the program listing on the printer as opposed to the screen. If CMD 4 is omitted, the printer outputs 'PROGRAM PRINTOUT' alone and the program is LISTed on the screen.

Note. On completion of LIST, control is automatically returned to direct mode, therefore line 40 is never reached. The statement contained in line 40 should be RETURNed in direct mode to restore the command channel and CLOSE logical file 4.

The use of CBM ASCII control codes, in conjunction with PRINT#, enables us to set the parameters for printing. Before we write a BASIC program to print specified characters to the printer we must first define the characters in four ways:

(i) Cursor up (Set 1, UPPER CASE/GRAPHICS) or Cursor down (Set 2, LOWER
   CASE/UPPER CASE) character set.
(ii) Reverse field on or Reverse field off.
(iii) Normal- or double-width character.
(iv) CBM ASCII code for character.

For example, to print the normal width, lower case character 'a' in reverse field we must select the lower case/upper case character set (cursor down), reverse field on and the CBM ASCII code for 'a'. Referring to Table 5.4 and Appendix 3, Table A2 the program would be

```
10  OPEN 4,4
20  PRINT#4, CHR$(17)CHR$(18)CHR$(65)
30  PRINT#4 : CLOSE4
```

which prints the required reverse field character.

On initialization, the printer is set to output normal-width characters. If we change the above program to

```
10  OPEN4,4
20  PRINT#4, CHR$(17)CHR$(18)CHR$(14)CHR$(65)
30  PRINT#4, CHR$(15)
40  PRINT#4 : CLOSE4
```

the double-width reverse field character 'a' is printed. Notice the addition of CHR$(15). This returns the printer to normal-width character output. The CLOSE command has no effect on control code printer modes.

The following program 'LO-DUMP' uses control codes to print an exact copy of the current screen display. It is numbered from 5000 up to enable its use as a GOSUB. The use of the graphics mode control code CHR$(8) in line 5190 is explained in the paragraph describing direct dot addressing.

Example

```
5000 REM**LO-DUMP****
5010 REM*DUMPS EXACT*
5020 REM*COPY SCREEN*
5030 REM*TO PRINTER *
5040 REM*************
5050 SC=4*(PEEK(36866)AND128)+64*(PEEK(36869)AND112):REM FIND SCREEN
5060 IF(PEEK(36869)AND15)=0THENP=145:REM SET1
5070 IF(PEEK(36869)AND15)=2THENP=17:REM SET2
5080 A(0)=2:FORI=1TO3:A(I)=I-1:NEXT
5090 OPEN4,4:CMD4
5100 FORR=0TO22
5110 FORC=0TO21
5120 SK=PEEK(SC+22*R+C):REM SCREEN CODE
5130 I=(SKAND96)/32
5140 CC=A(I)*32+(SKAND127):REM CHR$ CODE
5150 RF=146:IF(SKAND128)=128THENRF=18:REM REVERSE FIELD OFF/ON
5160 C$=CHR$(15)+CHR$(P)+CHR$(RF)+CHR$(CC)
5170 PRINT#4,C$;
5180 NEXTC
5190 PRINT#4,CHR$(8)CHR$(13);:REM NO VERT SPACE BETWEEN ROWS
5200 NEXTR
5210 PRINT#4,CHR$(15)CHR$(145)
5220 PRINT#4:CLOSE4:END
```

Figure 5.4, a picture of a dragon, was printed from a public domain program by PET BENELUX using LO-DUMP.

If character cells are numbered across a line from 0 to 79 the N*th* character cell can be selected by use of the control code CHR$(16). Thus

        10 OPEN 4, 4
        20 PRINT#4, CHR$(16)CHR$(51)CHR$(48) "VIC"
        30 PRINT#4 : CLOSE4

will result in 'VIC' being printed beginning in character cell 30, since 51 is the ASCII code for 3 and 48 the ASCII code for 0. Thus the use of CHR$(16) on the printer is analogous to the ordinary BASIC command SPC( ).

To address an individual pixel dot on a printer line, the printer is first set to *graphic* mode with CHR$(8). The control code CHR$(27) is then used in conjunction with CHR$(16). Following CHR$(8)CHR$(27)CHR$(16) the printer expects to receive two numbers, which together describe the column (0 to 479) in which the dot is to be printed. We may call these numbers HP (Hi-printer byte) and LP (Lo-printer byte). Thus if the dot is to be printed in column 258 we have HP = 1, LP = 2. Plainly HP is either 0 (columns 0 to 255) or 1 (columns 256 to 479).

Having selected the correct column, the required dot or dots are printed by assembling a vertical single column 'character'. This process is illustrated in Figure 5.5.

Figure 5.4 – Dragon.

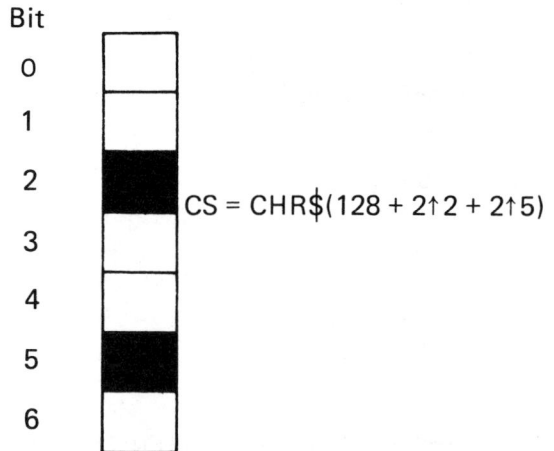

Bit

0
1
2
3
4
5
6

$CS = CHR\$(128 + 2\uparrow2 + 2\uparrow5)$

Figure 5.5 – A vertical byte for the printer.

Example

In this program individual dot addressing on the printer is illustrated by drawing a saw tooth wave, one character cell high, across the whole of one line. The required column is specified by the variable X and the vertical dot coordinate by Y ($0 \leqslant Y \leqslant 6$) measured downwards. As Y is computed the program displays the current value on the screen.

```
10 REM****PRINTER****
20 REM*DOT ADDRESSING*
30 OPEN4,4:CMD4
40 FORX=0TO479
50 HP=INT(X/256):LP=X-256*HP
60 A=INT(X/13):B=X-13*A:Y=INT(B/2):PRINTY
70 C$=CHR$(128+2↑Y)
80 IFB=12THENC$=CHR$(255)
90 PRINT#4,CHR$(8)CHR$(27)CHR$(16)CHR$(HP)CHR$(LP)C$;
100 NEXT
110 PRINT#4,CHR$(15)
120 PRINT#4:CLOSE4
```

Finally it should be mentioned that the printer will occasionally hang during a LIST. This can occur if either the disk drive or the printer is turned on *before* the VIC-20, or if a disk error has occurred before the LIST command is RETURNed. We have found no way to overcome this problem short of turning off the entire system and reloading the program. If the program has not yet been SAVEd the printer should be turned off and the disk re-initialized with OPEN15,8,15, "I". Any DEVICE NOT PRESENT ERROR will then be cleared and the program can be SAVEd to disk before powering down and reloading prior to a LIST.

6

Accessories

6.1 Introduction

In the previous chapter we described the principal peripheral devices which can transform the VIC-20 microcomputer into a fully integrated information processing system. In this chapter we shall take a brief look at some of the bewildering array of other accessories which can be added to a VIC-20, where they plug in and what they can do.

One of the striking aspects of the VIC-20 is its many and varied input/output ports. In addition to the cassette port and serial IEEE-488 port discussed in Chapter 5, the VIC-20 is fitted with a Games Port, a Memory Expansion Port and a User Port.

6.2 The games port

The games port is usually used to input data from a switch-based joystick to provide a means of control during graphics-based game programs. The input from a switch joystick is derived from the operation of five switches contained within the joystick. Four switches indicate a direction of movement and a fifth switch can be used for any additional purpose required by the program, usually as a FIRE button. Figure 6.1 shows the switch configurations with their outputs. All five switches are normally open circuit. S0 to S3 are closed when the stick control is pushed in their respective directions. In-between, 45° angles are represented by adjacent switch closures giving a combinational north-east, north-west, south-east or south-west output. Switch closures connect 0 volts to their respective I/O lines, the level of which can be read by PEEKing 37137, for SN SW, SS and F and 37152 for SE.

Before reading the contents of 37137 and 37152 it is first necessary to reset one Data Direction Register (DDR) in each of the two VIA 6522 chips to configure the VIC-20 to accept data from the games port. This can be accomplished by

POKE 37139, 0: POKE37154,127 : REM JOY PORT TO READ

The joystick is now an input device, *not* the keyboard, so these commands should only be used in a program which, having read the joystick, then restores the original configurations with

POKE 37154,255 : POKE37139,128 : REM RESTORE KEYBOARD/DISK†

A more detailed explanation of what is going on here is best left until section 6 which deals with the user port.

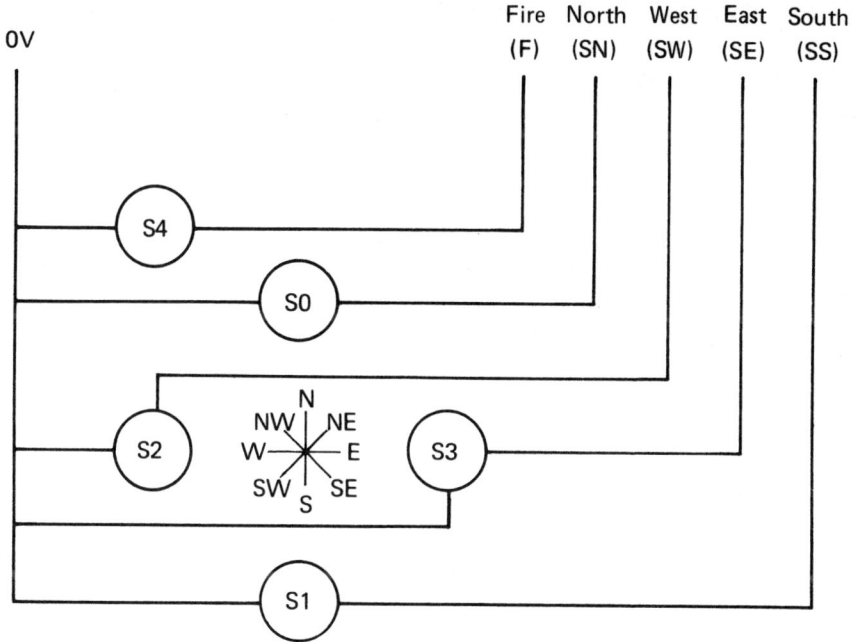

Fig. 6.1 – Switch joystick operation.

Having read the joystick input by PEEKing 37137 and 37152 the data is interpreted as follows

SN closed bit 2 = 0 ⎞
SS closed bit 3 = 0 ⎟ Address 37137
SW closed bit 4 = 0 ⎟
 F closed bit 5 = 0 ⎠
SE closed bit 7 = 0   Address 37152

We can isolate each bit for examination using AND (see Chapter 1, section 1). For example to determine whether SW is 0 (switch closed) or 1 (switch open)

S = PEEK (37137)
SW = (S AND 16)/16

Example
The following program uses a switch joystick to plot character cells of any selected color, across the screen. Use the RETURN key to terminate the program and select the color required using the color keys (but not CNTRL). The Fire button clears the screen.

---

†If the printer is turned on, any attempt to access the disk drive will now cause the system to hang; we frankly admit that this puzzles us. Turn the printer off to correct the situation.

```
10 REM***PICTURES*****
20 REM*JOYSTICK DEMO*
30 REM*USE NUMBERS TO*
40 REM*SELECT COLOUR*
50 REM*RETURN TO END *
100 PRINT""
110 POKE37139,0:POKE37154,127:REM SET JOY PORT TO READ
120 S=PEEK(37137)
130 SN=(SAND4)/4
140 SS=(SAND8)/8
150 SW=(SAND16)/16
160 F=(SAND32)/32
170 S=PEEK(37152)
180 SE=(SAND128)/128
190 POKE37154,255:POKE37139,128:REM RESTORE KEYBOARD/DISK
200 GETA$:IFCHR$(13)=A$THEN330
210 IFA$<>""THENC=VAL(A$)-1
220 IFC>9THENC=9
230 IFC<0THENC=0
240 W=Z
250 IFSW=0THENX=X-1:IFX<0THENX=0
260 IFSE=0THENX=X+1:IFX>21THENX=21
270 IFSN=0THENY=Y-1:IFY<0THENY=0
280 IFSS=0THENY=Y+1:IFY>22THENY=22
290 Z=22*Y+X
300 POKE7680+W,160:POKE38400+W,C:POKE7680+Z,42:POKE38400+Z,0
310 IFF=0THENPRINT""
320 GOTO110
330 PRINT"":END
```

The other popular accessories used in conjunction with the games port are a potentiometer joystick and pairs of game paddles. A potentiometer joystick is read in a quite different way from a switch joystick. As a consequence, programs written for one type of joystick will not work with the other type without some modification.

A potentiometer joystick is essentially two paddles, each consisting of a variable resistance with analogue to digital conversion. Each paddle returns a number in the range 0 to 255 to an address in the VIC chip registers. These values can be read directly without reconfiguring the DDR's of the VIA 6522 chips, thus

> Digitized value of PADDLE X lies in address 36872
> Digitized value of PADDLE Y lies in address 36873.

Unfortunately, to read the Fire button on each paddle it *is* necessary to reconfigure the DDRs:

> POKE 37139,0 : POKE 37154,127 : REM JOY PORT TO READ
> POKE 37154,255 : POKE 37139,128 : REM RESTORE KEYBOARD/DISK

Fire button operation is determined by

> PADDLE X Fire closed bit 4 = 0 Address 37137
>
> PADDLE Y Fire closed bit 7 = 0 Address 37152

These bits can be selected using the AND function as before. Thus

> S = PEEK(37137) : FX = (S AND 16)/16
>
> T = PEEK(37152) : FY = (T AND 128)/128

Another accessory which can be plugged into the game port is a light pen. A light pen consists of a light-sensitive photodiode which when the light pen is pressed against the CRT can detect a raster scan as it passes the point on the screen where the light pen is placed. Light pen data is input to the VIC 6561 chip via the VIAs. The 6561 chip keeps track of the scan position in two registers at

> Address 36870 X coordinate
> Address 36871 Y coordinate

When the light pen trigger input is brought low the VIC freezes the two registers. After the two registers are read by

> PEEK(36870) : PEEK(36871)

the trigger line is cleared so that a new scan input can again be placed in the registers.

Example

The following program uses a light pen to plot a reversed field red space in the character cell pointed to by the light pen. The X and Y coordinates returned by PEEKing 36870 and 36871 are not actually character cell coordinates, so a certain amount of normalizing is necessary to compute the cell coordinates. This is done in lines 30 and 40 of the program which also serves to illustrate the use of user-defined functions. Use of FNA(X), FNB(Y) is optional in this program not obligatory; the coordinates could just as easily be computed more conventionally. The precise numbers 47, 3.95, 38, 3.78 required to normalize the X,Y coordinates will vary from one CRT to another and must be determined by experiment. The program also PRINTs the computed X,Y character cell coordinates and the current contents of 36870 and 36871 in the top left corner of the screen.

```
10 REM*LIGHT PEN DEMO*
20 PRINT"⌂"
30 DEFFNA(X)=INT((PEEK(36870)-47)/3.95)
40 DEFFNB(Y)=INT((PEEK(36871)-38)/3.78)
50 X=FNA(X):Y=FNB(Y)
60 PRINT"⌂"X,Y,PEEK(36870),PEEK(36871)
70 POKE7680+22*Y+X,160:POKE38400+22*Y+X,2
80 GOTO50
```

Our experiments with a light pen were not altogether satisfactory. Accurate discrimination of the correct character cell was difficult owing to noticeable instability at the edge of the VIC-20 screen. Any light pen should be tested using the above program before purchase, to confirm that the degree of precision it offers is adequate for the intended application. If the light pen is to be used to select options for a menu-driven program there should be no difficulty, but other more demanding applications should be approached with caution. Since it is difficult to locate a character cell accurately, it is quite impractical to attempt to use a light pen to draw on a high resolution screen.

6.3 The memory expansion port

When the VIC-20 is first turned on the operating system checks for the presence of additional ROM or RAM as explained in Chapter 3, section 3.3. Additional memory is connected to the VIC-20 through the memory expansion port. Memory maps for the VIC-20 plus any one of the standard 3K, 8K or 16K expansion RAM packs are given in Chapter 3, Figure 3.1. If more than one expansion cartridge is required it is necessary to use a memory expansion board which provides several sockets. Each cartridge is preset to locate in a given part of memory, therefore when using an expansion board it is irrelevant which cartridge is plugged in where.

If 8K, 16K or 8K + 16K cartridges are used, the bottom of the user BASIC program area will be located at 4608. Addressing a further 3K (addresses 1024 to 4095) will *not* alter the 8K + configuration and in these circumstances the 3K block of RAM can only be used for machine code or POKE/PEEK arrays of data, since it lies below the bottom of user BASIC. It is no help to lower the bottom of memory as the video matrix cannot be located below 4096 and must be placed below 8191, see Chapter 3. The various configurations which can arise are given in Table 6.1.

Table 6.1 — Start addresses for different additional RAM configurations.

Additional RAM	MEMBOT	SCREEN START	COLOR START
NONE	4096	7680	38400
3K	1024	7860	38400
8K/16K/(8K + 16K)	4608	4096	37888
3K + 8K/16K/(8K + 16K)	4608	4096	37888

It should be noted that 8K and 16K RAM packs are both normally supplied to locate from 8192 upwards. Therefore if 8K + 16K is required, one of the RAM packs must be adjusted to locate differently. The usual practice is to resolder the links on the 8K RAM pack so that it locates from 24576 upwards (i.e. 'sits above' the 16K). This is a very simple adjustment and can be effected by following the manufacturer's instructions. After this modification the 8K RAM cannot be used as a *stand alone* extension of the user BASIC program area since BASIC demands an unbroken block of memory and there would be a gap in memory from 8192 to 24575. However, an 8K RAM pack modified in this way can always be used for machine code or POKE/PEEK arrays when no other RAM is present.

The memory expansion port can also be used to add facilities like the Super Expander Cartridge, Programmer's Aid and VICMON.

6.4 The Super Expander

The Super Expander Cartridge consists of ROM, which locates in the 8K block starting at 40960 and 3K of RAM which locates from 1024 to 4096. Therefore the Super Expander cannot be used in conjunction with a 3K RAM pack but can be used with a combination of 8K or 16K packs

The Super Expander is used to introduce high resolution graphics, color, and music commands into BASIC. Thus

```
10  GRAPHIC 2
20  COLOR 1,6,0,10
30  POINT 2,900,900
```

will format the screen to the high resolution mode used in the last program of Chapter 4 (160 X 176 pixel dot format), assign various colors as explained in Chapter 4, section 4.3, and plot a black pixel dot in the bottom right-hand corner of the screen.

When switched on with the Super Expander Cartridge in place the bottom of memory will be 1024 and the top of memory is lowered from 7679 to 7544 (so that PEEK(55) = 120, PEEK(56) = 29) giving 135 fewer bytes than a 3K RAM pack. This is because the machine code program in ROM needs some RAM to cope with the extra BASIC commands. Trying to raise the top of memory and claw back the last 135 bytes just throws the VIC-20 into a state of utter confusion, so don't bother.

The commands GRAPHIC 2 or GRAPHIC 3 leave the screen at 7680 and move the character matrix base location to 4096. To protect the character matrix from BASIC the top of memory is lowered by inserting the value 16 into addresses 52 and 56. Thus any program using the Super Expander high resolution modes and no other additional RAM cannot use more space than a unaugmented VIC-20.

Note that when re-entering normal graphic mode with GRAPHIC 0, the pointers at 52 and 56 remain set to 16 so that data in the character matrix continues to be protected.

Despite the fact that pixel dot coordinates are specified in the command POINT as numbers in the range 0 to 1023, the pixel dot format is the usual 160 rows by 176 columns; this can be a little confusing and seems rather unnecessary.

One might expect the character matrix to be used as a continuous block of memory as in the examples of Chapter 4. However, upon setting GRAPHIC 2 and POKEing 255 into all locations from 4096 to 7616 some rather curious gaps appear. Possibly this extra memory is needed to allow for normal characters to appear on a high resolution screen. Plainly, straightforward bit-mapping is not used since the program

```
10  GRAPHIC 2 : SCNCLR
20  FOR I = 0 TO 1023
30  FOR J = 0 TO 1023
40  POINT 2,I,J
50  NEXT : NEXT
```

produces long delays before each new vertical line is drawn.

Although POINT will plot a pixel dot on the screen there is no 'UNPOINT' command to unplot it. It should also be noted that it is impossible to PAINT both sides of a diagonal line without disturbing the line.

Other quibbles with the Super Expander are that SOUND has no sustain, and the notation for storing tunes is rather strange.

To summarize: if you are not bothered about understanding high resolution graphics then use the Super Expander to write some fun programs and as an extra 3K of RAM. If, on the other hand, you have the time and inclination to work through Chapters 4, 7 and 8 then you will be in a position to write your own machine code routines and end up doing it all much better.

6.5 The Programmer's Aid

The Programmer's Aid is just what it says, a great help if you are developing long programs. It consists of ROM which locates in the block 24576 upwards and so should not be used with more than 3K + 16K of additional RAM. To turn the Programmer's Aid on RETURN the command

SYS 28681

The functions RENUMER, FIND, CHANGE etc. then become part of BASIC. The most useful of all the new commands is MERGE which enables programs to be combined from tape or disk.

Once turned on the Programmer's Aid lowers the top of memory by one page, which you can verify with ? PEEK(56), but it does not similarly lower the pointer for strings (? PEEK(52)), which is a little untidy. When turned off with KILL it does *not* restore these pointers to their original values. This is very untidy.

In the page it reserves at the top of memory the Programmer's Aid places machine code routines for the function keys such as LIST, RUN etc. It does *not* clear these on KILL but POKEing the entire page with zeros eliminates these routines and clears the function keys for other use.

The command CHANGE which replaces 'old BASIC code' by 'new BASIC code' throughout a program needs great care in its use. Suppose you wish to replace the variable SC throughout an entire program by the variable SK. Begin with FINDSC. This will cause every line containing SC to be listed on the screen. The symbols SC will be 'found' wherever they appear including REM statements. If you now execute CHANGESC,SK *all* occurrences of SC discovered by FIND will have SC replaced by SK. The advantage in using FIND before CHANGE is that you can see what will be CHANGEd. It is also wise to use FINDSK before CHANGEing SC to SK, just in case you have used SK and forgotten about it. It is not possible to CHANGE code which contains a comma, since this will be taken as the delimiter used by the CHANGE instruction; nor is it possible to CHANGE code which contains inverted commas, since these are used by CHANGE in string substitution as in CHANGE "AJJ", "VIC". The command CHANGE will only make one substitution at a time. If SC occurs on the same line twice CHANGE will make two runs through the line and list the results of both passes on the screen. Problems can arise if the 'new code' contains the 'old code' as a subset and such a CHANGE is best avoided.

The screen scrolling routine in the Programmer's Aid is suspect and can produce garbled code. If the program looks odd it is best to LIST it.

Regardless of these various minor snags the fact remains that if you are developing long BASIC programs then you need the Programmer's Aid or similar 'toolkit'.

6.6 The machine code monitor VICMON

If you want to understand the VIC-20 beyond BASIC programming level then VICMON or an equivalent monitor is the single most important accessory you can buy. Like the Programmer's Aid, VICMON locates itself in the 8K block which begins at 24576 ($6000); therefore in theory the two are mutually incompatible.

The function of a machine code monitor is to enable the programmer to assemble, disassemble, save and load machine code programs to tape or disk. In fact VICMON comes equipped with many other helpful functions; for example the ability to single step through a machine code program.

You enter the world of VICMON by RETURNing the command

SYS 6 * 4096 .

Officially you can exit the monitor and return to BASIC by RETURNing

. X

However, VICMON uses lots of zero page locations and although the VIC-20 may initially appear healthy, upon your return the chances are that it is in a thoroughly confused state. To avoid problems of this kind the command .E can be used to enable a virtual zero page in some other part of memory, for example .E 1000 will reserve 256 bytes beginning at $1000. If the VIC is confused after exiting to BASIC SYS 64802 will normalize the situation without losing any machine code program in RAM, although any BASIC program will be lost.

VICMON can also be used to dump memory or disassembled code to the printer. All the machine code program listings in this book were produced by the following method.

(a) *Before* entering the monitor RETURN the command
        OPEN 4,4 : CMD 4

(b) Enter the monitor with
        SYS 6 * 4096

(c) To list a memory dump in hexadecimal, say from $1500 to $15FF, RETURN
        .M 1500 15FF

(d) To list disassembled code in the same range RETURN
        .D 1500 15FF

Like all other machine code monitors VICMON is fussy about spaces; it prints a '?' when you make a syntax error.

The main problem in learning machine code is getting started as there are very few good books for beginners. However, in Chapters 7 and 8 and Appendix 2 we give several simple routines which can be entered and saved using VICMON. These should whet your appetite. Remember that 6502 machine code once learnt, can be used to program any 6502-based microcomputer.

6.7 The user port

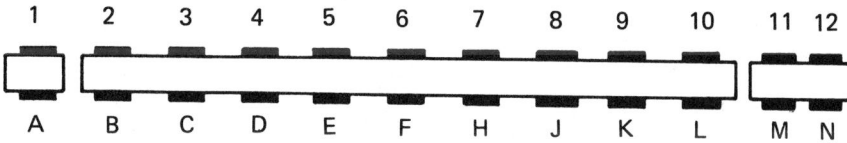

*CB1 & 2 = Control B, VIA1.

Pin	Signal	Function	Pin	Signal	Function
1	0V	Power supply, maximum	A	0V	
2	+5V	current 100 mA	B	CB1*	Sets I/O configuration
3	RESET	Causes cold start when pulled low	C	PB0	
4	JOY 0		D	PB1	
5	JOY 1	Connected to			
6	JOY 2	games port	F	PB3	8 bit data bus to
7	Light pen/JOY 4	6522 VIA Port A			6522 VIA 1, Port B
			H	PB5	
8	Cass. switch	Sense line	J	PB5	
9	Serial ATN in		K	PB6	
10	+9V		L	PB7	
11	0V	Power supply, maximum	M	CB2*	Sets I/O configuration
12	0V	current 100 in A	N	0V	

Figure 6.2 – The user port.

The user port consists of a 24 pin PCB edge connector whose I/O capabilities are controlled by the 6522 chips. Figure 6.2 gives the user port pin configurations together with a table of their functions. Pins 1 and 12 provide connections that enable the I/O facilities of the VIC-20 to be used with a variety of devices. A 24-contact female PCB connector is required for use with the user port and these are available from most specialist electronic suppliers. It should be noted that some of the lines of the user port are used by the games port and this places certain restraints on the simultaneous use of the games port and the user port.

Pins A to N provide an 8-bit data bus and associated control lines suitable for conversion, by the use of appropriate interfacing, to CBM parallel IEEE-488 or serial RS232C standard signals which would be a good trick if someone could make it work! A parallel IEEE-488 interface would enable the VIC-20 to control PET peripherals using similar commands to those given in Chapter 5 relating to the serial IEEE488 bus. The parallel IEEE-488 bus is described in detail in *PET and the IEEE-488 Bus,* Eugene Fisher and C. W. Jensen, Osborne/McGraw-Hill.

The user port can also be used to connect the VIC-20 to an RS-232 device such as a modem or most standard printers (RS-232 is a serial interface communications standard). However, since timing is critical it is not possible to use the disk, printer or cassette when accessing an RS-232 device. Control of the user port lines is achieved by instructions to the two 6522 VIA chips.

Each VIA has two registers and two DDRs (Data Direction Registers). Their addresses are:

		Address	DDR Address
VIA No. 1	PORT A	37136	37138
	PORT B	37137	37139
VIA No. 2	PORT A	37152	37155
	PORT B	37135	37154

Each bit of a single VIA register (or PORT) can be configured for input or output by setting the corresponding bit in its associated DDR (input = 0, output = 1).

Essential timing functions are also performed by the VIA 6522s; for example in generating the $\overline{\text{IRQ}}$ which causes a keyboard scan every 1/60 second.

A detailed analysis of the two VIA 6522 chips can be found in the *VIC Revealed* (Nick Hampshire, Computabits Ltd., 1981) and the MOS Technology *MCS 6522* data sheet. For the user port in relation to an RS-232 device the reader is referred to the article 'VIC communication: the RS–232 interface' by Jim Butterfield and Jim Law in *Compute!,* **4,** 8, August 1982.

7

System architecture

7.1 Introduction

The short history of computers is one of immense and rapid advances in technology. The first computers, built in the late 1940s and early 1950s to perform lengthy scientific computations, were large, slow, expensive and unreliable. It is a sobering thought that nowadays an equivalent machine can be bought on a watch!

Following the invention of the transistor the first integrated circuits appeared in the early 1960s. By the middle 1960s new production processes had substantially increased the amount of circuitry which could be put on a single chip, enabling the first generation of chip based, hand-held calculators to be made available by the end of that decade.

Calculator chips were able to take data from a small keyboard, perform specific arithmetic operations and exhibit the result on an illuminated display. These chips need neither high speed, because human response was involved before each operation, nor large memory, since few numbers needed to be stored. They were also inexpensive when made by the million. However, calculator chips were neither flexible nor extendable, making it difficult for manufacturers to add new functions.

The first true microprocessor to appear was the INTEL 4004, designed as a flexible calculator chip. The INTEL 4004 worked on blocks of 4 bits, using data and a stored program to produce the required results. It was also able to handle different forms of input and output (I/O), enabling a manufacturer to use the same component for many distinct applications. This flexibility is the basis for the now widespread use of microprocessors, although more specialized chips are being continually developed.

The 6502 microprocessor, used as a the basic component of the VIC-20, was introduced in 1976 by MOS Technology Inc.

7.2 VIC-20 architecture

Figure 7.1 is a block diagram of the VIC-20 system showing the operational organization of the principal components, which are:

(i)   The 6502 microprocessor   (CPU)
(ii) The 6561/6560 Video Interface Chip   (VIC)
(iii) Two 6522 Versatile Interface Adapters (VIAs)
(iv) Associated RAM and ROM   (Memory)

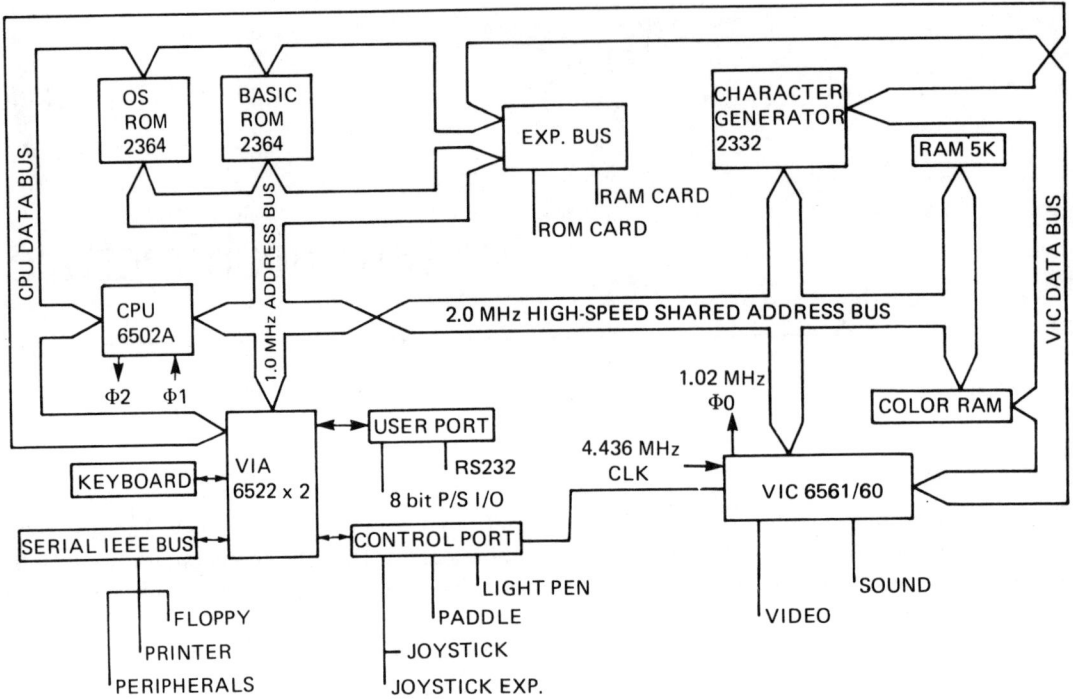

Fig. 7.1 – VIC-20 architecture.

The 6502 is an 8-bit microprocessor, meaning that during each instruction or operation cycle 8 bits of data are operated upon or transferred simultaneously. One complete cycle consists of the following steps: first the instruction is fetched from memory, then the instruction is decoded by the control logic, and finally it is executed. By the time an instruction reaches the 6502 it is already in binary machine code so that 'decoding' in this context is a switching process within the integrated circuit.

The 6561 VIC chip and the two VIA chips provide the VIC-20s means of communicating with the user and peripheral devices. The 6561 controls the video display and sound generation, and in addition can input data from a light pen and a potentiometer joystick. A detailed description of the 6561 control registers is given in Chapter 3. All remaining I/O operations are handled by the two 6522 VIAs and include the keyboard, user port, cassette deck, restore key, and switch joystick. In addition, the 6522 VIAs control the two principal channels for communication with other peripheral devices. These may loosely be described as a serial channel, that is information is transmitted serially bit by bit, and a parallel channel in which information is transmitted in 'parallel' form, 8 bits simultaneously. The serial communications port is known as an RS232 port, a designation which refers to an industrial standard.

The RS232 port can be used, for example, to connect the VIC-20 to a modem. The relevant industrial standard for a parallel communications channel is known as an IEEE-488 port, through which data can be transmitted on 8 lines simultaneously.

There is a possible source of confusion in discussing IEEE implementation on the VIC-20. Unlike PET computers, in which the IEEE standard is implemented, in the VIC-20 a stripped down version of the IEEE is used in which data is, in actuality, transmitted *serially* along a single line. Thus a simplified version of IEEE data transfer is emulated rather than actually performed. From the user's viewpoint this distinction is not apparent, except insofar as data transfer occurs at a slower rate. The VIC-20 uses its serial IEEE port to communicate with the VIC 1540 disk drive and the VIC 1515 printer. If full IEEE implementation is required then an IEEE Expansion Module is rumoured to be available which, for example, would enable the VIC-20 to use PET peripherals.

The other principal component of the VIC-20 is the RAM and ROM which constitutes the system memory.

The term *random access memory* was originally used to describe memory in which the access time is address independent, that is the time taken to read the contents of a randomly selected address is known and constant. Nowadays we tend to take this property of high-speed memory for granted and the phrase has come to mean memory which can be both read from and written to.

The 5K bytes of RAM used in an unexpanded VIC-20 consists of 10 MOS 2114 chips each organized as 1024 4-bit blocks. The access time for these chips is of the order of 300 nanoseconds. As we know 1K byte of this RAM is used by the operating system for working storage (addresses 0 to 1023), 3½K byte for user BASIC (addresses 4096 to 7679), and ½K byte for the video matrix (addresses 7680 to 8191). In addition one further 1024×4 bit chip is used to provide 1K nybble of RAM at addresses 37888 to 38911 as storage for the two possible locations of the color matrix. The color RAM can be accessed directly by the VIC 6561 (in a continuous block if required).

Read only memory, as the name implies, is memory which can only be read from. ROMs come in different forms; the first, which is used to hold the BASIC Interpreter, Kernal routines, and the Character matrix have their contents determined during the manufacture process according to a pattern which the manufacturer creates. This implies that each ROM containing different information is, in effect, a different chip. The second form of ROM, used for example in games cartridges, comes as a blank chip upon which information can be 'burnt in' by a special machine. This type of ROM is called Programmable Read Only Memory (PROM). Whilst the contents of a PROM are normally stable some PROMs are erased by exposure to intense ultraviolet light to give a completely clean chip which can then be reprogrammed, such a PROM is called an EPROM (Erasable PROM). None of these types of ROM lose their contents when power is removed; they are said to be *non-volatile.*

In order to communicate with other components of the VIC-20 system, the 6502 microprocessor must be able to accomplish the following:

(a) Select the required component.
(b) Select the correct part of that component.
(c) Control the direction of the data flow.
(d) Read or Write the data itself.

To keep the number of interconnecting electrical paths within reasonable bounds, all system components are connected to one another by means of three *buses.* These are made up of sets of parallel wires along which information can pass represented as voltages. Since the system is digital only two voltage levels are used: '1' and '0' are represented by +5 volts and 0 volts respectively. The *address bus* consists of 16 lines enabling any one of $2^{16} = 65536$ possible addresses to be accessed. Since the contents of any address consists of 8 bits the *data bus* consists of 8 bi-directional data lines.

The third bus is the *control bus* which consists of signal lines to control the direction and timing of data transfer between the processors and memory or peripheral devices. The important lines on this bus are as follows.

Read/Write (R/$\overline{W}$)

This line controls the direction of data transfer. When the R/$\overline{W}$ line is high (+5V), all data transfers will take place from memory to the processor, a read operation. If the R/$\overline{W}$ line is low (0V), then the processor will write data out of memory. It is conventional to indicate that an operation is implemented when the corresponding control line is low by putting a bar over its symbol; thus R/$\overline{W}$ indicates that a write occurs when the R/$\overline{W}$ line is low.

Reset ($\overline{RST}$)

When this control line goes low the 6502 and all system components are reset to their initial configuration, that is a restart.

Non-maskable interrupt ($\overline{NMI}$)

This line is used to interrupt the normal execution of a program and jump to another pre-arranged program. As the name implies there is no machine code instruction which can be used to prevent this automatic response to a non-maskable interrupt. The reset line takes priority over a nonmaskable interrupt.

Interrupt request ($\overline{IRQ}$)

This is much the same as the non-maskable interrupt, except that the machine code instruction SEI (*Set interrupt disable*) can be used to prevent any response to the $\overline{IRQ}$ line going low, that is an $\overline{IRQ}$ can be *masked*. Normal response to an $\overline{IRQ}$ is resumed upon execution of the instruction CLI (*Clear interrupt disable*). The non-maskable interrupt line takes priority over the interrupt request line.

7.3 Interrupts and their applications

To examine the uses of interrupts we should at least be aware that the 6502 microprocessor has 6 registers, whose functions will be briefly described in Chapter 8, they are:

1. An 8-bit accumulator   (A)
2. An 8-bit X index register.   (X)
3. An 8-bit Y index register.   (Y)
4. A 16-bit program counter. (PC)
5. An 8-bit stack pointer.   (SP)
6. An 8-bit status register.   (P)

The most fundamental of these registers is the program counter since it contains the address where the next instruction to be executed can be found.

The 6502 checks the current status of the interrupt system at the end of each instruction cycle Interrupts allow the microprocessor to respond to unpredictable events, such as power failure or peripherals being ready to send or accept data, very much more rapidly than would be the case if every possible source were periodically checked. Interrupts are also used to force execution of periodic service routines, such as checking the keyboard every 1/60 second.

When an interrupt occurs and, in the case of an $\overline{\text{IRQ}}$ interrupt, is not disabled the response of the 6502 is as follows. Firstly, the Program Counter and the Status Register are saved on the stack. Next the 6502 sets the interrupt disable flag (bit 2 of the Status Register), thereby masking further $\overline{\text{IRQ}}$ interrupts for the time being. Finally, the microprocessor fetches an address from a specified pair of memory locations, puts that address on the Program Counter and proceeds to execute the program indicated.

Apart from the two kinds of interrupt already mentioned there is a third, a software interrupt, which is performed upon execution of the machine code instruction BRK (Force break).

The locations at which the 6502 finds the address to be placed on the Program Counter are given below:

Interrupt	Address found at	Address (ROM)
$\overline{\text{NMI}}$	$FFFA $FFFB	$FEA9
$\overline{\text{IRQ}}$	$FFFE $FFFF	$FF72
BRK	$FFFE $FFFF	$FF72

What happens next is both important and useful to the programmer. We look first at the program which begins at $FEA9 and is executed if an $\overline{\text{NMI}}$ interrupt occurs. It is very simple and says: SEI (Set Interrupt disable), then proceed to execute the program whose address is stored in $0318 and $0319. The point to grasp is that $0318 and $0319 are RAM locations and *therefore their contents can be changed by the user*. Locations $0318 and $0319 are called $\overline{\text{NMI}}$ *RAM vector locations* because their contents, the actual vectors, point to the address which contains the next instruction to be executed.

Interrupt	Vector location (address)	Normal vector
$\overline{\text{NMI}}$	$0318 $0319	$FEAD
$\overline{\text{IRQ}}$	$0314 $0315	$EABF
BRK	$0316 $0317	$FED2

If an $\overline{\text{IRQ}}$ or BRK interrupt occurs then program execution first jumps to $FF72. The program which begins at $FF72 is a little longer than the equivalent program for an $\overline{\text{NMI}}$ interrupt. In the case of an $\overline{\text{IRQ}}$ or BRK we want to be able to resume execution of the program which was running before the interrupt occurred, regardless of any change which the user may make in the interrupt routine. Hence the program at $FF72 first saves the Accumulator, X Index Register and Y Index Register on the stack, since these were *not* saved by the 6502 when the interrupt occurred. Next the program determines whether the interrupt was caused by an $\overline{\text{IRQ}}$ or a BRK. It does this by examining the Status Register which the 6502 saved to the stack when the interrupt first occurred. If the interrupt is an $\overline{\text{IRQ}}$ then program execution jumps to the address stored in $0314 and $0315. If the interrupt is a BRK, execution jumps to the address stored in $0316 and $0317.

Why all the jumping about? Why not, for example, proceed straight to $FEAD in the event of an $\overline{\text{NMI}}$? The answer lies in the RAM vector. If the entire interrupt routine were in ROM the user would have no control over the program initiated by an interrupt. As it is, the provision of vectors in RAM allows the user to substitute his own interrupt routines. This is an extremely powerful programming technique but, inevitably, one which requires great care in its implementation.

A *system wedge* is a machine code program inserted into the normal system firmware which either modifies or monitors the system operation. There are two types of system wedge which can be readily implemented on the VIC-20: an *interrupt wedge* and a *CHARGET wedge*. An interrupt wedge operates by changing the corresponding RAM vector, to point to a routine defined by the user. The routine CHARGET (or GETCHAR or CHRGET) is the operating system routine which during normal program (or direct mode) execution reads the next keyword taken from the BASIC input buffer prior to translation into machine code. On power up this routine is written into RAM, at addresses $0073 to $008A. By altering CHARGET it is possible to create a system wedge which, for example, can introduce a new command into BASIC. An example of a CHARGET wedge is given in the *VIC Revealed* (Nick Hampshire, Computabits Ltd., 1981) and we shall not pursue the topic here (although there is a brief discussion of CHARGET in Chapter 8).

Three routines are required to create any system wedge.

1.   The wedge must be initialized. For an interrupt wedge this means altering the corresponding RAM vector, for a CHARGET wedge it means inserting a jump address into the CHARGET routine which points to the user-provided machine code.

2.   The wedge code itself. This code performs the function which amends or replaces the system function into which it is inserted. Normally if an interrupt wedge is used the wedge code will be terminated with a jump to the service routine which would have been executed had the RAM vector not been changed. Thus for an $\overline{\text{IRQ}}$ interrupt the wedge code would normally end with JMP $EABF.

3.   When the wedge code is no longer required it must be disabled by returning the RAM vectors to normal or restoring the original CHARGET routine.

Before giving an example of an interrupt wedge we must first explain that the 6502 microprocessor has four special instructions designed to manipulate its interrupt system, these are:

SEI (Set interrupt disable). This sets bit 2 of the Status Register and thus disables the maskable interrupt.
CLI (Clear interrupt disable). This clears bit 2 of the Status Register and thus enables the maskable interrupt.
BRK (Force break) sets the Break command flag, bit 4 of the Status Register, saves the Program Counter and the Status Register on the stack, disables the maskable interrupt, and places the contents of addresses $FFFE and $FFFF in the Program Counter.
RTI (Return from interrupt). The original values are returned to the Program Counter and the Status Register (including the interrupt bit). Note RTI differs from RTS (Return from subroutine) in that RTI restores the Status Register whereas RTS does not, moreover RTI does *not* add 1 to the return address as does RTS.

Example
The following program is a simple example of an $\overline{\text{IRQ}}$ wedge. It displays a single character (0 to 9) 10-second counter in the top left corner of the screen. The program uses locations $1CF0 and $1CF1 to store a cycle counter, so if run in conjunction with a BASIC program the top of memory should be lowered below $1CF0. After the wedge has been initialized by SYS7424 the 10-second counter will run continuously, in conjunction with whatever else the VIC-20 happens to be doing.[†] until the wedge is disbled by SYS7488. The program is given in Assembler which can be entered and saved using VIC-MON.

[†] Of course if 'whatever else the VIC-20 happens to be doing' resets the $\overline{\text{IRQ}}$ RAM vector the wedge will require re initialization.

10-SECOND COUNTER

```
·,  1D00 SEI              SET INTERRUPT DISABLE                          ↑
·,  1D01 LDA #$17    ⎫    Reset IRQ RAM vector Lo-byte
·,  1D03 STA $0314  ⎬
·,  1D06 LDA #$1D    ⎫    Reset IRQ RAM vector Hi-byte
·,  1D08 STA $0315  ⎬
                                                                   INSERT
·,  1D0B LDA #$00    ⎫    Store 0 in cycle counter                WEDGE
·,  1D0D STA $1CF0  ⎬
·,  1D10 LDA #$30    ⎫    Store initial screen character
·,  1D12 STA $1CF1  ⎬
·,  1D15 CLI              CLEAR INTERRUPT DISABLE
·,  1D16 RTS              Return to stack (back to BASIC)                ↓
```

```
      ·,  1D17 INC $1CF0         Increment cycle counter                ↑
      ·,  1D1A LDA $1CF0    ⎫
      ·,  1D1D CMP #$3C     ⎬    Is cycle counter equal to #$3C (dec 60)
No  ·,  1D1F BNE $1D3D    ⎭    (1 second)?
      ·,  1D21 LDA #$00     ⎫    Reset cycle counter to 0
      ·,  1D23 STA $1CF0  ⎬
      ·,  1D26 INC $1CF1         Increment screen character           UPDATE
      ·,  1D29 LDA $1CF1    ⎫    Is screen character greater than       AND
      ·,  1D2C CMP #$3A     ⎬    character '9'?                        PRINT
No. ·,  1D2E BNE $1D32   ⎭                                          COUNTER
      ·,  1D30 LDA #$30         Load accumulator with character '0'
└→·,  1D32 STA $1CF1         Store correct screen character
      ·,  1D35 STA $1E00         Display character on screen
      ·,  1D38 LDA #$00    ⎫    Set color (black)
      ·,  1D3A STA $9600  ⎬
──→·,  1D3D JMP $EABF ────→ CONTINUE WITH NORMAL IRQ ROUTINE             ↓
```

```
·,  1D40 SEI              SET INTERRUPT DISABLE                          ↑
·,  1D41 LDA #$BF    ⎫    Reset IRQ RAM vector Lo-byte
·,  1D43 STA $0314  ⎬
·,  1D46 LDA #$EA    ⎫    Reset IRQ RAM vector Hi-byte             DISABLE
·,  1D48 STA $0315  ⎬                                             WEDGE
·,  1D4B CLI              CLEAR INTERRUPT DISABLE
·,  1D4C RTS              Return to stack (back to BASIC)                ↓
```

```
·,  1D4D BRK
·,  1D4E BRK
·,  1D4F SBC $E5DC        Garbage
·
```

Whilst on the subject of RAM vectors we should mention that, in addition to the interrupt service routines, many other important Kernal routines have their own RAM vectors. Before using these it is often helpful to first disassemble the routine in question, to discover how it works, and then construct your own modifying code. The RAM vector addresses are 788($0314) to 815 ($032F), see Appendix 3, Table A1.

Example
The following program disables RUN/STOP and RUN/STOP + RESTORE. When RUN/STOP is pressed $FE is placed in $91 by the normal keyscan routine. The Kernal subroutine which tests the STOP flag is subsequently called from one of several possible places within the operating system, for example it is the first check made by the controlling loop $C7AE to $C7EA which runs BASIC. The Kernal TESTSTOP subroutine has its own RAM vector at $0328 and $0329. We therefore change this RAM vector to point to a routine which tests if $91 contains $FE, and if so changes the contents to $FF (which is a harmless value) before allowing TESTSTOP to continue.

Note that many input/output service routines use the RAM vectors and then reset them. Thus, for example, using the disk drive will reset the TESTSTOP vector and render this program ineffective until the wedge is reinstated.

TESTSTOP WEDGE

The wedge is inserted with SYS 7424 and disabled with SYS 7450

```
.,  1D00 SEI              SET INTERRUPT DISABLE                                    ↑
.,  1D01 LDA #$0D  ⎫      Reset TESTSTOP RAM vector Lo-byte                        │
.,  1D03 STA $0328 ⎬                                                          INSERT
.,  1D06 LDA #$1D  ⎫      Reset TESTSTOP RAM vector Hi-byte                   WEDGE
.,  1D08 STA $0329 ⎬                                                              │
.,  1D0B CLI              CLEAR INTERRUPT DISABLE                                  │
.,  1D0C RTS              Return to stack (back to BASIC)                          ↓
```
```
.,  1D0D LDA $91         Load flag                                                 ↑
.,  1D0F CMP #$FE  ⎫     Has STOP key been pressed (flag on)?              WEDGE
.,  1D11 BNE $1D17 ⎬                                                              │
.,  1D13 LDA #$FF        Store $FF in $91 (flag off!)                             │
.,  1D15 STA $91                                                                  │
.,  1D17 JMP $F770 → CONTINUE WITH NORMAL TESTSTOP                                ↓
```
```
.,  1D1A SEI             SET INTERRUPT DISABLE                                     ↑
.,  1D1B LDA #$70  ⎫     Reset TESTSTOP RAM vector Lo-byte                        │
.,  1D1D STA $0328 ⎬                                                              │
.,  1D20 LDA #$F7  ⎫     Reset TESTSTOP RAM vector Hi-byte                 DISABLE
.,  1D22 STA $0329 ⎬                                                       WEDGE
.,  1D25 CLI             CLEAR INTERRUPT DISABLE                                   │
.,  1D26 RTS             Return to stack (back to BASIC)                           ↓
```
```
.,  1D27 BRK
.,  1D28 BRK
```

A BASIC loader for this program is given below. When RUN this loader will insert all of the above machine code into the correct memory locations.

```
10 POKE55,0:POKE56,29
20 POKE51,0:POKE52,29:CLR
30 DATA120,169,13,141,40,3,169,29,141,41
40 DATA3,88,96,165,145,201,254,208,4,169
50 DATA255,133,145,76,112,247,120,169,112,141
60 DATA40,3,169,247,141,41,3,88,96,0,0,0
70 CC=0:FORI=7424TO7465
80 READJ:POKEI,J:CC=CC+J:NEXT
90 IFCC=4537THENPRINT"OK"
100 IFCC<>4537THENPRINT"DATA STATEMENT ERROR"
110 END
```

7.4 The Interpreter

The programming language BASIC with which we are familiar is not, as you know, the 'native' language of the 6502 microprocessor, which can only understand 6502 machine code. Therefore, at some stage between entering a BASIC program and RUNing it, the program must be translated into 6502 machine code. Up to this point, when referring to the background processing which goes on continuously in the VIC-20, we have talked vaguely about the 'operating system'. The time has come to reveal that the principal software component of the 'operating system' is in fact a huge machine code program called the BASIC *Interpreter*. To help it in its work the Interpreter has available a large library of other machine code routines, which it can call upon as the need arises. This library is called the *Kernal* and we shall take a look at it in the next section.

In its way the BASIC Interpreter is one of the great achievements of our generation, certainly without the Interpreter, or something conceptually equivalent, microcomputers as we know them could not exist. Imagine having a railway system with 2^{16} stations, that runs itself so that the trains never collide! Representing, as it does, thousands of manhours of work, we can do little more than briefly describe the main functions of the Interpreter. However, if you become conversant with Assembler (a convenient symbolic representation for machine code), with the aid of VICMON you can study the Interpreter yourself. The interpreter lives in ROM between addresses 49152 ($C000) and 57344 ($DFFF).

When computing was in its infancy all programs had to be written as a sequence of 0s and 1s. Plainly this is a very tedious, time-consuming and error-prone process. Even writing programs in Assembly language is open to the same objections. To meet this problem various high level languages were developed. A *high level* language, such as FORTRAN, PASCAL or BASIC, is a programming language which is more closely related to English than to Assembler or machine code.

When, for example, a FORTRAN program has been written for a mainframe computer the entire program must then be translated into machine code, a process known as *compilation*. Compilation is carried out by a huge machine code program called a *compiler* which has to be developed in conjunction with the high level language. Most compilers run a syntax check before beginning any serious translating and it is at this stage that the error messages usually start to appear. From the user's point of view this arrangement is less than satisfactory, mainly because if you make a syntax error in your program you don't get to know about it until the program is compiled: there is a lack of interactive editing at the time of entering the program. From the computer's viewpoint too there are problems, mainly relating to how much RAM is needed. Not only has the computer to store and run the compiler, it also has to hold the high level program whilst creating the machine code equivalent. Typically a mainframe compiler can use several hundred kilobytes of RAM.

The program language BASIC (Beginner's All-purpose Symbolic Instruction Code) was developed at Dartmouth College, New York, in the 1960s as an easy-to-learn and easy-to-use (high level) language. BASIC was designed to be as close to English as could sensibly be expected, at the same time providing the user with a reasonable degree of interactive editing.

The essential difference between an interpreter and a compiler is that an interpreter does not try to translate the entire program in one fell swoop. Instead, when RUN time comes, the interpreter translates the first program statement, executes the correponding machine code and then goes back to fetch the next program statement and so on. The advantage of this technique is that two copies of the program, one in the high level language and one in machine code, need never have to coexist in RAM simultaneously. A disadvantage is that translating each program line before it can be executed is time consuming and often inefficient, since the same line may be translated many times during a complete RUN of the program. Thus RUNing a program with a interpreter might be 100 times slower than RUNing the compiled equivalent. Still, the fact remains that it was the concept of an interpreter which made microcomputers like the VIC-20 possible and, as we know, the idea works very well.

The other principal function of the interpreter is to provide interactive editing of BASIC programs on a line by line basis. When a program is being entered from the keyboard the *Editor*, an associate of the Interpreter, takes control, allowing you to edit any line until the RETURN key is pressed. When this is done the line is translated, not into machine code, but into compressed text, changing all BASIC keywords and logical operators into one-byte tokens as explained in Chapter 3. Next the Interpreter searches memory, in the user BASIC program area, for a program line with the same line number. If such a line is found it is replaced by the new line; if not, the line is inserted in the appropriate place in memory in relation to the other existing lines. The process of text compression is reversed by execution of the command LIST which translates all keyword tokens back into the ASCII codes of the original text and transmits this information to an output device, usually the screen. The reasons for this intermediate phase of storing the program in compressed text, are that it takes up less RAM in this form and secondly, at RUN time, it makes the process of translation into machine code faster.

7.5 The Kernal

The Kernal is located in ROM at the very top of VIC-20 memory, addresses 57344 ($E000) to 65535 ($FFFF). It is made up of a series of machine code routines, which perform a variety of different functions. Many of these routines are in fact subroutines, terminated by RTS and designed so that they can be called upon from a user-written machine code program. The existence of this large library of machine code programs is therefore of enormous value to the programmer. From the viewpoint of the programmer the Kernal is a Jump Table which can be used to call upon the input, output and memory management subroutines normally employed by the operating system. Moreover a program written using Kernal subroutines, whilst being more compact, does not thereby lose portability between Commodore machines, since the jump addresses for Kernal subroutines called by such a program remain the same.

To use a Kernal subroutine you must first make all preliminary steps demanded by that particular subroutine. This may involve passing various parameters to the 6502 registers or first calling other Kernal subroutines.

Example

As a simple illustration we consider the Kernal subroutine PLOT which can read or set the position of the cursor on the screen, If PLOT is called with the carry bit clear (i.e. bit 0 of the 6502 Status Register equal to 0) then the cursor will be moved to the (U,V) position $(0 \leqslant U \leqslant 21, 0 \leqslant V \leqslant 22)$, where U and V are the contents of the Y Index Register and X Index Register respectively. Thus to set the cursor in row 10 column 11 we could use the following program

```
CLC          ;  Clear carry flag
LDX    #$09  ;  Set V coordinate equal to 9
LDY    #$0A  ;  Set U coordinate equal to 10
JSR    $FFF0 ;  Call PLOT
```

Other examples of the use of Kernal subroutines can be found in Appendix 2. Kernal subroutines which involve input or output operations return error codes if problems are encountered. A return from a Kernal subroutine with the carry bit set in the 6502 Status Register indicates that an error was encountered in processing. The Accumulator will contain the error number (value of ST). Good programming practice requires that your program check the error status, before continuing, after an I/O operation.

The specific requirements of any Kernal subroutine must be fully known before any attempt can be made to implement it. These requirements are common to all Commodore computers and very well documented, see for example the *Vic Revealed* (Nick Hampshire, Computabits Ltd. (1981) or the *VIC-20 Programmer's Reference Guide* (A. Finkel *et al.,* Commodore Business Machines Inc. and Howard W. Sams & Co. Inc., 1982), so we shall not repeat them here. The following is a list of user-callable Kernal routines.

```
.,  FF8A  JMP  $FD52      RESTOR   Restore default I/O RAM vector
.,  FF8D  JMP  $FD57      VECTOR   Read/set I/O RAM vectors
.,  FF90  JMP  $FE66      SETMSG   Control Kernal message
.,  FF93  JMP  $FEC0      SECOND   Set secondary address after LISTEN
.,  FF96  JMP  $FECE      TKSA     Send secondary address after TALK
.,  FF99  JMP  $FE73      MEMTOP   Read/set the top of memory
.,  FF9C  JMP  $FE82      MEMBOT   Read/set the bottom of memory
.,  FF9F  JMP  $EB1E      SCNKEY   Scan keyboard
.,  FFA2  JMP  $FE6F      SETTMO   Set time out on serial bus
.,  FFA5  JMP  $EF19      ACPTR    Input byte from serial port
.,  FFA8  JMP  $EEF4      CIOUT    Output byte from serial port
.,  FFAB  JMP  $EEF6      UNTLK    Command serial bus to untalk
.,  FFAE  JMP  $EF04      UNLSN    Command serial bus to unlisten
.,  FFB1  JMP  $EE17      LISTEN   Command devices on the serial bus to listen
.,  FFB4  JMP  $EE14      TALK     Command serial bus device to talk
.,  FFB7  JMP  $FE57      READST   Read I/O status word
.,  FFBA  JMP  $FE50      SETLFS   Set logical first and second address
.,  FFBD  JMP  $FE49      SETNAM   Set file name
.,  FFC0  JMP  ($031A)    OPEN     Open a specified logical file
.,  FFC3  JMP  ($031C)    CLOSE    Close a specified logical file
.,  FFC6  JMP  ($031E)    CHKIN    Open channel for input
.,  FFC9  JMP  ($0320)    CHKOUT   Open channel for output
.,  FFCC  JMP  ($0322)    CLRCHN   Close input and output channels.
```

```
., FFCF JMP ($0324)   CHRIN    Input character from channel
., FFD2 JMP ($0326)   CHROUT   Output character to channel
., FFD5 JMP $F542     LOAD     Load specified RAM from device
., FFD8 JMP $F675     SAVE     Save specified RAM to device
., FFDB JMP $F767     SETTIM   Set real time clock
., FFDE JMP $F760     RDTIM    Read real time clock
., FFE1 JMP ($0328)   STOP     Scan stop key
., FFE4 JMP ($032A)   GETIN    Get character from keyboard buffer
., FFE7 JMP ($032C)   CLALL    Close all channels and files
., FFEA JMP $F734     UDTIM    Increment real time clock
., FFED JMP $E505     SCREEN   Return X,Y organization of screen
., FFF0 JMP $E50A     PLOT     Read/set X,Y cursor position†
., FFF3 JMP $E500     IOBASE   Returns base address of devices
.
```

---

† N.B. Takes account of any linked lines, which can cause complications when using the screen editor.

8

Introduction to
machine code programming

8.1 Introduction

This chapter is a brief introduction to 6502 machine code programming on the VIC-20. A machine code program consists of a sequence of bytes sone of which represent instructions and others being data. In this form a machine code program is rather difficult to follow, obviously it would be helpful to distinguish the bytes which represent instructions (op-codes) from those which represent data (operands). The letters which we substitute for the op-codes are called *instruction mnemonics,* for example the instruction which clears the carry bit on the 6502 has op-code $18 and mnemonic CLC. Rather than performing these substitutions by hand it makes sense to get the computer to do it for us. A program which substitutes op-codes for mnemonics is called an *assembler* because it assembles machine code. Using an assembler it is possible to enter a machine code program in mnemonic form. Conversely a program which works through a block of RAM containing machine code and displays mnemonics for op-codes is called a *disassembler*. A machine code program written in mnemonic form is called an *Assembly language* program and is often loosely described as being written in Assembler. For all but the simplest of machine code programs it is quite impractical to work without the use of an assembler and disassembler, and therefore VICMON, or an equivalent monitor, must be regarded as an essential prerequisite.

Machine code instructions are rather simple, in the sense that an individual instruction cannot achieve a great deal. Any particular instruction can only change the contents of a memory location or alter one of the internal registers of the 6502 microprocessor. There are two main advantages of programming in machine code rather than BASIC. Firstly machine code programs run very fast indeed when compared to BASIC, this is because there is no need for a machine code program to be interpreted. Secondly, the machine code programmer has total control over the machine and its operations. This last weapon is double-edged; in being able to exercise total control the helping hand of the operating system disappears and it becomes necessary to spell out every step in precise detail. In order to do this the programmer must possess considerable knowledge of how the VIC-20 system works.

The only way to learn machine code programming is to actually do it yourself. It can be both extremely satisfying and very infuriating; the essential requirement is patience.

8.2 Programming model of the 6502

The 6502 microprocessor contains six registers which are available to the programmer. They are shown diagrammatically in Figure 8.1.

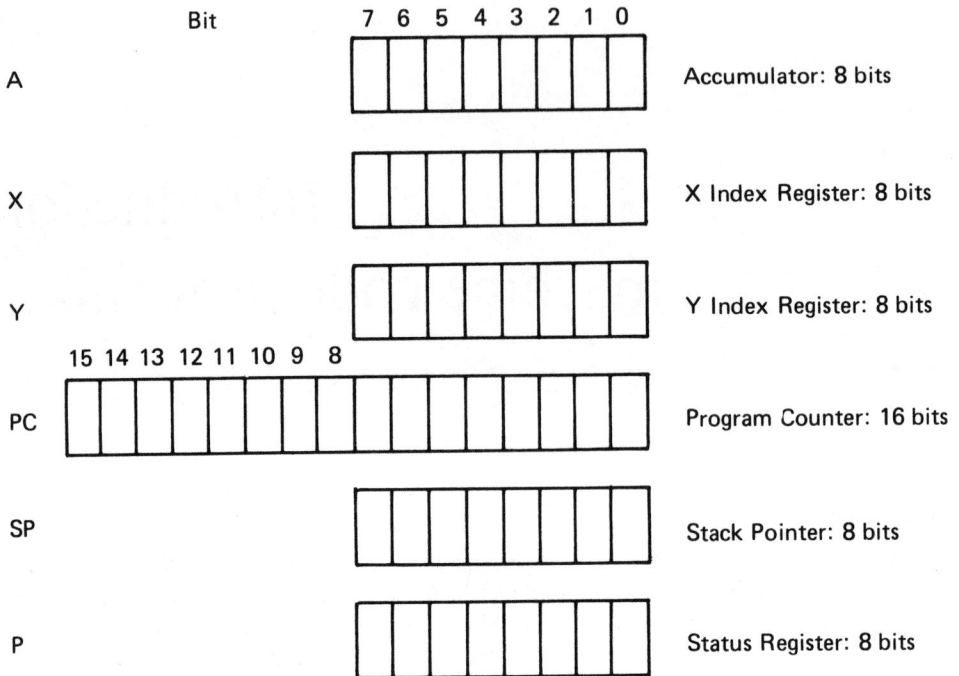

Fig. 8.1 — Programming model of the 6502.

We shall now examine each of these registers in detail.

The Accumulator

This is arguably the most important register in the 6502 microprocessor. It is the *only* internal register in which data may be placed and then subjected to arithmetic or logical operations. Apart from this its main use is as temporary storage whilst moving data from one location to another. This second function is duplicated by the X and Y Index Registers.

Examples

In this and all following examples Assembly language mnemonics are used. A complete list of the 6502 instruction set can be found at the end of this chapter.

        LDA #$0A   Load accumulator with decimal 10
        STA $1800   Store accumulator in $1800

Similarly

        LDX #$0A   or LDY #$0A
        STX $1800   STY $1800

The X *and* Y *Index Registers*
Like the accumulator these registers can hold data but their principal function is to hold short offsets, which can be used as pointers to specific memory locations, or counters. Each Index Register has instructions which can be used to increment (add 1) or decrement (subtract 1) its contents:

INX   Increment X Index Register   (Similarly INY),
DEX   Decrement X Index Register   (Similarly DEY).

The Index Registers are not identical in their functions but a discussion of the ways in which they differ is best postponed to the section on addressing modes.

The Program Counter
The Program Counter is a 16-bit register which holds the address of the next instruction to be executed. It works much the same way as memory locations 57 and 58 in BASIC, except that the Program Counter points to the next 6502 instruction rather than a current BASIC line number.

The cycle time of the 6502 microprocessor is determined by an external quartz oscillator, similar to the ones which drive electronic watches. The 8.86 MHz signal is divided to provide the 1.1 MHz signal which drives the 6502. The 6502 uses the externally applied signal to derive its own internal timings, required to coordinate the progression of activities within the microprocessor. The first step of an instruction cycle is to out the R/$\overline{W}$ line high, to indicate a read operation, and place the contents of the program counter on the address bus. The microprocessor then reads the contents of the address into its own internal *Instruction* register. This is an 8-bit register, not available to the programmer, which is used to hold the instruction whilst it is decoded by the internal control logic. At this point the Program Counter is incremented by one so that it points to the next relevant byte, which may be data or the next op-code.

During the second step the instruction itself is executed. This could involve moving more data from memory, as in a load accumulator instruction, or the instruction could be complete in itself. As different operations require differing amounts of data no instructions are actually completed within one cycle of the 6502 clock. As each byte is 'consumed' the Program Counter is incremented, so that by the time a complete instruction has been executed the Program Counter once again points to the next op-code.

Obviously if the externally applied frequency is altered, the internal cycle time of the 6502 will alter accordingly but, for reasons which are beyond the scope of the present discussion, there is an upper limit on the speed at which the 6502 can be driven.

The existence of the Program Counter enables the microprocessor to step sequentially through a program from start to finish. However, by itself this is not enough; an essential feature of any computer program is the ability to test conditions and vary the subsequent computation according to the outcome of the test. We also need some way of breaking the normal program sequence, performing another program sequence (a subroutine) and returning to the point immediately following the original point of departure. The Stack Pointer and the stack provide the means of jumping to a subroutine and subsequently returning. The Status Register provides the means whereby decisions can be made.

The Stack Pointer
The Stack Pointer is used mainly to handle interrupts and subroutines. Its contents point to an address on page 1, in the stack. The *stack* is a 255 byte buffer, organized on a 'last in, first out' principle, which begins at location $511 and is filled *downwards* from that address. Each time data is placed onto the stack the Stack Pointer is decremented by one. Similarly, as data is removed, the Stack Pointer is incremented. If an interrupt occurs or a subroutine is called, the contents of the Program Counter are placed in two successive bytes onto the stack and the Stack Pointer decremented appropriately.

A subroutine is called by the instruction JSR which pushes the contents of the Program Counter onto the stack to await retrieval. The address which follows the JSR is then placed in the Program Counter which causes execution to jump to the specified subroutine. The return from subroutine instruction RTS uses the Stack Pointer to retrieve the original address from the stack, thereby incrementing the Stack Pointer appropriately, and places this address in the Program Counter. RTS also increments the Program Counter by one to point to the next instruction following the original JSR.

The stack can also be used by the programmer for temporary storage, possibly for data used by a subroutine. To facilitate operations of this type the 6502 has several stack specific instructions such as

PHA   Push Accumulator onto stack.
PLA   Pull Accumulator from stack.
PHP   Push Status Register onto stack.
PLP   Pull Status Register from stack.

Each of these instructions ends by adjusting the stack pointer appropriately.

In some situations the programmer may need to change the contents of the Stack Pointer, which can be accomplished via the instructions

TSX   Transfer Stack Pointer to X Index Register.
and   TXS   Transfer X Index Register to Stack Pointer.

Normally the Stack Pointer is adjusted automatically and these last two instructions should be used with some care, since a fairly spectacular crash can result from their cavalier use!

The Status Register
As has been indicated the 8-bit Status Register provides the means whereby decisions can be made. Each bit of this register has its own special significance as indicated in Figure 8.2.

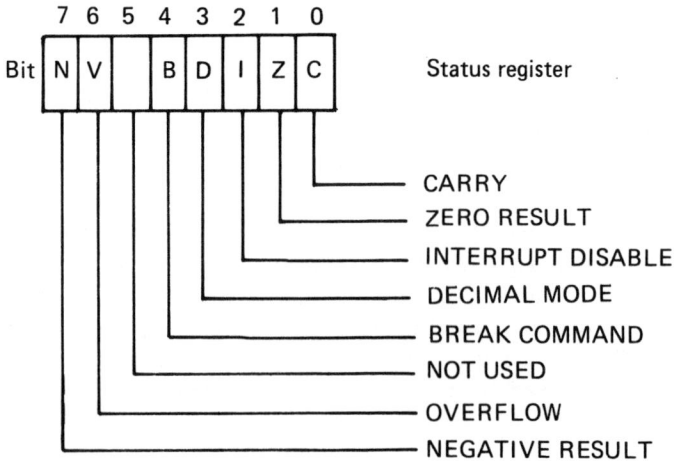

Fig. 8.2 – Status Register.

Carry
The Carry bit is used to indicate that the result of an arithmetic operation has generated a carry; the bit is set to 1 if a carry has been generated and cleared to 0 otherwise. It should be noted that the 6502

carry flag's meaning is inverted in subtraction operation. After SBC (Subtract memory from accumulator with Borrow) the Carry bit is cleared if a borrow was required and set if not. The Carry bit can be set or cleared by the programmer using the instructions

> SEC   Set Carry
> CLC   Clear Carry

and, in addition to the compare and load instructions, is also included in the instructions

> ROL   Rotate Accumulator or memory Left through Carry
> ROR   Rotate Accumulator or memory Right through Carry
> LSR   Logical Shift Right of Accumulator or memory.
> ASL   Arithmetic Shift Left of Accumulator or memory.

Examples

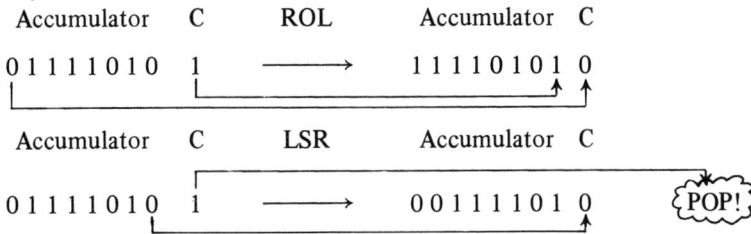

Zero result

This flag is automatically set by the microprocessor during any data movement or calculation operation when the 8 bits which are the result of the operation are all 0. The Z flag cannot be set or cleared by an instruction but can be affected by any of the instructions ADC, AND, ASL, BIT, CMP, CPY, CPX, DEC, DEX, DEY, EOR, INC, INX, INY, LDA, LDX, LDY, LSR, ORA, PLA, PLP, ROL, RTI, SBC, TAX, TXA, TYA (a list which may be useful).

Interrupt disable

The functions of this bit of the Status Register and the associated instructions SEI and CLI have already been illustrated in Chapter 7. If the interrupt bit is set, by SEI, then $\overline{\text{IRQ}}$ interrupts will be ignored. If the interrupt bit is cleared, by CLI, then an $\overline{\text{IRQ}}$ interrupt will be effective. The interrupt bit is automatically set when an $\overline{\text{IRQ}}$ interrupt occurs.

Decimal mode

The decimal mode flag is used to control whether Addition (ADC) and Subtraction (SBC) are performed using binary orf decimal arithmetic. When set by the SED instruction all subsequent arithmetic operations are performed in decimal arithmetic using blocks of 4 bits to specify a decimal digit.

Example

Decimal mode addition:

$$
\begin{array}{r}
0\,0\,0\,0\,0\,1\,0\,1 \quad (5) \\
+ \quad 0\,0\,0\,0\,1\,0\,0\,0 \quad (8) \\
\hline
0\,0\,0\,1\,0\,1\,1\,1 \quad (13)
\end{array}
$$

The decimal flag can be cleared by the CID instruction which returns all operations to binary. The only instructions which affect the decimal mode flag are CLD, PLP, RTI and SED.

Break command
The break command flag is set only by the 6502 and is used to determine during an interrupt sequence whether or not the interrupt was caused by a BRK instruction or by a real interrupt, see section 7.3. This bit is set by the BRK command and then saved with the Status Register, it is cleared to 0 otherwise.

Overflow
The overflow flag is used in signed binary arithmetic to monitor the validity of the sign bit (bit 7) following the ADC and SBC instructions. In signed binary arithmetic, numbers in the range -128 to $+127$ are represented using bits 0 to 6; if the number is positive, bit $7 = 0$; if the number is negative, bit $7 = 1$. The microprocessor recognizes, by knowledge of bit 7 for each of the two numbers, what the resultant bit 7 *must* be. If bit 7 is incorrect the overflow bit is set.

   A useful feature of the 6502 is that the overflow flag can be used to reflect the condition of bit 6 in a selected address. After the instructions BIT $1000, which ANDs the contents of $1000 with the accumulator, the contents of $1000 and the accumulator are unchanged but the Z flag is set according to the result of the logical AND operation, and the N and V flags according to bits 7 and 6 of the contents of $1000. When used in this way the overflow flag has nothing to do with signed arithmetic but is just another flag which the programmer can exploit. The overflow bit is cleared by the instruction CLV.

Negative
This bit is used to show the sign of the result of an operation. It will acquire the value of bit 7 of the result of any arithmetic or logical operation. This means, for example, that after a signed addition we can determine the sign of the result by sampling the N flag directly rather than finding a way to isolate bit 7. The N flag is 1 if the result is negative and 0 otherwise. The N flag cannot be directly controlled by the programmer since it represents the status of the last data movement. Instructions which affect the N flag are ADC, AND, ASL, BIT, CMP, CPY, CPX, DEC, DEX, DEY, EOR, INC, INX, INY, LDA, LDX, LDY, LSR, ORA, PLA, PLP, ROL, SBC, TAX, TAY, TSX, TXA and TYA.

To summarize: the 6502 microprocessor treats the flags discussed above as a single 8-bit register. One of these flags is controllable by the programmer only, some by both the programmer and the microprocessor, and others by the microprocessor only. The contents of the Status Register provide the basis for all decisions concerning whether to branch to another part of the program or not. The eight branch instructions are

BPL	Branch on result Positive.	Testing the N flag.
BMI	Branch on result Negative.	Testing the N flag.
BCC	Branch on Carry Clear.	Testing the C flag.
BCS	Branch on Carry Set.	Testing the C flag.
BEQ	Branch on result zero.	Testing the Z flag.
BNE	Brancy on result Not Zero.	Testing the Z flag.
BVS	Branch on overflow Set.	Testing the V flag.
BVC	Branch on overflow Clear.	Testing the V flag.

8.3 Addressing modes
Each 6502 instruction consists of a one-byte op-code followed by a 0, 1 or 2 byte operand. Clearly a one-byte op-code permits 256 possible instructions, of which 151 are used leaving 105 unassigned.

   Basically there are 56 different instructions, but most can be used in several of 13 distinct addressing modes. *Addressing mode* is the term used to describe how the 6502 decides which part of memory the particular instruction and operand must be applied to.

Immediate mode (2 bytes): Instruction, operand
In immediate addressing the instruction operates directly on the second byte. Thus

        LDA #$FF   (A9 FF)

loads $FF 'immediately' into the Accumulator. The # sign is used to signify the immediate addressing mode.

Absolute mode (3 bytes): instruction, address
In absolute addressing the second and third bytes contain the least significant and most significant bytes, respectively, of an address. The instruction then operates on the contents of this address. Thus

        AND $1F7E   (2D 7E   1F)

will AND the contents of the Accumulator with the contents of $1F7E and place the result in the Accumulator.

Zero page (2 bytes): instruction, Lo-byte of address
Zero page addressing is a shortened form of absolute addressing that can be used when the relevant memory location is on the lowest page (addresses $00 to $FF). The missing Hi-byte of the address is assumed to be $00. Because this byte does not need to be generated or decoded, zero page addressing is slightly faster than absolute addressing. Thus

        STA $27   (85   27)

will store the contents of the Accumulator in address $0027.

Implied mode (1 byte): instruction
In this addressing mode the register on which the instruction operates is implied by the instruction itself. Thus CLC, SEC, CLI, SEI etc. require no operand.

Relative addressing (2 bytes): instruction, offset
Branch-on condition instructions use the relative addressing mode; a single byte offset is treated as a signed binary number which is added to the Program Counter (after the Program Counter has been incremented). This allows displacements in the range -126 to $+129$. Thus in theory BCC $05 requests the Assembler to generate a BCC instruction that will load the Program Counter with its current value plus 5 if the Carry bit is 0. Because working out the required offset soon becomes a tiresome chore in practice VICMON does this for you. Thus

        BCC $18A6   (90   offset)

will cause program execution to jump to $18A6 if the Carry bit is clear *provided* the offset, from the current address, required to reach $18A6 lies within the permitted range (if it doesn't VICMON will respond with '?').

Indirect addressing (3 bytes): instruction, address
This addressing mode, sometimes called absolute indirect, applies only to the JMP instruction. It is used where the need arises to jump program execution to a truly computed address. In Assembly language indirect addressing is indicated by brackets. Thus

        JMP ($31FE)   (6C FE   31) will load the Program Counter with an address whose Lo byte is the contents of $31FE and whose Hi-byte is the contents of $31FF. Never let an indirect address cross a page boundary, as in JMP ($31FF), here the 6502 will fetch the Hi-byte of the address not from $3200 but from $3100.

We next consider those addressing modes which can be used in conjunction with the index registers. These are the most powerful addressing modes available, allowing the programmer to access, sequentially elements of a block or table, as with the FOR ... TO ... STEP loop in BASIC. It is in this context that instructions, such as INX, which increment or decrement the index registers really become useful.

Absolute indexed (3 bytes): instruction, address
When an instruction is used in this mode the contents of a specified index register are added to the given address to get the effective address. Thus if the X Index Register contains the value $1B the instruction

> LDA $1000, X   (BD   00   10)

will load the Accumulator with the contents of $101B. Instructions which allow absolute indexing by X are ADC, AND, ASL, CMP, DEC, EOR, INC, LDA, LDY, LSR, ORA, ROL, SBC and STA. Instructions which allow absolute indexing by Y are ADC, AND, CMP, EOR, LDA, LDX, ORA, SBC and STA.

Zero page indexed (2 bytes): instruction, Lo-byte of address
Zero page indexed addressing is a shortened form of absolute indexed addressing that can be used when the relevant memory location is on page zero. The missing Hi-byte of the given address is assumed to be $00. Thus if the X Index Register contains the value $13 the instruction

> LDA $20, X   (B5   20)

will load the Accumulator with the contents of $0033. If the base address plus X exceeds $FF (the greatest zero page address) no carry is generated and a zero page wrap around will occur. Except in the case of LDX and STX which *can* be indexed by Y, zero page indexed addressing is only available in conjunction with the X Index Register.

Example
This program illustrates the use of the absolute indexed addressing mode. The object of the exercise is to move 256 or fewer bytes from one memory block to another. In the particular case given 17 bytes are copied from the block $1600 − $1610 to the block $1700 − $1710.

Enter and save the following program using VICMON making sure you have remembered to put $10 in $1800. The program can be tested by placing known values in $1600 − $1610, checking the contents of $1700 to $1710, and then running the program by RETURNing

> . G 1819

If all is well the initial VICMON display should return, since the program ends with BRK (RTS will take you back to BASIC − not recommended!). Next examine the contents of $1700 to $1710 to check that the copy operation has been executed correctly.

```
        MEMORY DUMP
. :1800 10 00 00 00 00    $1800 contains COUNT ($10)
. :1805 00 00 00 00 00
. :180A 00 00 00 00 00    COUNT  One less than number of bytes to be
. :180F 00 00 00 00 00               copied (0 ≤ COUNT ≤ 255)
. :1814 00 00 00 00 00
.
```

TINYCOPY

```
    .,  1819 LDX $1800     Load COUNT into X Index Register
┌──→.,  181C LDA $1600,X  ⎫ Copy
│   .,  181F STA $1700,X  ⎭
│   .,  1822 DEX           Decrement X
│No .,  1823 BNE $181C     Is X = 0 ?
└── .,  1825 LDA $1600    ⎫
    .,  1828 STA $1700    ⎭ Copy last byte
    .,  182B BRK           (Return to VICMON)
    .,  182C NOP
```

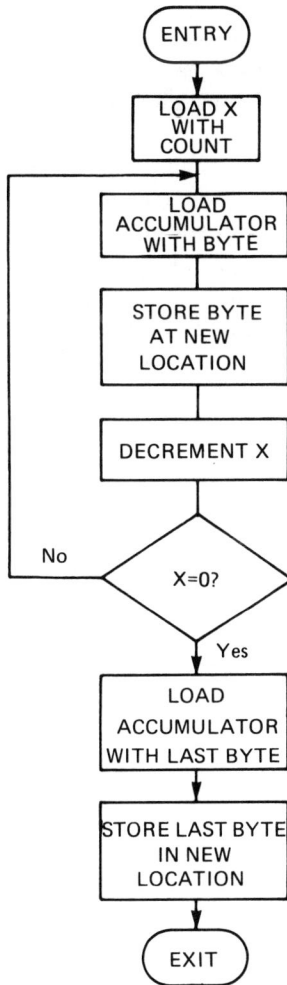

Fig. 8.3 — Moving 256 or fewer bytes.

A flowchart for TINYCOPY is given in Figure 8.3. Note that the initial X Index Register value is COUNT, which is one less than the number of bytes moved. Whatever the value of COUNT the program will always copy the contents of $1600 into $1700, indeed if COUNT = 0 this is done twice!

The essential features of the program TINYCOPY can be summarized without reference to specific memory locations. We can replace absolute addresses by labels or tokens. In this form the program listing looks as follows.

```
        LDX   COUNT    ; INITIALIZE COUNTER
NEXT    LDA   FROM,X   ; MOVE BYTE TO ACCUMULATOR
        STA   DEST,X   ; STORE BYTE IN NEW LOCATION
        DEX            ; DECREMENT COUNTER
        BNE   NEXT     ; COUNTER = 0? IF NO GOTO NEXT
        LDA   FROM     ; MOVE LAST BYTE TO ACCUMULATOR
        STA   DEST     ; STORE BYTE IN NEW LOCATION
        BRK            ; FINISHED
```

A program listed in this way is said to be expressed in *symbolic form*. Professional microprocessor development systems even permit a program to be *entered* in symbolic form, complete with comments. Of course VICMON can't cope with symbolic form at all, but nevertheless it is a good way to prepare the early drafts of a program on paper.

Whilst TINYCOPY is a useful illustration of absolute indexed addressing it has two significant limitations. Firstly the start address FROM and target address DEST must actually be specified in the program, which means it cannot easily be used as a subroutine in which these addresses are supplied as variables. Secondly, at most 256 bytes can be copied. In our next example we shall dispose of both these objections and create an all-purpose COPY routine.

The final and most powerful of all addressing modes are Indexed Indirect and Indirect Indexed. Before examining these two modes we should take a closer look at the concept of indirect addressing which was briefly mentioned in connection with JMP.

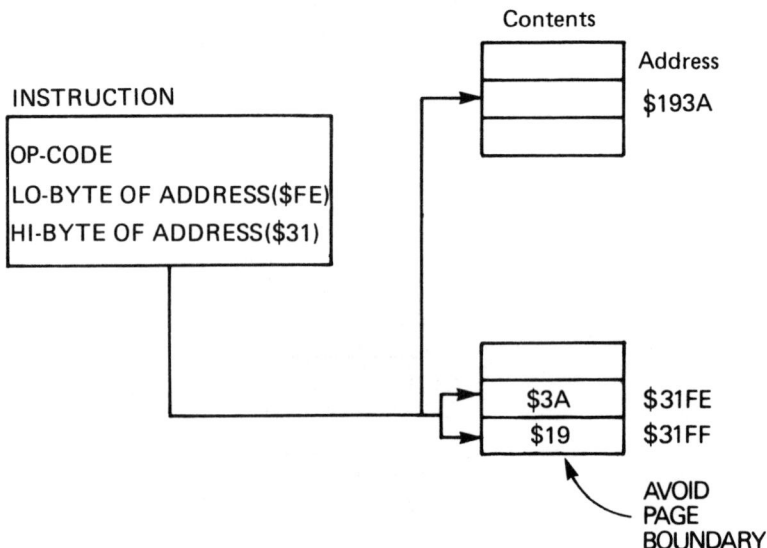

Fig. 8.4 — Indirect addressing.

The underlying idea behind indirect addressing is illustrated in Figure 8.4. Following the instruction op-code an address is specified, in this illustration $31FE. The *effective* address is then constructed from the contents of the specified address *and* the contents of the address immediately following it. The final two addressing modes combine indexing with indirect addressing and can be used by instructions other than JMP.

Indexed Indirect (2 bytes): instruction, Lo-byte of address
Indexed Indirect addressing can only be used in conjunction with the X Indirect Register. It uses a form of indirect zero page addressing combined with indexing. Thus if the X Index Register contains the value $2A then the instruction.

      LDA   ($01, X)   (A1   01)

will load the Accumulator with the contents of an address whos Lo-byte is contained in $002B and whose Hi-byte is contained in $002C.

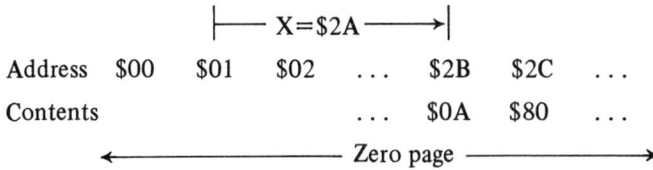

	$	\longleftarrow$ X=$2A $\longrightarrow	$			
Address	$00	$01	$02	...	$2B	$2C	...
Contents				...	$0A	$80	...

$$\longleftarrow \text{——————— Zero page ———————} \longrightarrow$$

Figure 8.5 – Indexed indirect addressing.

Figure 8.5 further illustrates the example given. The contents of the X Index Register are used as an offset from the zero page locations specified, in this case location $01. The effective address is determined by the contents of $2B and $2C. Thus if address $2B contains the value $0A and the address $2C contains $80 then the instruction

      LDA   ($01, X)

has the same effect as

      LDA $800A .

The principal use of indexed indirect addressing is in accessing tables of data or lists of addresses for the Program Counter. If the indexed address is greater than $FF it is wrapped back to the start of zero page. Instructions which allow the use of indexed indirect addressing are ADC, AND, CMP, EOR, LDA, ORA, SBC, and STA.

Indirect indexed (2 bytes): instruction, Lo-byte of address
This is the last and arguably the most powerful of the addressing modes. Using indirect indexed addressing it is possible to create a pointer to any part of memory. This addressing mode can only be used in conjunction with the Y Index Register. Suppose the Y Index Register contains $10. Then the instruction

      STA ($01) , Y   (91   01)

will store the Accumulator in an effective address $10 bytes beyond the address pointed to by the contents of $01 and $02. Figure 8.6 should serve to clarify matters.

Index

$\vdash\!\!-\!\!- Y = \$10 \longrightarrow\!|$

| Address | $00 | $01 | $02 | ... | $1A04 | ... | $1A14 |

Contents $04 $1A

Pointer   Effective address

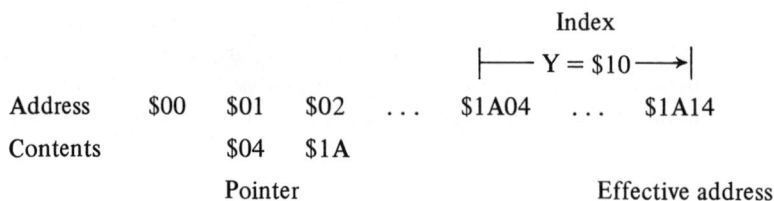

Figure 8.6 – Indirect indexed addressing.

Example
In this example indirect indexed addressing is used to copy any specified block of RAM to a block beginning at a specified address. Unlike TINYCOPY which copied from the top down this program copies from the bottom up; considerations of this kind become important when the two RAM blocks overlap. The RAM to be copied is specified by a START address and an END address with START $\leqslant$ END. The beginning of the RAM which is to contain the copy is address DESST (destination start).

The program is set up as a subroutine which can be called from BASIC by SYS 6250. The 6 bytes which describe START, END and DESST are stored as:

Address Dec	Hex	Comment
6153	$1809	Copy – from START Lo-byte
6154	$180A	Copy – from START Hi-byte
6155	$180B	Copy – from END Lo-byte
6156	$180C	Copy – from END Hi-byte
6165	$1815	Copy – to DESST Lo-byte
6166	$1816	Copy – to DESST Hi-byte

If called from BASIC then values should first be set up by POKEing the required bytes into addresses 6153 etc. A flowchart for COPY is given in Figure 8.7.

COPY

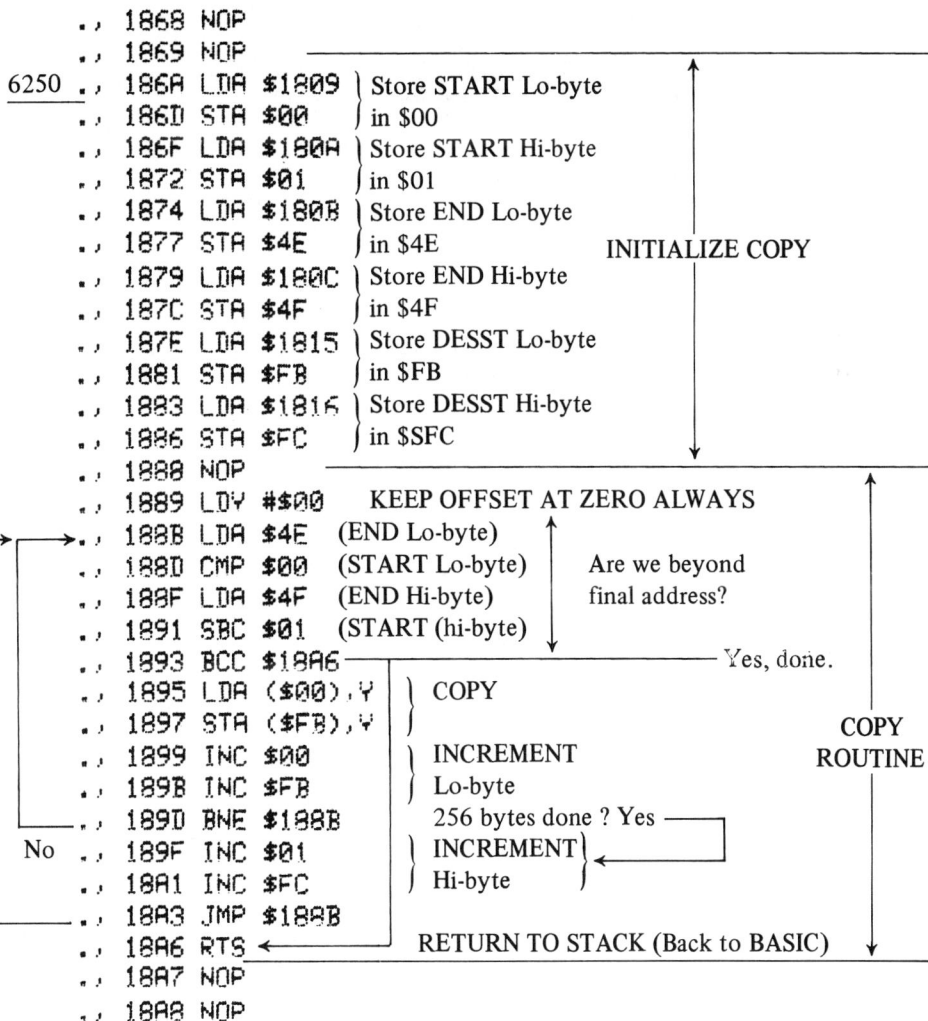

```
.,  1868 NOP
.,  1869 NOP
6250 .,  186A LDA $1809 ⎫ Store START Lo-byte
.,  186D STA $00    ⎭ in $00
.,  186F LDA $180A ⎫ Store START Hi-byte
.,  1872 STA $01    ⎭ in $01
.,  1874 LDA $180B ⎫ Store END Lo-byte
.,  1877 STA $4E    ⎭ in $4E        INITIALIZE COPY
.,  1879 LDA $180C ⎫ Store END Hi-byte
.,  187C STA $4F    ⎭ in $4F
.,  187E LDA $1815 ⎫ Store DESST Lo-byte
.,  1881 STA $FB    ⎭ in $FB
.,  1883 LDA $1816 ⎫ Store DESST Hi-byte
.,  1886 STA $FC    ⎭ in $SFC
.,  1888 NOP
.,  1889 LDY #$00    KEEP OFFSET AT ZERO ALWAYS
.,  188B LDA $4E    (END Lo-byte)
.,  188D CMP $00    (START Lo-byte)      Are we beyond
.,  188F LDA $4F    (END Hi-byte)        final address?
.,  1891 SBC $01    (START (hi-byte)
.,  1893 BCC $18A6 ─────────────────── Yes, done.
.,  1895 LDA ($00),Y ⎫ COPY
.,  1897 STA ($FB),Y ⎭                        COPY
.,  1899 INC $00    ⎫ INCREMENT           ROUTINE
.,  189B INC $FB    ⎭ Lo-byte
.,  189D BNE $188B    256 bytes done ? Yes
No .,  189F INC $01    ⎫ INCREMENT
.,  18A1 INC $FC    ⎭ Hi-byte
.,  18A3 JMP $188B
.,  18A6 RTS ◄──────── RETURN TO STACK (Back to BASIC)
.,  18A7 NOP
.,  18A8 NOP
```

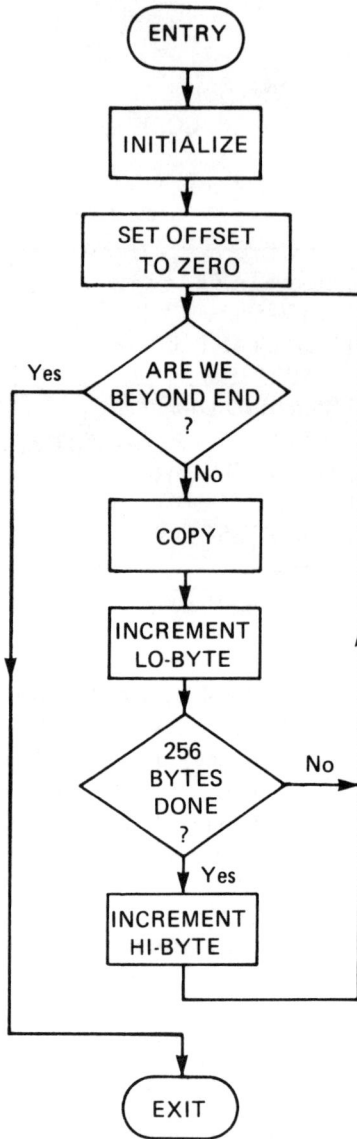

Fig. 8.7 – Flow chart of COPY.

8.4 CHARGET and wedges

We have referred on a number of occasions to the machine code routine CHARGET. When a BASIC program is RUNing the compressed text of each program line is copied from user BASIC RAM into the BASIC input buffer. The function of CHARGET is quite simple, it merely scans through the compressed text contained in the BASIC input buffer, ignoring spaces, until a byte of text is encountered. The byte of text, which may represent a character or a keyword code, is placed in the Accumulator and program execution then returns to the Interpreter, where the text is interpreted. Thus CHARGET is the vital link between the BASIC program and the Interpreter. The routine lives in RAM from $0073 to $008A. By modifying CHARGET it is possible to add new functions and commands to BASIC.

Although quite short CHARGET has several interesting features. It is a self-modifying routine which in normal operation changes an absolute mode address that points to the next byte in the BASIC input buffer. The self-modifying nature of the routine requires that it is located in RAM, which in turn means that a copy must be kept in ROM and written into RAM when the VIC-20 is first turned on. A listing of CHARGET is given below.

CHARGET

```
          ., 0073 INC $7A      Increment POINTER Lo-Byte
  No  ., 0075 BNE $0079     Is Lo-byte = 0?
          ., 0077 INC $7B      Increment POINTER Hi-byte
          ., 0079 LDA $0207     NOTE Lo-byte ($07) in $7A. Hi-byte ($02) in $7B
          ., 007C CMP #$3A      ⎫ Is ASCII code greater than $39?
          ., 007E BCS $008A ⎯ Yes ⎬ (see (a) below)
          ., 0080 CMP #$20      ⎫
  Yes ., 0082 BEQ $0073     ⎬ Is character a space?
          ., 0084 SEC          ⎭
          ., 0085 SBC #$30      ⎫
          ., 0087 SEC          ⎬ Adjust Carry bit as in (b) and (c).
          ., 0088 SBC #$D0      ⎭
          ., 008A RTS ⎯⎯⎯⎯⎯ Done
```

It should be noted that upon emerging from CHARGET the Carry bit is clear or set according to the following conditions

(a) If the character originally encountered has a CBM ASCII code greater than 57 ($39), i.e. above the character '9', the Carry bit will be set.

(b) If the CBM ASCII code of the character is in the range 48 to 57 ($30 to $39), i.e. corresponds to a numerical character, the Carry bit will be clear.

(c) If the CBM ASCII code of the character is less than 57 ($39), i.e. below the character '0', the Carry bit will be set.

A very simple modification of CHARGET is to remove the code in $80 to $83 which checks for a space. This will make BASIC programs RUN very slightly faster but produce a SYNTAX ERROR if a space is encountered. To effect this modification the contents of $80 to $83 are replaced by NOP (No Operation) instructions, the op-code being $EA. We can do this with

POKE 129,234 : POKE 128,234 : POKE131,234 : POKE130,234

(no spaces!). A listing of the new version is given below. Note that since CHARGET is used whenever a BASIC command is executed, any modification of CHARGET from BASIC requires extreme care as the routine must make sense at every stage.

CHARGET WITH NO SPACE CHECK

```
., 0073 INC $7A
., 0075 BNE $0079
., 0077 INC $7B
., 0079 LDA $0207
., 007C CMP #$3A
., 007E BCS $008A
., 0080 NOP
., 0081 NOP
., 0082 NOP
., 0083 NOP
., 0084 SEC
., 0085 SBC #$30
., 0087 SEC
., 0088 SBC #$D0
., 008A RTS
```

In order to add a new command to BASIC via CHARGET the usual approach is to intercept CHARGET at its start with a JMP to an appropriate wedge routine, which identifies the new command and performs the appropriate machine code. The new command can be identified by defining a new keyword, in which case it will be necessary to check for the corresponding character string, or by using a single character such as '!' which is not normally used by BASIC. If a single character is used the wedge code need only check for this 'keyword' symbol. If the new command is not found the flow of the program must continue as normal through CHARGET. (See R. West, Programming the PET/CBM, for further details).

8.5 Machine code Hi-resolution PLOTSUB

The following Assembly language listing duplicates in machine code the BASIC high resolution PLOTSUB given in the last program of Chapter 4. It can be used from BASIC as illustrated by the final BASIC program PLOTSUB TEST. Alternatively by applying the technique outlined in section 8.4 it could be used to create three high resolution keywords (INIT, PLOT, RESTORE) as new BASIC commands. Only a slight modification is required to create a fourth command UNPLOT which removes a specified pixel dot.

Machine code PLOTSUB

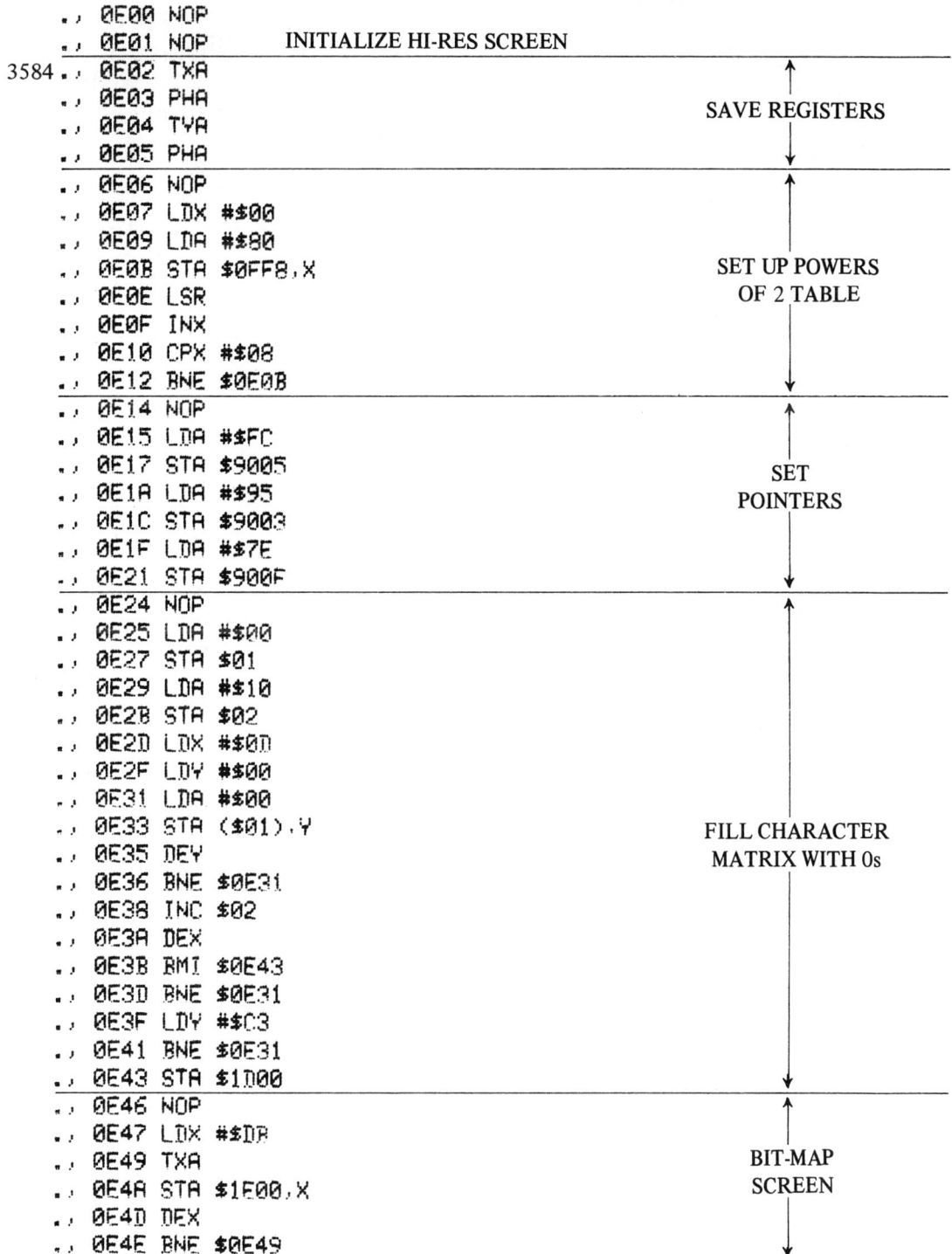

```
        .,  0E00  NOP
        .,  0E01  NOP            INITIALIZE HI-RES SCREEN
3584 .,  0E02  TXA                                                    ↑
        .,  0E03  PHA                                      SAVE REGISTERS
        .,  0E04  TYA
        .,  0E05  PHA                                                 ↓
        .,  0E06  NOP                                                 ↑
        .,  0E07  LDX  #$00
        .,  0E09  LDA  #$80
        .,  0E0B  STA  $0FF8,X                             SET UP POWERS
        .,  0E0E  LSR                                        OF 2 TABLE
        .,  0E0F  INX
        .,  0E10  CPX  #$08
        .,  0E12  BNE  $0E0B                                          ↓
        .,  0E14  NOP                                                 ↑
        .,  0E15  LDA  #$FC
        .,  0E17  STA  $9005                                    SET
        .,  0E1A  LDA  #$95                                   POINTERS
        .,  0E1C  STA  $9003
        .,  0E1F  LDA  #$7E
        .,  0E21  STA  $900F                                          ↓
        .,  0E24  NOP                                                 ↑
        .,  0E25  LDA  #$00
        .,  0E27  STA  $01
        .,  0E29  LDA  #$10
        .,  0E2B  STA  $02
        .,  0E2D  LDX  #$0D
        .,  0E2F  LDY  #$00
        .,  0E31  LDA  #$00
        .,  0E33  STA  ($01),Y                             FILL CHARACTER
        .,  0E35  DEY                                     MATRIX WITH 0s
        .,  0E36  BNE  $0E31
        .,  0E38  INC  $02
        .,  0E3A  DEX
        .,  0E3B  BMI  $0E43
        .,  0E3D  BNE  $0E31
        .,  0E3F  LDY  #$C3
        .,  0E41  BNE  $0E31
        .,  0E43  STA  $1D00                                          ↓
        .,  0E46  NOP                                                 ↑
        .,  0E47  LDX  #$DB
        .,  0E49  TXA                                          BIT-MAP
        .,  0E4A  STA  $1F00,X                                 SCREEN
        .,  0E4D  DEX
        .,  0E4E  BNE  $0E49                                          ↓
```

Listing continues next page

```
      ., 0E50 NOP                                      ↑
      ., 0E51 LDX #$DB                          FILL COLOR
      ., 0E53 LDA #$00                          MATRIX WITH
      ., 0E55 STA $9600,X                        0s (BLACK)
      ., 0E58 DEX
      ., 0E59 BNE $0E55                                ↓
      ., 0E5B NOP                                      ↑
      ., 0E5C PLA
      ., 0E5D TAY                               RESTORE REGISTERS
      ., 0E5E PLA                                 AND RETURN
      ., 0E5F TAX
      ., 0E60 RTS                                      ↓
      ., 0E61 NOP
      ., 0E62 NOP        RESTORE NORMAL SCREEN
3683  ., 0E63 LDA #$AE                                 ↑
      ., 0E65 STA $9003
      ., 0E68 LDA #$F0
      ., 0E6A STA $9005                             RESET
      ., 0E6D LDA #$1B                            POINTERS
      ., 0E6F STA $900F
      ., 0E72 RTS                                      ↓
3706  ., 0E73 NOP
      ., 0E74 NOP
      ., 0E75 NOP              PLOTSUB
      ., 0E76 TXA                                      ↑
      ., 0E77 PHA
      ., 0E78 TYA                               SAVE REGISTERS
      ., 0E79 PHA                                      ↓
      ., 0E7A CLC                                      ↑
      ., 0E7B LDA $0FF6
      ., 0E7E ADC #$60                          CHECK Y AND X
      ., 0E80 BCS $0E5C                          IN RANGE. IF
      ., 0E82 LDA $0FF7                        NOT EXIT PLOTSUB
      ., 0E85 ADC #$50
      ., 0E87 BCS $0E5C                                ↓
      ., 0E89 NOP                                      ↑
      ., 0E8A LDA $0FF6
      ., 0E8D LSR
      ., 0E8E LSR                        COMPUTE U = INT(Y/16)
      ., 0E8F LSR
      ., 0E90 LSR
      ., 0E91 STA $0FF5                                ↓
```

Listing continues next page

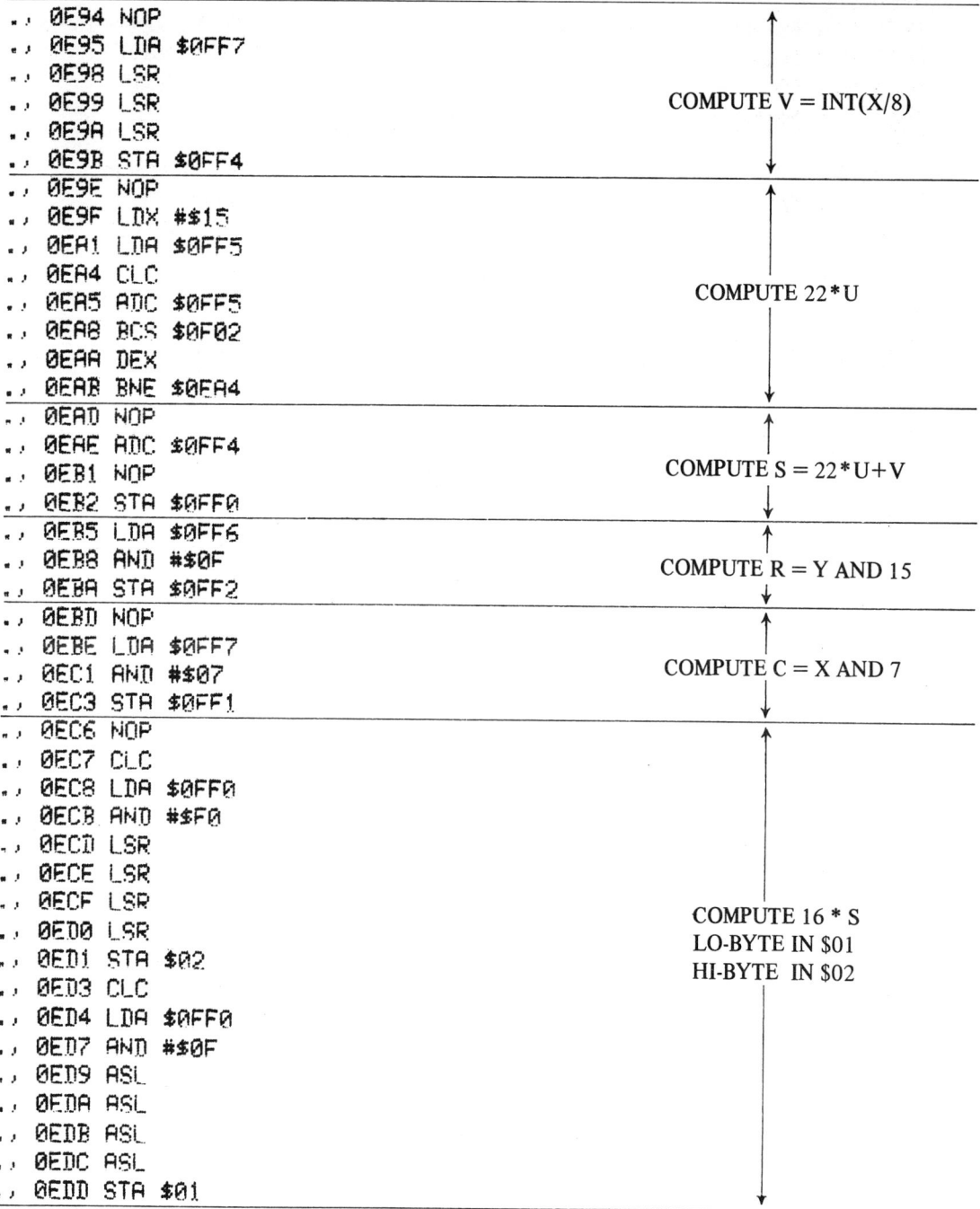

```
.,  0E94  NOP
.,  0E95  LDA  $0FF7
.,  0E98  LSR
.,  0E99  LSR                      COMPUTE V = INT(X/8)
.,  0E9A  LSR
.,  0E9B  STA  $0FF4
.,  0E9E  NOP
.,  0E9F  LDX  #$15
.,  0EA1  LDA  $0FF5
.,  0EA4  CLC
.,  0EA5  ADC  $0FF5              COMPUTE 22*U
.,  0EA8  BCS  $0F02
.,  0EAA  DEX
.,  0EAB  BNE  $0EA4
.,  0EAD  NOP
.,  0EAE  ADC  $0FF4
.,  0EB1  NOP                      COMPUTE S = 22*U+V
.,  0EB2  STA  $0FF0
.,  0EB5  LDA  $0FF6
.,  0EB8  AND  #$0F                COMPUTE R = Y AND 15
.,  0EBA  STA  $0FF2
.,  0EBD  NOP
.,  0EBE  LDA  $0FF7
.,  0EC1  AND  #$07                COMPUTE C = X AND 7
.,  0EC3  STA  $0FF1
.,  0EC6  NOP
.,  0EC7  CLC
.,  0EC8  LDA  $0FF0
.,  0ECB  AND  #$F0
.,  0ECD  LSR
.,  0ECE  LSR
.,  0ECF  LSR
.,  0ED0  LSR
.,  0ED1  STA  $02                 COMPUTE 16 * S
.,  0ED3  CLC                      LO-BYTE IN $01
.,  0ED4  LDA  $0FF0               HI-BYTE  IN $02
.,  0ED7  AND  #$0F
.,  0ED9  ASL
.,  0EDA  ASL
.,  0EDB  ASL
.,  0EDC  ASL
.,  0EDD  STA  $01
```

Listing continues next page

```
.,  0EDF  NOP
.,  0EE0  CLC
.,  0EE1  LDA #$10
.,  0EE3  ADC $02
.,  0EE5  STA $02
.,  0EE7  LDA $0FF2
```
COMPUTE $4096 + 16 * S = M$
LO-BYTE IN $01
HI-BYTE IN $02

```
.,  0EEA  CLC
.,  0EEB  ADC $01
.,  0EED  BCC $0EF1
.,  0EEF  INC $02
.,  0EF1  STA $01
```
COMPUTE $M + R$
LO-BYTE IN $01
HI-BYTE IN $02

```
.,  0EF3  NOP
.,  0EF4  LDX $0FF1
.,  0EF7  LDA $0FF8,X
```
GET CORRECT BIT FROM LOOKUP TABLE
(C%(C) IN ACCUMULATOR)

```
.,  0EFA  LDY #$00        Pure indirect (offset = 0)
.,  0EFC  NOP
.,  0EFD  ORA ($01),Y     C%(C) OR PEEK(M + R)
.,  0EFF  STA ($01),Y     POKE M + R, . . .
```
PLOT PIXEL DOT

```
.,  0F01  NOP
.,  0F02  PLA
.,  0F03  TAY
.,  0F04  PLA
.,  0F05  TAX
```
RESTORE REGISTERS

```
.,  0F06  NOP
.,  0F07  RTS
```
RETURN

```
.,  0F08  NOP
.,  0F09  NOP
.,  0F0A  NOP
```

.

Variable List

$0FF0	S	Zero page requirements
$0FF1	C	$01 and $02
$0FF2	R	
$0FF3	Unused	
$0FF4	V	
$0FF5	U	
$0FF6	Y	
$0FF7	X	
$0FF8	$2 \uparrow 7$	
$0FF9	$2 \uparrow 6$	
$0FFA	$2 \uparrow 5$	
$0FFB	$2 \uparrow 4$	C%(C)
$0FFC	$2 \uparrow 3$	TABLE
$0FFD	$2 \uparrow 2$	
$0FFE	$2 \uparrow 1$	
$0FFF	$2 \uparrow 0$	

```
10 REM PLOTSUB TEST
20 PRINT""
30 SYS3584
40 FORX=0TO175
50 Y=80-INT(90*EXP(-X/40)*SIN(8*π*X/175))
60 POKE4087,X:POKE4086,Y
70 SYS3706
80 NEXT
90 GETA$:IFA$=""THEN90
100 SYS3683
110 PRINT""
120 END
```

8.6 6502 instruction set

Table 8.1 – Alphabetic sequence.

ADC	Add Memory to Accumulator with Carry		**JSR**	Jump to New Location Saving Return Address
AND	"AND" Memory with Accumulator			
ASL	Shift Left One Bit (Memory or Accumulator)		**LDA**	Load Accumulator with Memory
			LDX	Load Index X with Memory
			LDY	Load Index Y with Memory
BCC	Branch on Carry Clear		**LSR**	Shift Right One Bit (Memory or Accumulator)
BCS	Branch on Carry Set			
BEQ	Branch on Result Zero			
BIT	Test Bits in Memory with Accumulator		**NOP**	No Operation
BMI	Branch on Result Minus		**ORA**	"OR" Memory with Accumulator
BNE	Branch on Result not Zero		**PHA**	Push Accumulator on Stack
BPL	Branch on Result Plus		**PHP**	Push Processor Status on Stack
BRK	Force Break		**PLA**	Pull Accumulator from Stack
BVC	Branch on Overflow Clear		**PLP**	Pull Processor Status from Stack
BVS	Branch on Overflow Set			
			ROL	Rotate One Bit Left (Memory or Accumulator)
CLC	Clear Carry Flag		**ROR**	Rotate One Bit Right (Memory or Accumulator)
CLD	Clear Decimal Mode			
CLI	Clear Interrupt Disable Bit		**RTI**	Return from Interrupt
CLV	Clear Overflow Flag		**RTS**	Return from Subroutine
CMP	Compare Memory and Accumulator			
CPX	Compare Memory and Index X		**SBC**	Subtract Memory from Accumulator with Borrow
CPY	Compare Memory and Index Y		**SEC**	Set Carry Flag
DEC	Decrement Memory by One		**SED**	Set Decimal Mode
DEX	Decrement Index X by One		**SEI**	Set Interrupt Disable Status
DEY	Decrement Index Y by One		**STA**	Store Accumulator in Memory
			STX	Store Index X in Memory
EOR	"Exclusive-Or" Memory with Accumulator		**STY**	Store Index Y in Memory
INC	Increment Memory by One		**TAX**	Transfer Accumulator to Index X
INX	Increment Index X by One		**TAY**	Transfer Accumulator to Index Y
INY	Increment Index Y by One		**TSX**	Transfer Stack Pointer to Index X
			TXA	Transfer Index X to Accumulator
JMP	Jump to New Location		**TXS**	Transfer Index X to Stack Pointer
			TYA	Transfer Index Y to Accumulator

The following notation applies to this summary:

A	Accumulator
X, Y	Index Registers
M	Memory
P	Processor Status Register
S	Stack Pointer
√	Change
—	No Change
+	Add
∧	Logical AND
—	Subtract
∀	Logical Exclusive Or
↑	Transfer from Stack
↓	Transfer to Stack
→	Transfer to
←	Transfer to
V	Logical OR
PC	Program Counter
PCH	Program Counter High
PCL	Program Counter Low
OPER	Operand
#	Immediate addressing mode

Note. At the top of each table is located in parentheses a reference number (Ref: XX) which directs the user to that section in the *MCS6500 Microcomputer Family Programming Manual* in which the instruction is defined and discussed.

ADC   *Add Memory to Accumulator with Carry*   ADC

Operation: $A + M + C \rightarrow A, C$

N Z C I D V
√ √ √ – – √

(Ref: 2.2.1)

Addressing Mode	- Assembly Language Form		OP CODE	No. Bytes	No. Cycles
Immediate	ADC	# Oper	69	2	2
Zero Page	ADC	Oper	65	2	3
Zero Page, X	ADC	Oper, X	75	2	4
Absolute	ADC	Oper	6D	3	4
Absolute, X	ADC	Oper, X	7D	3	4*
Absolute, Y	ADC	Oper, Y	79	3	4*
(Indirect, X)	ADC	(Oper, X)	61	2	6
(Indirect), Y	ADC	(Oper), Y	71	2	5*

* Add 1 if page boundary is crossed.

AND   *"AND" Memory with Accumulator*   AND

Logical AND to the accumulator

Operation: $A \wedge M \rightarrow A$

N Z C I D V
√ √ – – – –

(Ref: 2.2.3.0)

Addressing Mode	Assembly Language Form		OP CODE	No. Bytes	No. Cycles
Immediate	AND	# Oper	29	2	2
Zero Page	AND	Oper	25	2	3
Zero Page, X	AND	Oper, X	35	2	4
Absolute	AND	Oper	2D	3	4
Absolute, X	AND	Oper, X	3D	3	4*
Absolute, Y	AND	Oper, Y	39	3	4*
(Indirect, X)	AND	(Oper, X)	21	2	6
(Indirect), Y	AND	(Oper), Y	31	2	5

* Add 1 if page boundary is crossed.

ASL   ASL *Shift Left One Bit (Memory or Accumulator)*   ASL

Operation: $C \leftarrow \boxed{7\,6\,5\,4\,3\,2\,1\,0} \leftarrow 0$

N Z C I D V
√ √ √ – – –

(Ref: 10.2)

Addressing Mode	Assembly Language Form	OP CODE	No. Bytes	No. Cycles
Accumulator	ASL A	0A	1	2
Zero Page	ASL Oper	06	2	5
Zero Page, X	ASL Oper, X	16	2	6
Absolute	ASL Oper	0E	3	6
Absolute, X	ASL Oper, X	1E	3	7

BCC   BCC *Branch on Carry Clear*   BCC

Operation: Branch on $C = 0$

N Z C I D V
– – – – – –

(Ref: 4.1.1.3)

Addressing Mode	Assembly Language Form	OP CODE	No. Bytes	No. Cycles
Relative	BCC Oper	90	2	2*

* Add 1 if branch occurs to same page.
* Add 2 if branch occurs to different page.

BCS   BCS *Branch on Carry Set*   BCS

Operation: Branch on $C = 1$

N Z C I D V
– – – – – –

(Ref: 4.1.1.4)

Addressing Mode	Assembly Language Form	OP CODE	No. Bytes	No. Cycles
Relative	BCS Oper	B0	2	2*

* Add 1 if branch occurs to same page.
* Add 2 if branch occurs to next page.

BEQ   BEQ *Branch on Result Zero*   BEQ

Operation: Branch on $Z = 1$

N Z C I D V
– – – – – –

(Ref: 4.1.1.5)

Addressing Mode	Assembly Language Form	OP CODE	No. Bytes	No. Cycles
Relative	BEQ Oper	F0	2	2*

* Add 1 if branch occurs to same page.
* Add 2 if branch occurs to next page.

BIT   BIT *Test Bits in Memory with Accumulator*   BIT

Operation: $A \wedge M, M_7 \rightarrow N, M_6 \rightarrow V$

Bit 6 and 7 are transferred to the status register.
If the result of $A \wedge M$ is zero then $Z = 1$, otherwise
$Z = 0$

N Z C I D V
M_7 √ – – – M_6

(Ref: 4.2.1.1)

Addressing Mode	Assembly Language Form	OP CODE	No. Bytes	No. Cycles
Zero Page	BIT Oper	24	2	3
Absolute	BIT Oper	2C	3	4

BMI   BMI *Branch on Result Minus*   BMI

Operation: Branch on $N = 1$

N Z C I D V
– – – – – –

(Ref: 4.1.1.1)

Addressing Mode	Assembly Language Form	OP CODE	No. Bytes	No. Cycles
Relative	BMI Oper	30	2	2*

* Add 1 if branch occurs to same page.
* Add 2 if branch occurs to different page.

BNE   BNE *Branch on Result not Zero*   BNE

Operation: Branch on $Z = 0$

N Z C I D V
– – – – – –

(Ref: 4.1.1.6)

Addressing Mode	Assembly Language Form	OP CODE	No. Bytes	No. Cycles
Relative	BNE Oper	D0	2	2*

* Add 1 if branch occurs to same page.
* Add 2 if branch occurs to different page.

BPL   BPL *Branch on Result Plus*   BPL
Operation: Branch on N = Ø   N Z C I D V
                                              − − − − − −
(Ref: 4.1.1.2)

Addressing Mode	Assembly Language Form	OP CODE	No. Bytes	No. Cycles
Relative	BPL Oper	1Ø	2	2*

* Add 1 if branch occurs to same page.
* Add 2 if branch occurs to different page.

BRK   BRK *Force Break*   BRK
Operation: Forced Interrupt PC + 2 ↓ P ↓   N Z C I D V
                                               − − − 1 − −
(Ref: 9.11)

Addressing Mode	Assembly Language Form	OP CODE	No. Bytes	No. Cycles
Implied	BRK	ØØ	1	7

1. A BRK command cannot be masked by setting I.

BVC   BVC *Branch on Overflow Clear*   BVC
Operation: Branch on V = 0   N Z C I D V
                                               − − − − − −
(Ref: 4.1.1.8)

Addressing Mode	Assembly Language Form	OP CODE	No. Bytes	No. Cycles
Relative	BVC Oper	5Ø	2	2*

* Add 1 if branch occurs to same page.
* Add 2 if branch occurs to different page.

BVS   BVS *Branch on Overflow Set*   BVS
Operation: Branch on V = 1   N Z C I D V
                                               − − − − − −
(Ref: 4.1.1.7)

Addressing Mode	Assembly Language Form	OP CODE	No. Bytes	No. Cycles
Relative	BVS Oper	7Ø	2	2*

* Add 1 if branch occurs to same page.
* Add 2 if branch occurs to different page.

CLC   CLC *Clear Carry Flag*   CLC
Operation: Ø → C   N Z C I D V
                                               − − Ø − − −
(Ref: 3.0.2)

Addressing Mode	Assembly Language Form	OP CODE	No. Bytes	No. Cycles
Implied	CLC	18	1	2

CLD   CLD *Clear Decimal Mode*   CLD
Operation: Ø → D   N Z C I D V
                                               − − − − Ø −
(Ref: 3.3.2)

Addressing Mode	Assembly Language Form	OP CODE	No. Bytes	No. Cycles
Implied	CLD	D8	1	2

CLI   CLI *Clear Interrupt Disable Bit*   CLI
Operation: Ø → I   N Z C I D V
                                               − − − Ø − −
(Ref: 3.2.2)

Addressing Mode	Assembly Language Form	OP CODE	No. Bytes	No. Cycles
Implied	CLI	58	1	2

CLV   CLV *Clear Overflow Flag*   CLV
Operation: Ø → V   N Z C I D V
                                               − − − − − Ø
(Ref: 3.6.1)

Addressing Mode	Assembly Language Form	OP CODE	No. Bytes	No. Cycles
Implied	CLV	B8	1	2

CMP   CMP *Compare Memory and Accumulator*   CMP
Operation: A − M   N Z C I D V
                                               √ √ √ − − −
(Ref: 4.2.1)

Addressing Mode	Assembly Language Form	OP CODE	No. Bytes	No. Cycles
Immediate	CMP #Oper	C9	2	2
Zero Page	CMP Oper	C5	2	3
Zero Page, X	CMP Oper, X	D5	2	4
Absolute	CMP Oper	CD	3	4
Absolute, X	CMP Oper, X	DD	3	4*
Absolute, Y	CMP Oper, Y	D9	3	4*
(Indirect, X)	CMP (Oper, X)	C1	2	6
(Indirect), Y	CMP (Oper), Y	D1	2	5*

* Add 1 if page boundary is crossed.

CPX   CPX *Compare Memory and Index X*   CPX
Operation: X − M   N Z C I D V
                                               √ √ √ − − −
(Ref: 7.8)

Addressing Mode	Assembly Language Form	OP CODE	No. Bytes	No. Cycles
Immediate	CPX #Oper	EØ	2	2
Zero Page	CPX Oper	E4	2	3
Absolute	CPX Oper	EC	3	4

CPY   CPY *Compare Memory and Index Y*   **CPY**

Operation: Y − M

N Z C I D V
√ √ √ − − −

(Ref: 7.9)

Addressing Mode	Assembly Language Form	OP CODE	No. Bytes	No. Cycles
Immediate	CPY # Oper	C0	2	2
Zero Page	CPY Oper	C4	2	3
Absolute	CPY Oper	CC	3	4

DEC   DEC *Decrement Memory by One*   **DEC**

Operation: M − 1 → M

N Z C I D V
√ √ − − − −

(Ref: 10.7)

Addressing Mode	Assembly Language Form	OP CODE	No. Bytes	No. Cycles
Zero Page	DEC Oper	C6	2	5
Zero Page, X	DEC Oper, X	D6	2	6
Absolute	DEC Oper	CE	3	6
Absolute, X	DEC Oper, X	DE	3	7

DEX   DEX *Decrement Index X by One*   **DEX**

Operation: X − 1 → X

N Z C I D V
√ √ − − − −

(Ref: 7.6)

Addressing Mode	Assembly Language Form	OP CODE	No. Bytes	No. Cycles
Implied	DEX	CA	1	2

DEY   DEY *Decrement Index Y by One*   **DEY**

Operation: Y − 1 → Y

N Z C I D V
√ √ − − − −

(Ref: 7.7)

Addressing Mode	Assembly Language Form	OP CODE	No. Bytes	No. Cycles
Implied	DEY	88	1	2

EOR   EOR *"Exclusive-Or" Memory with Accumulator*   **EOR**

Operation: A ∀ M → A

N Z C I D V
√ √ − − − −

(Ref: 2.2.3.2)

Addressing Mode	Assembly Language Form	OP CODE	No. Bytes	No. Cycles
Immediate	EOR # Oper	49	2	2
Zero Page	EOR Oper	45	2	3
Zero Page, X	EOR Oper, X	55	2	4
Absolute	EOR Oper	4D	3	4
Absolute, X	EOR Oper, X	5D	3	4*
Absolute, Y	EOR Oper, Y	59	3	4*
(Indirect, X)	EOR (Oper, X)	41	2	6
(Indirect),Y	EOR (Oper), Y	51	2	5*

* Add 1 if page boundary is crossed.

INC   INC *Increment Memory by One*   **INC**

Operation: M + 1 → M

N Z C I D V
√ √ − − − −

(Ref: 10.6)

Addressing Mode	Assembly Language Form	OP CODE	No. Bytes	No. Cycles
Zero Page	INC Oper	E6	2	5
Zero Page, X	INC Oper, X	F6	2	6
Absolute	INC Oper	EE	3	6
Absolute, X	INC Oper, X	FE	3	7

INX   INX *Increment Index X by One*   **INX**

Operation: X + 1 → X

N Z C I D V
√ √ − − − −

(Ref: 7.4)

Addressing Mode	Assembly Language Form	OP CODE	No. Bytes	No. Cycles
Implied	INX	E8	1	2

INY   INY *Increment Index Y by One*   **INY**

Operation: Y + 1 → Y

N Z C I D V
√ √ − − − −

(Ref: 7.5)

Addressing Mode	Assembly Language Form	OP CODE	No. Bytes	No. Cycles
Implied	INY	C8	1	2

JMP   JMP *Jump to New Location*   **JMP**

Operation: (PC + 1) → PCL
        (PC + 2) → PCH   (Ref: 4.0.2)
                     (Ref: 9.8.1)

N Z C I D V
− − − − − −

Addressing Mode	Assembly Language Form	OP CODE	No. Bytes	No. Cycles
Absolute	JMP Oper	4C	3	3
Indirect	JMP (Oper)	6C	3	5

JSR   JSR *Jump to New Location Saving Return Address*   **JSR**

Operation: PC + 2 ↓, (PC + 1) → PCL
               (PC + 2) → PCH
               (Ref: 8.1)

N Z C I D V
− − − − − −

Addressing Mode	Assembly Language Form	OP CODE	No. Bytes	No. Cycles
Absolute	JSR Oper	20	3	6

LDA　　　　LDA *Load Accumulator with Memory*　　　**LDA**

Operation: M → A　　　　　　　　　　　　　　N Z C I D V

　　　　　　　(Ref: 2.1.1)　　　　　　　　　✓ ✓ – – – –

Addressing Mode	Assembly Language Form	OP CODE	No. Bytes	No. Cycles
Immediate	LDA # Oper	A9	2	2
Zero Page	LDA Oper	A5	2	3
Zero Page, X	LDA Oper, X	B5	2	4
Absolute	LDA Oper	AD	3	4
Absolute, X	LDA Oper, X	BD	3	4*
Absolute, Y	LDA Oper, Y	B9	3	4*
(Indirect, X)	LDA (Oper, X)	A1	2	6
(Indirect), Y	LDA (Oper), Y	B1	2	5*

* Add 1 if page boundary is crossed.

LDX　　　　LDX *Load Index X with Memory*　　　**LDX**

Operation: M → X　　　　　　　　　　　　　　N Z C I D V

　　　　　　　(Ref: 7.0)　　　　　　　　　　✓ ✓ – – – –

Addressing Mode	Assembly Language Form	OP CODE	No. Bytes	No. Cycles
Immediate	LDX # Oper	A2	2	2
Zero Page	LDX Oper	A6	2	3
Zero Page, Y	LDX Oper, Y	B6	2	4
Absolute	LDX Oper	AE	3	4
Absolute, Y	LDX Oper, Y	BE	3	4*

*　Add 1 when page boundary is crossed.

LDY　　　　LDY *Load Index Y with Memory*　　　**LDY**

Operation: M → Y　　　　　　　　　　　　　　N Z C I D V

　　　　　　　(Ref: 7.1)　　　　　　　　　　✓ ✓ – – –– –

Addressing Mode	Assembly Language Form	OP CODE	No. Bytes	No. Cycles
Immediate	LDY # Oper	A0	2	2
Zero Page	LDY Oper	A4	2	3
Zero Page, X	LDY Oper, X	B4	2	4
Absolute	LDY Oper	AC	3	4
Absolute, X	LDY Oper, X	BC	3	4*

* Add 1 when page boundary is crossed.

LSR　　LSR *Shift Right One Bit (Memory or Accumulator)*　　**LSR**

Operation: 0 → [7 6 5 4 3 2 1 0] → C　　　N Z C I D V

　　　　　　　(Ref: 10.1)　　　　　　　　　　0 ✓ ✓ – – –

Addressing Mode	Assembly Language Form	OP CODE	No. Bytes	No. Cycles
Accumulator	LSR A	4A	1	2
Zero Page	LSR Oper	46	2	5
Zero Page, X	LSR Oper, X	56	2	6
Absolute	LSR Oper	4E	3	6
Absolute, X	LSR Oper, X	5E	3	7

NOP　　　　　　NOP *No Operation*　　　　　**NOP**

Operation: No Operation (2 cycles)　　　　N Z C I D V

　　　　　　　　　　　　　　　　　　　　　– – – – – –

Addressing Mode	Assembly Language Form	OP CODE	No. Bytes	No. Cycles
Implied	NOP	EA	1	2

ORA　　　ORA *"OR" Memory with Accumulator*　　　**ORA**

Operation: A V M → A　　　　　　　　　　　N Z C I D V

　　　　　　　(Ref: 2.2.3.1)　　　　　　　　✓ ✓ – – – –

Addressing Mode	Assembly Language Form	OP CODE	No. Bytes	No. Cycles
Immediate	ORA # Oper	09	2	2
Zero Page	ORA Oper	05	2	3
Zero Page, X	ORA Oper, X	15	2	4
Absolute	ORA Oper	0D	3	4
Absolute, X	ORA Oper, X	1D	3	4*
Absolute, Y	ORA Oper, Y	19	3	4*
(Indirect, X)	ORA (Oper, X)	01	2	6
(Indirect), Y	ORA (Oper), Y	11	2	5

* Add 1 on page crossing

PHA　　　　PHA *Push Accumulator on Stack*　　　**PHA**

Operation: A ↓　　　　　　　　　　　　　　　N Z C I D V

　　　　　　　(Ref: 8.5)　　　　　　　　　　– – – – – –

Addressing Mode	Assembly Language Form	OP CODE	No. Bytes	No. Cycles
Implied	PHA	48	1	3

PHP　　　PHP *Push Processor Status on Stack*　　　**PHP**

Operation: P↓　　　　　　　　　　　　　　　N Z C I D V

　　　　　　　(Ref: 8.11)　　　　　　　　　　– – – – – –

Addressing Mode	Assembly Language Form	OP CODE	No. Bytes	No. Cycles
Implied	PHP	08	1	3

PLA　　　　PLA *Pull Accumulator from Stack*　　　**PLA**

Operation: A ↑　　　　　　　　　　　　　　　N Z C I D V

　　　　　　　(Ref: 8.6)　　　　　　　　　　✓ ✓ – – – –

Addressing Mode	Assembly Language Form	OP CODE	No. Bytes	No. Cycles
Implied	PLA	68	1	4

PLP

PLP *Pull Processor Status from Stack*   **PLP**

Operation: P ↑

N Z C I D V

(Ref: 8.12)   From Stack

Addressing Mode	Assembly Language Form	OP CODE	No. Bytes	No. Cycles
Implied	PLP	28	1	4

ROL

ROL *Rotate One Bit Left (Memory or Accumulator)*   **ROL**

Operation: [7 6 5 4 3 2 1 Ø] ← [C] ←   M or A

N Z C I D V
√ √ √ − − −

(Ref: 10.3)

Addressing Mode	Assembly Language Form	OP CODE	No. Bytes	No. Cycles
Accumulator	ROL A	2A	1	2
Zero Page	ROL Oper	26	2	5
Zero Page, X	ROL Oper, X	36	2	6
Absolute	ROL Oper	2E	3	6
Absolute, X	ROL Oper, X	3E	3	7

ROR

ROR *Rotate One Bit Right (Memory or Accumulator)* **ROR**

Operation: → C → [7 6 5 4 3 2 1 Ø] →

N Z C I D V
√ √ √ − − −

(Ref: 10.4)

Addressing Mode	Assembly Language Form	OP CODE	No. Bytes	No. Cycles
Accumulator	ROR A	6A	1	2
Zero Page	ROR Oper	66	2	5
Zero Page,X	ROR Oper,X	76	2	6
Absolute	ROR Oper	6E	3	6
Absolute,X	ROR Oper,X	7E	3	7

Note: ROR instruction will be available on MCS650X microprocessors after June, 1976.

RTI

RTI *Return from Interrupt*   **RTI**

Operation: P↑ PC↑

N Z C I D V
From Stack

(Ref: 9.6)

Addressing Mode	Assembly Language Form	OP CODE	No. Bytes	No. Cycles
Implied	RTI	4Ø	1	6

RTS

RTS *Return from Subroutine*   **RTS**

Operation: PC↑, PC + 1 → PC

N Z C I D V
− − − − − −

(Ref: 8.2)

Addressing Mode	Assembly Language Form	OP CODE	No. Bytes	No. Cycles
Implied	RTS	6Ø	1	6

SBC

SBC *Subtract Memory from Accumulator with Borrow* **SBC**

Operation: A − M − $\overline{C}$ → A

N Z C I D V
√ √ √ − − √

Note: $\overline{C}$ = Borrow   (Ref: 2.2.2)

Addressing Mode	Assembly Language Form	OP CODE	No. Bytes	No. Cycles
Immediate	SBC # Oper	E9	2	2
Zero Page	SBC Oper	E5	2	3
Zero Page, X	SBC Oper, X	F5	2	4
Absolute	SBC Oper	ED	3	4
Absolute, X	SBC Oper, X	FD	3	4*
Absolute, Y	SBC Oper, Y	F9	3	4*
(Indirect, X)	SBC (Oper, X)	E1	2	6
(Indirect), Y	SBC (Oper), Y	F1	2	5*

* Add 1 when page boundary is crossed.

SEC

SEC *Set Carry Flag*   **SEC**

Operation: 1 → C

N Z C I D V
− − 1 − − −

(Ref: 3.0.1)

Addressing Mode	Assembly Language Form	OP CODE	No. Bytes	No. Cycles
Implied	SEC	38	1	2

SED

SED *Set Decimal Mode*   **SED**

Operation: 1 → D

N Z C I D V
− − − − 1 −

(Ref: 3.3.1)

Addressing Mode	Assembly Language Form	OP CODE	No. Bytes	No. Cycles
Implied	SED	F8	1	2

SEI

SEI *Set Interrupt Disable Status*   **SEI**

Operation: 1 → I

N Z C I D V
− − − 1 − −

(Ref: 3.2.1)

Addressing Mode	Assembly Language Form	OP CODE	No. Bytes	No. Cycles
Implied	SEI	78	1	2

STA

STA *Store Accumulator in Memory*   **STA**

Operation: A → M

N Z C I D V
− − − − − −

(Ref: 2.1.2)

Addressing Mode	Assembly Language Form	OP CODE	No. Bytes	No. Cycles
Zero Page	STA Oper	85	2	3
Zero Page, X	STA Oper, X	95	2	4
Absolute	STA Oper	8D	3	4
Absolute, X	STA Oper, X	9D	3	5
Absolute, Y	STA Oper, Y	99	3	5
(Indirect, X)	STA (Oper, X)	81	2	6
(Indirect), Y	STA (Oper), Y	91	2	6

STX   STX *Store Index X in Memory*   **STX**

Operation: X → M   N Z C I D V

(Ref: 7.2)   − − − − − −

Addressing Mode	Assembly Language Form	OP CODE	No. Bytes	No. Cycles
Zero Page	STX Oper	86	2	3
Zero Page, Y	STX Oper, Y	96	2	4
Absolute	STX Oper	8E	3	4

STY   STY *Store Index Y in Memory*   **STY**

Operation: Y → M   N Z C I D V

(Ref: 7.3)   − − − − − −

Addressing Mode	Assembly Language Form	OP CODE	No. Bytes	No. Cycles
Zero Page	STY Oper	84	2	3
Zero Page, X	STY Oper, X	94	2	4
Absolute	STY Oper	8C	3	4

TAX   TAX *Transfer Accumulator to Index X*   **TAX**

Operation: A → X   N Z C I D V

(Ref: 7.11)   √ √ − − − −

Addressing Mode	Assembly Language Form	OP CODE	No. Bytes	No. Cycles
Implied	TAX	AA	1	2

TAY   TAY *Transfer Accumulator to Index Y*   **TAY**

Operation: A → Y   N Z C I D V

(Ref: 7.13)   √ √ − − − −

Addressing Mode	Assembly Language Form	OP CODE	No. Bytes	No. Cycles
Implied	TAY	A8	1	2

TSX   TSX *Transfer Stack Pointer to Index X*   **TSX**

Operation: S → X   N Z C I D V

(Ref: 8.9)   √ √ − − − −

Addressing Mode	Assembly Language Form	OP CODE	No. Bytes	No. Cycles
Implied	TSX	BA	1	2

TXA   TXA *Transfer Index X to Accumulator*   **TXA**

Operation: X → A   N Z C I D V

(Ref: 7.12)   √ √ − − − −

Addressing Mode	Assembly Language Form	OP CODE	No. Bytes	No. Cycles
Implied	TXA	8A	1	2

TXS   TXS *Transfer Index X to Stack Pointer*   **TXS**

Operation: X → S   N Z C I D V

(Ref: 8.8)   − − − − − −

Addressing Mode	Assembly Language Form	OP CODE	No. Bytes	No. Cycles
Implied	TXS	9A	1	2

TYA   TYA *Transfer Index Y to Accumulator*   **TYA**

Operation: Y → A   N Z C I D V

(Ref: 7.14)   √ √ − − − −

Addressing Mode	Assembly Language Form	OP CODE	No. Bytes	No. Cycles
Implied	TYA	98	1	2

Starship

1 Introduction

Although, as we have tried to show, a microcomputer is far more than a game-playing device, nearly everyone enjoys a good 'Startrek' game. Starship was one of the first programs that we wrote for our VIC-20 and originally it needed about 12K of RAM to run. It was no easy task to reduce the program to run on a VIC plus the Super Expander Cartridge, which gives fewer bytes than a VIC plus 3K, but we guessed that this was what most of our readers would want. The program listed below will run on a VIC plus any RAM pack.

Unlike all the other programs in this book, which we have tried to make easy to follow, Starship is packed as tightly as possible, has no REMs and is practically unreadable. It just barely runs with the Super Expander and should be entered exactly as listed. Using low line numbers saves about 50 bytes in the program text; it is that tight.

However, if you have more RAM and a Programmer's Aid you can easily RENUMBER in tens and insert REMs with the aid of the following explanation. The way is then clear for you to add your own routines and expand the program.

2 General explanation

Figure A1(a) shows the 'reports' board (it is more fun in color). The data display in the top left of the screen is more or less self-explanatory.

The ship generates energy by controlled fusion of interstellar hydrogen ions collected by a 'scoop' magnetic field. Its drive is a Bussard ramjet which ejects highly energized particles produced by the fusion generators, this enables speeds close to that of light to be approached. The less said about 'warping', which kicks the ship across vast interstellar distances from one sector of space to another, the better. Of course the ship's LOG date differs from GMT because of relativistic time dilation and random effects of warping.

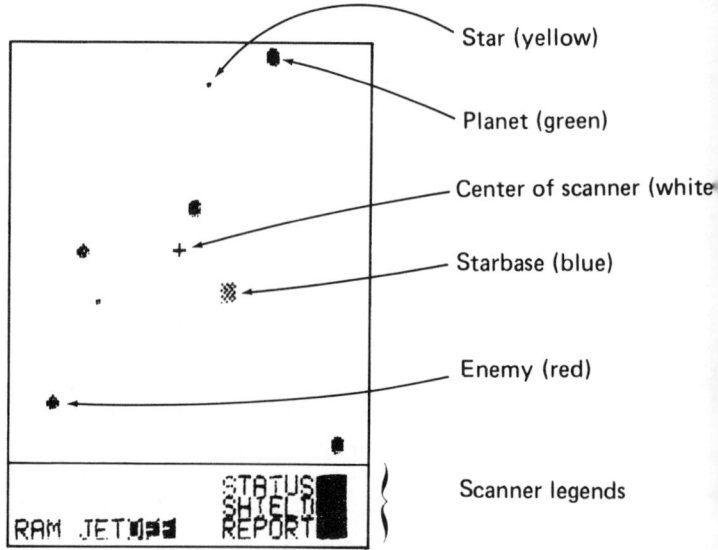

(a) Reports   (b) Scanner (color on black)

Figure A1

The top right of the reports board indicates damage to one or more vital systems. If the color bar on the right is green, the system is functioning; amber indicates the system is damaged but will be repaired, given time, by the ship's damage control devices; red indicates a total failure which can only be repaired by a starbase. Damage is progressive, moving through amber to red.

Shield damage means you can no longer transfer energy back and forth between the energy banks and the shield; therefore, if you are under attack, the shield energy can only decrease. If you are fired upon and the shield energy is insufficient to absorb the attack, the ship will be destroyed. The shield cannot, incidentally, protect you from being rammed.

Ramjet damage turns the drive off, fusion amber means energy is generated at half the usual rate, fusion red means no energy is being generated (get to a starbase quickly!). Phaser damage means you cannot shoot back and warp damage means you cannot warp. This last is important since warping is the only thing you can do which the enemy cannot. The enemy incidentally are mindless automata, remnants of some long-forgotten galactic war, which attack on sight. They occur as groups of between two and seven in roughly a third of the sectors of space.

The middle four lines of the reports board are free to display any suitable message, lots of room for expansion in this direction.

In the lower part of the reports board sensor-scan information is displayed, three numbers for each of the 70 sectors of normal space. The first of these three is the number of planets, the second is the number of stars (starbases count as stars) and the third, yes you guessed it, is the number of enemy. The sector you are currently in is displayed in reverse field, and whilst every other sector is printed in blue, those which contain a starbase are printed in green. Sectors adjacent to the one currently occupied are automatically sensor-scanned whenever the reports board is called, the information is cumulatively updated as the ship moves about the galaxy. The only way to move from one sector to another is by warping.

The reports board is 'time-out' and you can return to the fray by hitting the space bar. The main controls are:

S : *Shield.* Will ask you to INPUT a shield level between 0 and 9999, subject to available reserves. Setting the shield for less than its current value transfers the balance to the energy banks.

C : *Course.* Will first ask you to INPUT an angle and then a 'factor' (speed) between 1 and 9. Energy consumption depends on the factor. At higher factors the ship can outrun enemy provided the ramjet is not hit.

D : *Drive* off.

P : *Phaser.* Will ask you to INPUT an angle.

W : *Warp.* Will ask for X sector coordinate and Y sector coordinate. Each warp consumes 5000 units.

R : *Reports.* Exit with space bar.

Course and phaser angles are set in degrees according to conventional mathematical usage.

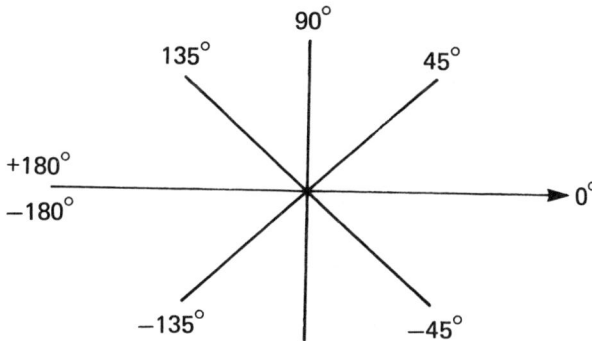

$$90°$$
$$135° \qquad 45°$$
$$+180°$$
$$-180° \qquad\qquad\qquad\qquad 0°$$
$$-135° \qquad -45°$$

The normal display is the scanner, Figure A1(b). Here the center of the screen represents the ship; planets, stars, starbases and enemy move about as they might on a radar screen. The *status, shield level* and *report* indicators (bottom right) are color-coded bars as in the reports board damage section. These indicators are set according to the following rules.

Status	Red if enemy present in sector.
	Red if red damage on any vital system.
	Amber if amber damage on any vital system.
	Amber if energy banks less than 5000 units.
	Green otherwise.
Shield level	Red if shield energy less than 1500 units.
	Amber if shield energy less than 3000 units.
	The probability of hit damage is increased at shield levels below 3000.
Report	Red if red damage exists.
	Amber if status amber.
	Green otherwise.
	The report indicator, once set, is cleared to green only after the reports board has been called. On longer versions the report indicator can be used to signal that an incoming message has arrived.

To dock at a starbase you simply set course straight for it at low factor and leave the rest to the ship's computer.

Before you sally forth to be annihilated, one final word: beware the malevolent Zeds of the uncharted sectors, in which the normal laws of the galaxy do not apply.

3 Overall program plan

The galaxy lives in the cassette buffer at addresses 828 to 897, one byte for each of the 70 sectors. The sector with coordinates XS, YS ($0 \leqslant XS \leqslant 6, 0 \leqslant YS \leqslant 9$) has address $828 + 10 * XS + YS$. Each sector-data byte contains the following information.

Bits 0 to 1	Number of planets	(0 to 3).
Bits 2 to 3	Number of stars	(1 to 3).
Bits 4 to 6	Number of enemy	(0 to 7)
Bit 7	Is 1 if the sector has been visited or sensor-scanned and 0 otherwise.	

Given a seed number SS% ($1 \leqslant$ SS% $\leqslant 438$), fixed once-and-for-all at the beginning of the game, GOSUB WARP determines from XS, YS the following information.

1. Lines 51 to 53 generate the coordinates X%(I), Y%(I) of all 13 characters which may appear in the sector. WARP generates an apparently random set of positions for the characters on the screen, differing from sector to sector but the same each time a given sector is entered; WARP also avoids the scanner display center location (208), so that the ship cannot warp in on top of any enemy, planet or star.

2. For each of the 13 possible characters which may occur within a sector we need a screen code and a color code. Line 50 of WARP extracts from the relevant sector-data byte the number of planets, stars and enemy (C(0), C(1), C(2)) in the sector. Lines 54 to 56 then insert the correct 13 screen codes (81 = planet, 46 = star, 90 = enemy) into 13 consecutive cassette buffer locations, 898 to 910, and similarly the 13 correct color codes (5 = planet, 7 = star, 2 = enemy) in locations 911 to 923. If a planet, star or enemy is absent a black space is substituted. Thus addresses 898 to 923 contain all screen codes and colors for the 13 characters of the current sector, except if a starbase is present. In line 57 if the sector contains a starbase (i.e. if S = SB%(I) for some I between 1 and 3) the screen code 102 and color 3 are substituted for the first star; there is always at least one star in every sector.

The information set up by WARP is then used in lines 92 to 98 (MOVE/PRINT SCANNER) to generate the initial sector display. The routines MOVE/PRINT SCANNER and MOVE/ REPRINT ENEMY (lines 100 to 106) subsequently update the position coordinates X%(I), Y%(I) as the ship and enemy move. Thus the origin for all coordinates X%(I), Y%(I) is always the top left of the screen immediately after warping in to the given sector.

Those readers with a mathematical background may be intrigued to know why WARP avoids the centre location 208. Since the first 20 screen rows are used for the scanner display there are 440 (0 to 439) possible screen locations, and we wish to avoid one of them, thus leaving 439 available. It so happens that 439 is prime and 15 is a primitive root modulo 439, that is consecutive powers of 15 generate all possible residue classes modulo 439 except 0 (hence the occurrence of 15 in line 52). We decide to ignore the last screen location, 439, using only locations 0 to 438, and therefore compute screen locations modulo 439. Since $Q2 \not\equiv 0 \pmod{439}$ it follows that $Q3 \equiv Q2 + 208 \not\equiv 0 \pmod{439}$, in particular $Q3 \neq 208$.

4 Detailed program comments

The principal variables, strings and arrays used in Starship are given below followed by brief descriptive notes on each major subroutine.

T0	Time at which the program began execution; measured in jiffys (1/60 second) since the machine was turned on.
G0%	Hypothetical date of game start, LOG and GMT are equal to begin with.
W	Top bit of 36866, used to find the screen and color matrices and special effects in WARP.
R$	(Red on, Reverse field on, Two spaces, Reverse off, White on) Red string for use in scanner and reports.
0$	Orange or amber string for use in scanner and reports.
G$	Green string for use in scanner and reports.
P$	(Home, followed by 20 cursor downs) A position string for twentieth row.
S$	(Thirteen spaces) To wipe any message on the row reached by P$.
D$	(P$ + S$ + P$) To wipe row reached by P$ and reposition the cursor at the beginning of this row.
SC	Screen start address in memory.
CO	Color start address in memory.
V0	Volume.
S3	(36876) Sound oscillator 3.
S4	(36877) Sound oscillator 4.
CV	(36879) VIC color control register.
RE$	Report indicator color string on scanner. Takes values R$, 0$, or G$.
SL$	Shield level indicator color string on scanner. Takes values R$, 0$, or G$.
ST$	Status indicator color string on scanner. Takes values R$, 0$, or G$.
DC%	DC% = 0, not docked. DC% = 1, docked.
VS	Used to count through sector Y coordinates.
US	Used to count through sector X coordinates.
Z	Used to count through the sector-data byte addresses in the cassette buffer ($Z = 828 + 10 * US + VS$).
Q0	General-purpose variable, used once to construct the galaxy.
Q1, Q2, Q3	General purpose variables used once to construct the galaxy and again in WARP (no connection).
YD	Destination sector Y coordinate in WARP, phaser screen Y coordinate in OWN PHASERS (no connection).
XD	Destination sector X coordinate in WARP, phaser screen X coordinate in OWN PHASERS (no connection).
XS	Current sector X coordinate.
YS	Current sector Y coordinate.
S	Current sector-data byte address in cassette buffer ($S = 828 + 10 * XS + YS$).
WI	WI = 1, ship has just warped in to new sector, WI = 0 otherwise. Used to give one extra move when ship has just warped in.
IM	IM = 1, ramjet (impulse) on. IM = 0 ramjet off.
DD%	Cumulative date difference between LOG and GMT.
EN%	Number of surviving enemy in the current sector.
TX	Current translation in the X direction. When the ramjet is on the entire scanner display is repeatedly moved by this amount in the X direction.

TY   Current translation in the Y direction.
SL   General-purpose offset from SC for a current screen location.
A$ General-purpose control or variable string.
AL   Alive indicator. AL > 0 means the ship has been destroyed.

In addition to the main variables/strings listed above the following arrays are used.

MR$, $0 \leqslant I \leqslant 5$ Message report strings defined in lines 67 to 69 and used in REPORTS line 31.

SR$(I), $0 \leqslant I \leqslant 5$ System title (report) strings defined in lines 67 to 69 and used in REPORTS line 31.

V(I) $0 \leqslant I \leqslant 5$ Vital ship parameters.
      V(0)   Energy bank level.
      V(1)   Shield energy level.
      V(2)   Total number of enemy destroyed.
      V(3)   Total number of enemy remaining.
      V(4)   Date LOG.
      V(5)   Date GMT.
DM$(I), $0 \leqslant I \leqslant 5$. Damage indicator strings used in REPORTS line 31, and to refuse access to a damaged system. These strings take values R$, 0$ or G$.

MR$(I), $0 \leqslant I \leqslant 5$ Message report strings defined in lines 67 to 69 and used in REPORTS line 31.

C(K), $0 \leqslant K \leqslant 2$. Sector-data picked up from cassette buffer in REPORTS line 35 or WARP in line 50.
      C(0)   Number of planets in sector.
      C(1)   Number of stars in sector.
      C(2)   Number of enemy in sector.

X%(I), Y%(I), $0 \leqslant I \leqslant 12$. These arrays contain the current coordinates of all thirteen characters in the sector, whether on or off the screen.

SB%(I), $1 \leqslant I \leqslant 3$. Contains the cassette buffer address of the three sectors which have a starbase.

All GOSUBs have been placed at the beginning of the program to facilitate speedy access. The program therefore really begins on line 63.

63–66 INITIALIZE strings and variables.
67–69 INITIALIZE string arrays GOSUB DOCKED to initialize ship, GOSUB REPORTS to put an initial display on the screen.
70–73 CONSTRUCT GALAXY
Q1 Number of planets in sector, 0 to 3 with probability 7/10, 0 with probability 3/10.
Q2 Number of stars in sector, 1 to 3.
Q3 Number of enemy in sector, 2 to 7 with probability 3/10, 0 with probability 7/10.
Q0 Composite data-byte for sector.
Z Address of sector.
POKE Z, Q0 AND 127. Insert data-byte in current address, set top bit to zero since not
yet scanned or visited.
Distribute 3 starbases throughout galaxy.
Select initial sector randomly.
GOTO WARP with MI set to 1. Return to line 92.

74   *Main program* loop starts here.
74–75   *REPAIR DAMAGE* to ship
76–82   *UPDATE SCANNER* color indicators.
83–85   *UPDATE REPORTS* data
86–91   *GET CONTROL* and respond
92–98   *MOVE/'PRINT' SCANNER* display.
99–105 MOVE/'PRINT' ENEMY
106–108 ENEMY PHASERS.
109 No longer just warped in. If still alive return to 74.
110 Dead.

The routines MOVE/PRINT SCANNER display and MOVE/PRINT ENEMY perhaps demand further comment. The principal problem in displaying independently moving objects (enemy) on the screen is that of position conflict avoidance, i.e. two distinct characters occupying the same space on the screen. Ideally, when moving a character, one should check that the target character cell is empty. If it is not empty one should then search systematically through adjacent character cells until a satisfactory substitute is located. If no satisfactory substitute is found the character is not moved. This procedure is both lengthy and time-consuming in BASIC. The decision was therefore made to omit the conflict avoidance check. This is not to say the problem can be totally ignored. An enemy passing over a planet, or two enemy cohabiting the same character cell is not a serious problem until, that is, an enemy is destroyed. When an enemy is destroyed a space is substituted for its character code, and black for its color, in the appropriate two current sector display bytes (898 to 923 in the cassette buffer). Unless one is very careful it can then happen that a dead enemy, i.e. a space, is printed over an existing enemy, with the result that an enemy which is never visible when one can shoot it, can still destroy the ship by ramming. Other, less disastrous, problems can also occur. Thus in lines 94, 96 and 101, 104, apart from checking that the subsequent POKE is to screen memory, one must also avoid printing superfluous spaces.

An additional consideration is that whereas a given pair $X\%(I)$, $Y\%(I)$ define a unique $SL = 22 * Y\%(I) + X\%(I)$ (which may or may not give a location on the screen) the converse is not true. For example $208 = 22 * 9 + 10 = 22 * 10 - 12$, but the character with coordinates -12 and 10 should not be on the screen. In lines 94 and 101, concerned with printing a space over a character prior to moving it, this problem is ignored since no disastrous consequences would follow. However, in lines 96 and 104, concerned with printing a moved character, the problem cannot be ignored and so $X\%(I)$, $Y\%(I)$ have to be separately checked.

Having discussed the main body of the program we next turn to the GOSUBS.

2 Flash 'DAMAGE' on the screen to indicate the control requested is unavailable.

3 to 6 SET COURSE and factor if drive not damaged.

7 to 11 OWN PHASERS. If phasers not damaged 'get angle of fire' print blips on screen, check for hit. If enemy hit GOSUB ENEMY DESTROYED. Decrement energy.

12 to 15 ENEMY DESTROYED. Reverse field enemy. Count through enemy coordinates $X\%(L)$, $Y\%(L)$ to find which one (or more than one!) has been hit. Convert relevant sector display byte to space, black. Decrement number of enemy in sector. Adjust sector-data byte, enemy estimated, and enemy destroyed, accordingly.

16 to 20 SHIELD. Set shield level adjust energy balance suitably.

21 to 24 SCANNER LEGENDS.

25 to 29 SHIP HIT. Pick random energy loss 0 to 600. Decrement shield energy. Check if dead. Flash screen. If shield high and energy loss low avoid damage, otherwise pick system, damage it with damage being progressive through amber to red.

30 to 41 REPORTS. Print reports and sensor-scan board.

42 to 43 DOCKED. Reset energy levels. Repair all damage. Set scanner indicators to green. Set message.

44 to 62 WARP. If WARP not damaged check energy banks. If sufficient energy input destination sector coordinates XD, YD. If destination in range reset current sector coordinates XS, YS, compute sector-data byte address S. Decrement energy 5000 units, set WI, IM and random time dilation. Pull out C(0), C(1), C(2) from sector-data byte, reset top bit to indicate now visited. Compute screen coordinates of all 13 characters, reset current sector display bytes in 898 to 923. Set EN% to new value. Check if sector contains a starbase, if so substitute it for the first star in current sector display bytes 901 and 914. Special effects with due acknowledgement to Chris Palmer's Hypnotic (lines 59, 60)!

```
1 DIMX%(12),Y%(12):GOTO63
```

DAMAGE
```
2 PRINTD$+"█"+SR$(0):FORL=0TO300:NEXT:PRINTD$:RETURN
3 IFDM$(2)<>G$THENGOSUB2:RETURN
```

SET COURSE
```
4 PRINTD$;:INPUT"COURSE";A$:A=VAL(LEFT$(A$,4)):B=(INT(A/45-.5)+1)*π/4
5 PRINTD$;:INPUT"FACTOR";B$:C=.1*(VAL(LEFT$(B$,1))-1)+1.5
6 TX=-C*COS(B):TY=C*SIN(B):IM=1:PRINTD$:GOSUB21:RETURN
```

OWN PHASERS
```
7 IFDM$(4)<>G$THENGOSUB2:RETURN
8 PRINTD$;:INPUT"P/ANGLE";A$:R=VAL(A$)*π/180:GOSUB21:A=COS(R):R=-SIN(B)
9 FORK=1TO6STEP.5:XD=INT(10+K*1.42*A+.5):YD=INT(9+K*1.42*B+.5):SL=22*YD+XD
10 IFPEEK(SC+SL)=90THENGOSUB12
11 POKESC+SL,46:POKECO+SL,6:POKESC+SL,32:POKECO+SL,0:NEXT:PRINTD$:V(0)=V(0)-100:
RETURN
```

ENEMY DESTROYED
```
12 POKESC+SL,218:POKECO+SL,1:FORL=6TO12:IFXD<>X%(L)ORYD<>Y%(L)OR(PEEK(898+L)<>90
)THEN15
13 POKE898+L,32:POKE911+L,0:EN%=EN%-1:POKES,((16*EN%)AND112)OR(PEEK(S)AND143)
14 V(3)=V(3)-1:V(2)=V(2)+1
15 NEXT:RETURN
```

SHIELD
```
16 IFDM$(1)<>G$THENGOSUB2:RETURN
17 PRINTD$;:INPUT"SHIELD";A$:A=INT(VAL(A$)):IFA<0THENA=0
18 IFA>9999THENA=9999
19 K=(SGN(V(0)+V(1)-A)+1)/2:V(0)=K*(V(0)+V(1)-A):V(1)=K*A+(1-K)*(V(0)+V(1))
20 PRINTD$:RETURN
```

SCANNER LEGENDS
```
21 PRINTP$SPC(13)"█STATUS"+ST$;:PRINTSPC(14)SR$(1)+SL$;::PRINT" RAM JET";
22 IFIM=0THENPRINT" █OFF█";
23 IFIM=1THENPRINT" █ON█";
24 PRINTSPC(3)"█REPORT█"+RE$+"█";::POKECO+208,43:POKECO+208,1:RETURN
```

SHIP HIT
```
25 K=INT(600*RND(1)):V(1)=V(1)-K:IFV(1)<0THENA=2
26 POKECV,3:IFV(1)>3000ANDK<400THEN29
27 K=INT(5*RND(1))+1:IFDM$(K)=0$THENDM$(K)=R$
28 IFDM$(K)=G$THENDM$(K)=0$
29 FORK=0TO100:NEXT:POKECV,8:RETURN
```

Listing continues next page

```
30 PRINT"J";:POKECV,30:PRINT"L****COMPUTER    DATA L****";:FORI=0TO5:K=13-LEN(MR$
(I))
31 PRINTMR$(I)+RIGHT$(LEFT$(C$$,K-1)+STR$(V(I)),K)"J"TAB(14)SR$(I)+"";
32 NEXT:FORI=1TO4:PRINTM$(I)=W$:NEXT:PRINT"L****SENSOR  SCANL****";
33 FORVS=9TO0STEP-1:PRINTRIGHT$(STR$(VS),1)::FORUS=0TO6:Z=828+10*VS+US:K=PEEK(Z)
AND128
34 IF(ABS(XS-US)>10RABS(YS-VS)>1)AND((K<)128)0RMI=1THENPRINT"";:GOTO39
35 POKEZ,PEEK(Z)OR128:C(0)=PEEK(Z)AND3:C(1)=(PEEK(Z)AND12)/4:C(2)=(PEEK(Z)AND112)
>/16
```
REPORTS
```
36 FORK=1TO3:IFZ=SR%(K)THENPRINT"J";
37 NEXT:IFZ=STHENPRINT"J";
38 FORK=0TO2:PRINTRIGHT$(STR$(C(K)),1)::NEXT:PRINT"";
39 NEXTUS:NEXTVS:FORK=0TO6:PRINTSPC(2)RIGHT$(STR$(K),1)::NEXT:IFMI=10RAL>0THENRE
TURN
40 GETA$:IFA$<>CHR$(32)THEN40
41 PRINT"J":POKECV,8:RETURN
```
DOCKED
```
42 V(0)=30000:V(1)=5000:FORI=1TO5:DM$(I)=G$:NEXT:RE$=G$:SL$=G$:ST$=G$:DC%=0
43 M$(1)="DOCKED":M$(2)="REPAIRS COMPLETE":M$(3)="SEEK OUT AND DESTROY":RETURN
44 IFDM$(5)<>G$THENGOSUB2:RETURN
45 PRINTD$;:IFV(0)<5000THENPRINT"LOW ENERGY":FORL=0TO300:NEXT:PRINTD$:RETURN
46 INPUT"SECTOR/X";A$:PRINTD$;:INPUT"SECTOR/Y";B$:PRINTD$
47 XD=VAL(LEFT$(A$,1)):YD=VAL(LEFT$(B$,1))
48 IF(XS-XD)↑2+(YS-YD)↑2>10THENPRINTD$+"  OUT  OF  RANGE":FORL=0TO300:NEXT:PRINTD$:
RETURN
49 XS=XD:YS=YD:S=828+10*XS+YS:V(0)=V(0)-5000:WI=1:IM=0:DD%=INT(10*RND(1))+DD%
50 C(0)=PEEK(S)AND3:C(1)=(PEEK(S)AND12)/4:C(2)=(PEEK(S)AND112)/16:POKES,PEEK(S)0
R128
51 Q1=SS%*(10*XS+YS+1):FORI=0TO12:02=01-439*INT(01/439)
52 03=02+208-439*INT((02+208)/439):01=15*02
53 Y%(I)=INT(03/22):X%(I)=03-22*Y%(I):POKE898+I,32:POKE911+I,0
54 IFI<3ANDI<C(0)THENPOKE898+I,81:POKE911+I,5
55 IFI>2ANDI-3<C(1)THENPOKE898+I,45:POKE911+I,7
56 IFI>5ANDI-6<C(2)THENPOKE898+I,90:POKE911+I,2
57 NEXT:EN%=C(2):FORI=1TO3:IFS=SR%(I)THENPOKE901+I,102:POKE914,3
```
WARP

```
58 NEXT:POKEV0,15:POKE54,214:A=0:B=22:C=1:IFMI=1THENPOKECV.8:PRINT"J"
59 FORI=ATOBSTEPC:POKES.238+T:POKE36864.12+T:POKE36865,38+T
60 POKE36866,22+W-T:POKE36867,174-2*T:NEXT:PRINT"J":A=22-B:C=-C:IFA=22THE
   N59
61 POKE54,0:POKEV.0:IFMI=1THENMI=2:WI=1:GOSUB21:GOTO92
62 RETURN
```

INITIALIZE VARIABLES/STRINGS
```
63 PRINT"J":T0=TI:G0%=2500+INT(500*RND(1)):V(4)=G0%:V(5)=v(4):MI=1:W=PEEK(36866)
   AND128
64 R$="":O$="":::G$="":P$=""
65 S$=::    ::W$="":D$=F$+S$+P$
66 SC=4*W+64*(PEEK(36869)AND112):C0=37888+4*W:V0=36878:S3=36876:S4=S3+1:CV=36879
```

INITIALIZE STRING ARRAYS
```
67 DATA"ENERGY "," DAMAGE "," SHIELD "," ENEMY(DFS)","RAMJET","ENEMY(EST)
   "
68 DATA"FUSION","DATE/LOG","PHASER","DATE/GMT","WARP  "
69 FORI=0TO5:READMR$(I):READSR$(I):NEXT:M$(4)="STAND BY":GOSUB30
```

CONSTRUCT GALAXY
```
70 SS%=INT(438*RND(1))+1:FORI=0TO6:FORVS=0TO9:Q1=INT(4*RND(1))*-(RND(2)<.7)
71 Q2=INT(3*RND(1))+1:Q3=(INT(6*RND(1))+2)*-(RND(2)<.3):V(3)=V(3)+Q3:Q0=Q1+4*Q2+
   16*Q3
72 Z=828+10*US+VS:POKEZ.Q0AND127:NEXTVS:NEXTUS:FORI=1TO3
73 SB%(I)=828+INT(24*RND(1))+23*(I-1):NEXT:XD=INT(7*RND(1)):VD=INT(10*RND(1)):GO
   TO49
```

REPAIR DAMAGE
```
74 FORI=1TO5:IFDM$(I)=0ANDRND(1)<.2THENDM$(I)=0$
75 NEXT:FORI=2TO5STEP3:IFDM$(I)=R$THENDM$(I)=0$
```

UPDATE SCANNER
```
76 NEXT:IFDM$(2)=0$THENIM=0
77 ST$=G$:IFV(0)<5000THENST$=0$:RE$=0$:IFV(0)<0THENAL=3
78 SL$=G$:IFV(1)<3000THENSL$=0$:IFV(1)<1500THENSL$=R$
79 FORI=1TO5:IFDM$(I)=0$THENA$=0$
80 IFDM$(I)=R$THENA$=R$:I=5
81 NEXT:IFA$=0$ORA$=R$THENST$=A$:RE$=A$
82 IFEN%>0THENST$=R$
```

UPDATE REPORTS
```
83 V(0)=V(0)-INT(22*(TX*2+TY*2)):DD%=DD%+1:IFV(3)=0THENRUN
84 IFDM$(3)=G$ORDM$(3)=0$THENV(0)=V(0)+200:IFDM$(3)=G$THENV(0)=V(0)+200:IFFV(3)=0THENRUN
85 GOSUB21:V(4)=G0%+INT((TI-T0)/3600):V(5)=V(4)+DD%:IFV(0)>10E4THENV(0)=10E4
```

Listing continues next page

```
GET CONTROL  86 GETA$:IFA$=""THENIM=0:GOSUB44:GOSUB21:WI=1
             87 IFA$="P"THENGOSUB7
             88 IFA$="S"THENGOSUB16
             89 IFA$="D"ANDIM=1THENIM=0:GOSUB21
             90 IFA$="C"THENGOSUB3:GOSUB21
             91 IFA$="R"THENGOSUB30:RE$=G$:GOSUB21

MOVE/PRINT   92 IFIM=0THENTX=0:TV=0
             93 FORI=0TO12:SL=22*V%(I)+X%(I):IFX%(I)=10ANDV%(I)=9AND(PEEK(898+I)=102)THENDC%=
                1
SCANNER      94 IFSL>=0ANDSL<44AND(SL<>208)ANDPEEK(898+I)<>32THENPOKESC+SL,32:POKECO+SL,0
             95 X%(I)=X%(I)+INT(TX+.5):V%(I)=V%(I)+INT(TV+.5)
             96 IFX%(I)<0ORX%(I)>21ORV%(I)<0ORV%(I)>19OR(PEEK(898+I)=32)THEN98
             97 SL=22*V%(I)+X%(I):POKESC+SL,PEEK(898+I):POKECO+SL,PEEK(911+I)
             98 NEXT:IFDC%=1THENGOSUB42:GOSUB30:RE$=G$:IM=0:GOSUB21:GOTO74

MOVE/PRINT   99 IFWI=10RENX=0THEN109
            100 FORI=6TO12:SL=22*V%(I)+X%(I)
ENEMY       101 IFSL>=0ANDSL<44AND(SL<>208)ANDPEEK(898+I)<>32THENPOKESC+SL,32:POKECO+SL,0
            102 IFPEEK(898+I)<>32THENX%(I)=X%(I)+SGN(10-X%(I)):V%(I)=V%(I)+SGN(9-V%(I))
            103 IFX%(I)=10ANDV%(I)=9AND(PEEK(898+I)=90)THENAL=1
            104 IFX%(I)<0ORX%(I)>21ORV%(I)<0ORV%(I)>19OR(PEEK(898+I)=32)THEN106
            105 SL=22*V%(I)+X%(I):POKESC+SL,PEEK(898+I):POKECO+SL,PEEK(911+I)

ENEMY       106 NEXT:FORI=6TO12:IFPEEK(911+I)<>20R((X%(I)-10)^2+(V%(I)-9)^2)>75THEN108
PHASERS     107 IF(RND(1)<.4THENGOSUB25
            108 NEXT
ALIVE?      109 WI=0:IFAL=0THEN74
DEAD        110 M$(2)="SHIP DESTROYED":GOSUB30:POKECV,112:FORI=0TO2000:NEXT:PRINT"⌂":POKECV,
                27
```

Hi-resolution routines

1. Introduction

We give below two Hi-resolution programs. The first enables a Hi-resolution picture to be drawn with an ordinary switch joystick. The picture can then be saved to disk (or tape) and retrieved by the program whenever needed. Creating a Hi-resolution picture with a joystick is not the optimal solution; ideally a graphics pad should be used, but on the other hand most of us already have a joystick.

Having created and saved a Hi-resolution picture with the first program, the second enables the picture to be reloaded and output to a VIC printer.

Both programs use a short machine code routine which lives on page 15 (3840 up). Details of the machine code, which should be entered using a machine code monitor, are given in the last section of this appendix. Both programs also assume the same screen and character matrix configuration used in the last example of Chapter 4; that is 10 rows of 16×8 character cells with the character matrix located from 4096 to 7616.

2. Creating a picture

To run this program successfully you will need

1. A 3K RAM pack or Super Expander Cartridge.
2. A switch joystick.
3. A disk drive or cassette.
4. A machine code monitor or at least a copy of the machine code program, entered and saved using a monitor.

In case you have not got access to an expansion board and a machine code monitor the last program in this appendix is a BASIC loader for the machine code routine.

If you plan to use cassette, which is slow because each Hi-resolution picture occupies more than 3½K of space, then make the following changes.

Omit line 170 and the GOSUB in lines 780–850.

Change line 200 to POKE 3853,1

Omit the calls for GOSUB 780 in lines 630 and 700 (you might instead check the ST value).

Let us assume you have entered and saved the BASIC program under the name HI-DRAW and the machine code routine under the name M/C HI-DRAW. The procedure for getting a combination of the two up and running is *firstly* load the machine code with

	LOAD "M/C HI-DRAW", 8, 1	(Disk),
or	LOAD "M/C HI-DRAW", 1, 1	(Tape).

The secondary address of 1 tells the VIC to load the program back in the memory locations from which it was originally saved (3840 up). At this point the end of program pointers are set high because the machine code ends somewhere on page 15, as you can see by peeking these locations and returning ?FRE(0). One could lower the pointers by returning NEW, which will not affect the machine code, but this is not really necessary because our next step is to load the BASIC program, which automatically resets all the pointers, with

	LOAD "HI-DRAW", 8	(Disk),
or	LOAD "HI-DRAW"	(Tape).

Now return RUN and provided there are no errors (unlikely!) you will be away drawing, saving and loading back Hi-resolution pictures.

```
10 REM**HI-RES DRAW**
20 REM* ERASE/DRAW  *
30 REM*WITH JOYSTICK*
40 REM*CLRSCR 'FIRE'*
50 REM*SAVE/LOAD PIC*
60 REM*TO DISK/TAPE *
70 REM*RETURN TO END*
80 REM*USE 3KRAMPACK*
90 REM***************
100 POKE55,255:POKE56,14:POKE51,255:POKE52,14:REM LOWER MEMTOP
110 FORI=0TO7:C%(I)=2^(7-I):NEXT
120 POKE36869,252:REM CM TO4096
130 POKE36867,149:REM 16*8 AND 10ROWS
140 POKE36879,27:REM COLOUR
150 SYS3993:REM CLR CM
160 GOSUB730
170 OPEN15,8,15,"I":GOSUB780
180 REM**DEVICE NB***
190 REM TAPE=1/DISK=8
200 POKE3853,8
210 REM***************
220 REM**BEGIN**
230 POKE37139,0:POKE37154,127:REM I/O TO READ
240 P=PEEK(37137)
```
Listing continues next page

```
250 JN=(PAND4)/4
260 JS=(PAND8)/8
270 JW=(PAND16)/16
280 JF=(PAND32)/32
290 P=PEEK(37152)
300 JE=(PAND128)/128
310 POKE37154,255:POKE37139,128:REM RESTORE I/O(FOR DISK/KEYBRD)
320 IFJF=0THENSYS3993
330 GETA$:IFA$=CHR$(13)THEN440
340 IFA$="E"THENE=1:REM ERASE
350 IFA$="D"THENE=0:REM DRAW
360 IFA$="S"THENGOSUB590
370 IFA$="L"THENGOSUB660
380 IFJN=0THENY=Y-1:IFY<0THENY=0
390 IFJS=0THENY=Y+1:IFY>159THENY=159
400 IFJE=0THENX=X+1:IFX>175THENX=175
410 IFJW=0THENX=X-1:IFX<0THENX=0
420 GOSUB490
430 GOTO220
440 PRINT"J":POKE36867,174:POKE36869,240:CLOSE15
450 POKE55,120:POKE56,29:POKE51,120:POKE52,29:END
460 REM*MEMTOP RESET *
470 REM*FOR SPR EXPND*
480 REM*****************
490 REM**PLOTSUB**
500 REM X=0TO175
510 REM Y=159TO0
520 V=INT(X/8):U=INT(Y/16)
530 S=22*U+V:PM=M:PC=C
540 R=YAND15:C=XAND7
550 M=4096+16*S+R
560 IFE=0THENPOKEM,PEEK(M)ORC%(C)
570 IFE=1THENPOKEM,PEEK(M)ORC%(C):POKEPM,PEEK(PM)AND(255-C%(PC))
580 RETURN
590 REM**SAVE SCREEN**
600 POKE36867,174:POKE36869,240:PRINT"J"
610 INPUT"HSC#(0TO255)";N
620 POKE3848,(N+48)AND255
630 SYS3872:GOSUB780
640 POKE36867,149:POKE36869,252:GOSUB730
650 RETURN
660 REM**LOAD SCREEN**
670 POKE36867,174:POKE36869,240:PRINT"J"
680 INPUT"HSC#(0TO255)";N
690 POKE3848,(N+48)AND255
700 SYS3955:GOSUB780
710 POKE36867,149:POKE36869,252:GOSUB730
```

Listing continues next page

```
720 RETURN
730 REM**BIT MAP SC**
740 FORS=0TO219
750 POKE7680+S,S
760 POKE38400+S,0
770 NEXT:RETURN
780 REM*ERROR CHANNEL*
790 INPUT#15,EN,EM$,ET,ES
800 IFEN=0THENRETURN
810 PRINT:PRINT"█ERROR█"EN:PRINTEM$:PRINT"TRACK"ET:PRINT"SECTOR"ES:PRINT
820 PRINT"PRESS █SPACE█ TO CONT"
830 GETB$:IFB$=""THEN830
840 IFB$<>" "THEN830
850 RETURN
```

Of course you do not have to draw pictures with a joystick. The BASIC program could be rewritten as a graph plotter, as in the last Example of Chapter 4, and the graphs could then be saved to tape or disk. Nor does machine code have to be used, it is just an awful lot faster and economical.

3. Hi-resolution output to the printer

To output a Hi-resolution picture to the VIC 1515 printer poses two main difficulties. Firstly the bits which represent the picture as stored in the character matrix are arranged in blocks of 16 bytes per character cell, each byte being one *horizontal* block of 8 bits; whereas the printer character cell format is 7 bits by X bits.[†] Secondly the printer uses *vertical* bytes to specify its character cell. If we add to these difficulties the constraints imposed by the physical limitations of the printer, namely once a carriage return has been printed *that* line cannot be modified, it becomes plain that a simple solution is unlikely to be available.

The program listed below starts constructing 7×7 (vertical) byte character cells in the top left corner of the screen, more precisely using the top 7 bits of the first 7 bytes of the character matrix. As each vertical byte is assembled it is stored in an array A%(I), $1 \leqslant I \leqslant 7$. When the array A%(I) is full, the composite high resolution character is constructed as C$ and output to the printer. The whole process is moved right 7 bits and repeated until the end of the first row (22 screen character cells equal to 26 printer character cells). At this point a carriage return is printed, the memory pointer to the character matrix S%(L) is adjusted accordingly, and the whole process is repeated. Figure A2 sums up the book-keeping problems.

As the 7×7 cell moves through the character matrix memory, at any given point it may overlap up to 4 of the 16×8 character matrix cells. It is therefore necessary to distinguish *left* vertical bytes and *right* vertical bytes, which in turn may be assembled from *top* horizontal bytes and *bottom* horizontal bytes. The offset in character matrix memory from the last top horizontal byte (working down) to the first bottom horizontal byte is 21 * 16.

The critical part of the printer routine is line 170 and lines 370 to 810, the remainder of the program is concerned with selecting the device for LOAD, loading a picture saved previously, and error checking for the disk if appropriate.

---

†Retrospective comment: it would have been much simpler to use the graphic mode to construct a 7×8 character cell rather than the 7×7 cell actually employed!

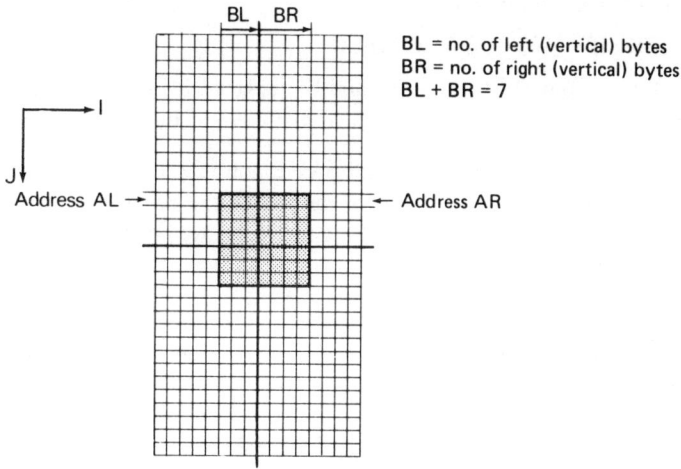

Fig. A2 — Character 'cells' in memory.

One final aspect of this program should be noted, this is the GOSUB in lines 5000–5060. This GOSUB is a useful technique for avoiding the necessity of loading the machine code routine separately with a

       LOAD "M/C HI-DRAW", 8,1   (Disk)
or   LOAD "M/C HI-DRAW", 1,1   (Tape),

before loading the BASIC program. If the following sequence is performed it will create a composite program, BASIC plus machine code, which can be loaded as any normal BASIC program.

1. First enter the BASIC program, inserting REM at the beginning of lines 90 and 220. This will enable the program to be debugged without risk of crashing the VIC. It is wise to SAVE the result.

2. Next remove the REMs on lines 90 and 220 and RETURN a CLR. Now LIST the program and PEEK the BASIC pointers in 45 to 50. Insert the corresponding values in lines 5010 to 5030. Note that if you have varied the program in the smallest detail, for example the insertion of an odd space, the values obtained will be different from those in the listing. You must have the 3K RAM pack in at this stage. Finally, for the purpose of illustration, we have done the same thing in line 5040 for the pointers in 174, 175 which relate to SAVE.[†] As a last step, recheck the values obtained by PEEKing 45 to 50; these values must equal those that occur in your program listing. Now SAVE the resulting BASIC program.

3. For the remaining stages you will need simultaneously a machine code monitor and a 3K RAM pack, which means using a memory expansion board. First LOAD the previously saved machine code program with

       LOAD "M/C HI-DRAW", 8,1   (Disk)
or   LOAD "M/C HI-DRAW", 1,1   (Tape).

Now load the program saved in step 2.

4. Finally enter VICMON with

       SYS 6 * 4096

---

†Actually this is pointless since SAVE resets these locations!

and SAVE the composite program with

    . S "HI-DUMP+M/C", 08,0401, 0FCC

Note 08 is the device number (Disk), which must be replaced by 01 if the SAVE is to tape, 0401 (hex) is the start of BASIC (dec 1025) and 0FCC (hex) is just beyond the end of the machine code.

When HI-DUMP + M/C is loaded the BASIC and SAVE pointers are high, but as soon as the program is RUN the pointers are set to the correct values for the end of the BASIC part of the program (by GOSUB 5000). Line 80 protects the machine code and character matrix from being overwritten by BASIC.

```
80 POKE55,255:POKE56,14:POKE51,255:POKE52,14:CLR:REM LOWER MEMTOP
90 GOSUB5000
100 PRINT"J":PRINT
110 PRINT" DO YOU WISH TO LOAD  FROM":PRINT
120 PRINT"  TAPE ▓T▒ OR DISK ▓D▒":PRINT
130 INPUT"DEVICE";D$
140 IFD$="T"THENPOKE3853,1:GOTO170
150 IFD$="D"THENPOKE3853,8:OPEN15,8,15,"I":GOSUB1000:GOTO170
160 GOTO130
170 DIMA%(7),P%(8),Q%(27),R%(24),S%(24)
180 PRINT"J":PRINT
190 PRINT"SPECIFY WHICH FILE NUMBER YOU WISH TO LOAD":PRINT
200 INPUT"HSC#(0TO255)";A$:N=VAL(A$)
210 POKE3848,(N+48)AND255:PRINT"J"
220 SYS3955:REM LOAD
230 IFD$="D"THENGOSUB1000:IFEN<>0THEN180
240 POKE36869,252:REM CM TO 4096
250 POKE36867,149:REM 16*8 AND 10 ROWS
260 REM*BITMAP SCREEN*
270 FORL=0TO219:POKE7680+L,L:POKE38400+L,0:NEXT
280 FORL=0TO2000:NEXT
290 REM*FLIPBACK*
300 POKE36867,174:POKE36869,240:PRINT"J"
310 PRINT"DO YOU WISH TO OUTPUT THIS TO A PRINTER(Y/N)OR QUIT(Q)?"
320 GETA$:IFA$=""THEN320
330 IFA$="Q"THEN860
340 IFA$="N"THEN180
350 IFA$="Y"THEN370
360 GOTO320
370 REM*SET DUMP*
380 FORJ=0TO7:P%(J)=2↑J:NEXT
390 FORL=1TO23
400 R%(L)=(7*(L-1))AND15
410 S%(L)=4096+22*16*INT(7*(L-1)/16)+R%(L):REM CM START FOR LINE L
420 NEXT
430 FORN=1TO26                            Listing continues next page
```

```
440 Q%(N)=16*7*INT((N-1)/8):REM CM OFFSET FOR CHAR N (ON ANY LINE)
450 NEXT
460 REM**START DUMP**
470 OPEN4,4:T=TI
480 FORL=1TO23
490 PRINT"]WORKING ON LINE"L:PRINT
500 PRINT"TIME TO COMPLETION     APPROX"INT(16-(TI-T)/3600)"MINS
510 Z=6:IFL=23THENZ=5
520 FORN=1TO26
530 BL=(N-1)AND7:BR=7-BL
540 IFBL=0THEN640
550 REM*ASSEMBLE LEFT (VERT) BYTES*
560 FORI=1TOBL:X=0:AL=S%(L)+16*(BL-1)+Q%(N)
570 FORJ=0TOZ
580 X=((PEEK(AL+J)ANDP%(BL-I))/P%(BL-I))*P%(J)+X
590 IFR%(L)+J=15THENAL=AL+21*16
600 NEXTJ
610 A%(I)=X
620 NEXTI
630 IFBR=0THEN720
640 REM*ASSEMBLE RIGHT (VERT) BYTES*
650 FORI=1TOBR:X=0:AR=S%(L)+16*(7-BR)+Q%(N)
660 FORJ=0TOZ
670 X=((PEEK(AR+J)ANDP%(8-I))/P%(8-I))*P%(J)+X
680 IFR%(L)+J=15THENAR=AR+21*16
690 NEXTJ
700 A%(BL+I)=X
710 NEXTI
720 IFN=26THENFORI=2TO7:A%(I)=0:NEXT
730 REM*CONSTRUCT N(TH) CHAR CELL*
740 C$=""
750 FORI=1TO7:C$=C$+CHR$(A%(I)+128):NEXT
760 PRINT#4,CHR$(8)C$;
770 NEXTN
780 PRINT#4,CHR$(13);
790 NEXTL
800 PRINT#4,CHR$(15)CHR$(13)
810 PRINT#4:CLOSE4
820 PRINT"]"
830 PRINT"DO YOU WISH TO CONT"
840 INPUT"(Y/N)";A$
850 IFA$="Y"THEN180
860 POKE55,120:POKE56,29:POKE51,120:POKE52,29:CLOSE15:END
870 REM*MEMTOP RESET *
880 REM*FOR SPR EXPND*
890 REM***************
1000 REM*ERROR CHANNEL*
```

Listing continues next page

```
1010 INPUT#15,EN,EM$,FT,ES:PRINT
1020 IFEN=0THENRETURN
1030 PRINT"∎ERROR#"EN:PRINTEM$:PRINT"TRACK"FT:PRINT"SECTOR"ES:PRINT"∎"
1040 PRINT"∎PRESS RETURN TO CONT"
1050 GETA$:IFA$<>CHR$(13)THEN1050
1060 RETURN
5000 REM*RESET BASIC*
5010 POKE45,133:POKE46,12
5020 POKE47,133:POKE48,12
5030 POKE49,133:POKE50,12
5040 POKE174,133:POKE175,12
5060 RETURN
```

4. The machine code routine

The machine code program below has three separate functions:

(i) to SAVE the entire block of RAM from 4096 to 7616 to disk (or tape) as a PRG file with file name HSC0, where the last character can be varied with a POKE to 3848;

(ii) to LOAD a previously saved PRG file with name HSC0 back into locations 4096 to 7616;

(iii) To fill the entire block of RAM from 4096 to 7616 with zeros, i.e. a routine to CLEAR a Hi-resolution screen quickly.

In fact the program will SAVE or LOAD any specified block of RAM to disk or tape, since the device number and the block of RAM saved or loaded can be changed with POKES. Since Kernal control and error messages are requested, when the program is used to SAVE or LOAD a Hi-resolution screen the character matrix should be relocated in ROM and the video matrix cleared before calls to these routines.

SAVE	is called by SYS 3872
LOAD	is called by SYS 3955
CLEAR	is called by SYS 3993

Commented data dump for M/C HI-DRAW

```
3840  .:0F00 00 10 C0 1D 04
3845  .:0F05 48 53 43 30 00
3850  .:0F0A 00 00 00 08 00
3855  .:0F0F 00 00 00 00 00
3860  .:0F14 00 00 00 00 00
```

Comment. A memory dump such as above can be output to the printer as follows

```
OPEN 4,4 : CMD 4 [RETURN]
SYS 6 * 4096      [RETURN]
.M 0F00, 0F14     [RETURN]
```

Address		Contents		Comment
Dec	Hex	Hex	Dec	
3840	0F00	00	0	CM start Lo-byte
3841	0F01	10	16	CM start Hi-byte
3842	0F02	C0	192	CM end Lo-byte
3843	0F03	1D	29	CM end Hi-byte
3844	0F04	04	4	Length of file name
3845	0F05	48	72	H
3846	0F06	53	83	S
3847	0F07	43	67	C
3848	0F08	30	48	0
3849	0F09	00	0	Unused
3850	0F0A	00	0	Unused
3851	0F0B	00	0	Unused
3852	0F0C	00	0	Unused
3853	0F0D	08	8	Device number (disk)
3854	3871	—	—	Unused

Commented program listing for M/C.

```
.,  0F1D  BRK                  ⎧ #$40 control messages (bit 6)
.,  0F1E  BRK                  ⎨ #$80 Kernal messages (bit 7)
.,  0F1F  BRK                  ⎩ #$C0 all messages (bits 7 and 8)
.,  0F20  LDA  #$C0    ──────
.,  0F22  JSR  $FF90          SET MESSAGES
.,  0F25  LDA  #$01          Logical file number
.,  0F27  LDX  $0F0D         Device number
.,  0F2A  LDY  #$0F          Secondary address
.,  0F2C  JSR  $FFBA         SET LOGICAL FIRST AND SECOND ADDRESS
.,  0F2F  LDA  $0F04         File name length                    OPEN 1,8,15,
.,  0F32  LDX  #$05          Start of file name, Lo-byte          "HSC0,PRG"
.,  0F34  LDY  #$0F          Start of file name, Hi-byte
.,  0F36  JSR  $FFBD         SET FILE NAME
.,  0F39  JSR  $FFC0         OPEN LOGICAL FILE
.,  0F3C  NOP
.,  0F3D  NOP
.,  0F3E  NOP
.,  0F3F  LDA  #$01          Logical file number
.,  0F41  LDX  $0F0D         Device number                         SAVE
.,  0F44  LDY  #$0F          Secondary address
.,  0F46  JSR  $FFBA         SET LOGICAL FIRST AND SECOND ADDRESS
.,  0F49  LDA  $0F04         File name length
.,  0F4C  LDX  #$05          Start of file name, Lo-byte
.,  0F4E  LDY  #$0F          Start of file name. Hi-byte
.,  0F50  JSR  $FFBD         SET FILE NAME
.,  0F53  LDA  $0F00      ⎫  Store Lo-byte of CM start
.,  0F56  STA  $00        ⎭  in $00
.,  0F58  LDA  $0F01      ⎫  Store Hi-byte of CM start
.,  0F5A  STA  $01        ⎭  in $01
.,  0F5D  LDA  #$00          Zero page offset (#$00 since first two locations used)
.,  0F5F  LDX  $0F02         CM end, Lo-byte
.,  0F62  LDY  $0F03         CM end, Hi-byte
.,  0F65  JSR  $FFD8         SAVE
.,  0F68  NOP
.,  0F69  NOP
.,  0F6A  LDA  #$01          Logical file number
.,  0F6C  JSR  $FFC3         CLOSE LOGICAL FILE
.,  0F6F  RTS               Return to stack (back to BASIC)
.,  0F70  BRK
.,  0F71  BRK
.,  0F72  BRK
.,  0F73  LDA  #$C0          All messages
.,  0F75  JSR  $FF90         SET MESSAGES
```

Listing continues next page

.,	0F78 LDA #$01	Logical file number	
.,	0F7A LDX $0F0D	Device number	
.,	0F7D LDY #$0F	Secondary address	
.,	0F7F JSR $FFBA	SET LOGICAL FIRST AND SECOND ADDRESS	
.,	0F82 LDA $0F04	File name length	
.,	0F85 LDX #$05	Start of file name, Lo-byte	LOAD
.,	0F87 LDY #$0F	Start of file name, Hi-byte	
.,	0F89 JSR $FFBD	SET FILE NAME	
.,	0F8C LDA #$00	load = #$00, verify = #$01	
.,	0F8E LDX $0F00	CM start, Lo-byte	
.,	0F91 LDY $0F01	CM start, Hi-byte	
.,	0F94 JSR $FFD5	LOAD	
.,	0F97 RTS	Return to stack (back to BASIC)	
.,	0F98 BRK		
.,	0F99 LDA $0F00	⎫ Store CM start Lo-byte in $00	
.,	0F9C STA $00	⎬	
.,	0F9E LDA $0F01	⎫ Stor CM start Hi-byte in $01	INITIALIZE
.,	0FA1 STA $01	⎬	CLEAR
.,	0FA3 LDA $0F02	⎫ Store CM end Lo-byte in $4E	
.,	0FA6 STA $4E	⎬	
.,	0FA8 LDA $0F03	⎫ Store CM end Hi-byte in $4F	
.,	0FAB STA $4F	⎬	
.,	0FAD NOP		
.,	0FAE LDY #$00	Keep index offset always at zero	
.,	0FB0 LDA $4E	CM end, Lo-byte	
.,	0FB2 CMP $00	Compare with contents $00	
.,	0FB4 LDA $4F	CM end, Hi-byte	
.,	0FB6 SBC $01	Compare with contents $01	
.,	0FB8 BCC $0FC7	Done? If yes then	
.,	0FBA LDA #$00	⎫ Store #$00 in address with Lo-byte equal	
.,	0FBC STA ($00),Y	⎬ to contents of $00, Hi-byte equal to contents $01	CLEAR
.,	0FBE INC $00	Increment Lo-byte	
.,	0FC0 BNE $0FB0	256 bytes done?	
.,	0FC2 INC $01	Increment Hi-byte	
.,	0FC4 JMP $0FB0	Jump	
.,	0FC7 RTS	Return to stack (back to BASIC)	
.,	0FC8 BRK		
.,	0FC9 BRK		
.,	0FCA BRK		
.,	0FCB ???	Garbage	
.,	0FCC ???	Garbage	
.,	0FCD ???		

For those who do not have access to an expansion board or machine code monitor the following BASIC program will load M/C HI-DRAW into 3840 to 4044. The program should be loaded and run (with a 3K RAM pack in place!) before loading either HI-DRAW or HI-DUMP.

```
10 REM*M/C LOADER FOR*
20 REM*  M/C HI-DRAW *
30 REM*USE 3K RAMPACK*
40 REM**************
50 DATA0,16,192,29,4
60 DATA72,83,67,48,0
70 DATA0,0,0,0,0,0,0
80 DATA0,0,0,0,0,0,0
90 DATA0,0,0,0,0,0,0
100 DATA0,169,192,32
110 DATA144,255,169,1
120 DATA174,13,15,160,15,32
130 DATA186,255,173,4
140 DATA15,162,5,160
150 DATA15,32,189,255
160 DATA32,192,255,234
170 DATA234,234,169,1
180 DATA174,13,15,160
190 DATA15,32,186,255
200 DATA173,4,15,162,5
210 DATA160,15,32,189
220 DATA255,173,0,15
230 DATA133,0,173,1,15
240 DATA133,1,169,0
250 DATA174,2,15,172,3
260 DATA15,32,216,255
270 DATA234,234,169,1
280 DATA32,195,255,96
290 DATA0,0,0,169,192
300 DATA32,144,255,169
310 DATA1,174,13,15
320 DATA160,15,32,186
330 DATA255,173,4,15
340 DATA162,5,160,15
350 DATA32,189,255,169
360 DATA0,174,0,15,172
370 DATA1,15,32,213
380 DATA255,96,0,173,0
390 DATA15,133,0,173,1
400 DATA15,133,1,173,2
410 DATA15,133,78,173
420 DATA3,15,133,79
```

Listing continues next page

```
430 DATA234,160,0,165
440 DATA78,197,0,165
450 DATA79,229,1,144
460 DATA13,169,0,145,0
470 DATA230,0,208,238
480 DATA230,1,76,176
490 DATA15,96,0,0,0
500 DATA0,32
1000 POKE51,255:POKE52,14:POKE55,255:POKE56,14
1010 CC=0:FORI=3840TO4044
1020 READX:POKEI,X
1030 CC=CC+X
1040 NEXT
1050 IFCC=17958THENPRINT"OK"
1060 IFCC<>17958THENPRINT"DATA STATEMENT ERROR"
1070 END
```

Tables

Table A1 — VIC-20 Memory Map First 1K Block[†]

HEX	DECIMAL	DESCRIPTION
0000	0	Jump for USR
0001–0002	1–2	USR vector
0003–0004	3–4	Float–Fixed vector
0005–0006	5–6	Fixed–Float vector
0007	7	Search character, ':' or endline
0008	8	Scan between quotes flag
0009	9	TAB, column save position of cursor on line
000A	10	0 = LOAD, 1 = VERIFY
000B	11	Input, buffer pointer/#subscript
000C	12	Default DIM flag
000D	13	Type: FF = string, 00 = numeric
000E	14	Type: 80 = integer, 00 = floating point
000F	15	DATA scan/LIST quote/memory flag
0010	16	Subscript/FNx flag
0011	17	0 = INPUT; $40 = GET; $98 = READ
0012	18	ATN sign/Comparison eval flag
0013	19	Current I/O prompt flag
0014–0015	20–21	Basic integer address for SYS,GOTO etc.
0016	22	Pointer: temporary string stack
0017–0018	23–24	Last temp string vector
0019–0021	25–33	Stack for temporary strings
0022–0025	34–37	Utility pointer area

†Compiled by Jim Butterfield.

Table A1 continued

HEX	DECIMAL	DESCRIPTION
0026–002A	38–42	Product area for multiplication
002B–002C	43–44	Pointer: Start of user BASIC (bottom of memory)
002D–002E	45–46	Pointer: Start of Variables
002F–0030	47–48	Pointer: Start of Arrays
0031–0032	49–50	Pointer: End of Arrays
0033–0034	51–52	Pointer: String storage (moving down)
0035–0036	53–54	Pointer: Top of active strings
0037–0038	55–56	Pointer: End of user BASIC (top of memory)
0039–003A	57–58	Current Basic line number
003B–003C	59–60	Previous Basic line number
003D–003E	61–62	Pointer: Basic statement for CONT
003F–0040	63–64	Current DATA line number
0041–0042	65–66	Current DATA item address
0043–0044	67–68	Input vector
0045–0046	69–70	Current variable name
0047–0048	71–72	Current variable address
0049–004A	73–74	Variable pointer for FOR/NEXT
004B–004C	75–76	Y-save; op-save; Basic pointer save
004D	77	Comparison symbol accumulator
004E	78–83	Misc. work area, Pointers, etc.
0054–0056	84–86	Jump vector for functions
0057–0060	87–96	Misc. numeric work area
0061	97	Accum#1: Exponent
0062–0065	98–101	Accum#1: Mantissa
0066	102	Accum#1: Sign
0067	103	Series evaluation constant pointer
0068	104	Accum#1 hi-order (overflow)
0069–006E	105–110	Accum#2: Exponent, Mantissa, etc
006F	111	Sign comparison, Acc#1 vs. Acc#2
0070	112	Accum#1 lo-order (rounding)
0071–0072	113–114	Cassette buffer length/Series pointer
0073–008A	115–138	CHARGET subroutine (Get Basic char)
007A–007B	122–123	Basic CHARGET vector (within subroutine)
008B–008F	139–143	RND seed value;
0090	144	Status word ST
00091	145	Keyswitch PIA: STOP (= $FE) and RVS flags
0092	146	Timing constant for tape
0093	147	Load = 0, Verify = 1
0094	148	Serial output: deferred char. flag (IEEE)
0095	149	Serial deferred character (IEEE)
0096	150	Tape EOT received
0097	151	Register save (IEEE)
0098	152	How many open files?
0099	153	Input device (normally 0)

Table A1 continued

HEX	DECIMAL	DESCRIPTION
009A	154	Output (CMD) device (normally 3)
009B	155	Tape character parity
009C	156	Byte-received flag/cassette dipole switch
009D	157	OS message flag: Direct = $80/RUN = 0
009E	158	Tape Pass 1 error log/char. buffer
009F	159	Tape Pass 2 error log corrected
00A0–00A2	160–162	Jiffy Clock (HML)
00A3	163	Serial bit count/EOI flag
00A4	164	Cycle count for serial I/O
00A5	165	Countdown, tape write/bit count
00A6	166	Pointer: tape buffer
00A7	167	Tape write ldr count/Read pass/inhibit (RS232)
00A8	168	Tape Write new byte/Read error/inhibit cnt (RS232)
00A9	169	Write start bit/Read bit err/stbit (RS232)
00AA	170	Tape Scan;Ld;End/byte assy (RS232)
00AB	171	Write lead length/Rd checksum/parity (RS232)
00AC–00AD	172–173	Pointer: tape buffer, scrolling
00AE–00AF	174–175	Tape end addresses/End of program for SAVE
00B0–00B1	176–177	Tape timing constants
00B2–00B3	178–179	Pointer: start of tape buffer
00B4	180	Tape timer (1 = enable); bit cnt (RS232)
00B5	181	Tape EOT/next bit to send (RS232)
00B6	182	Read character error/outbyte buffer (RS232)
00B7	183	# characters in file name
00B8	184	Current logical file
00B9	185	Current secondary address or R/W
00BA	186	Current device
00BB–00BC	187–188	Pointer: to file name
00BD	189	Write shift word/Read input char (RS232)
00BE	190	# blocks remaining to Write/Read
00BF	191	Serial word buffer
00C0	192	Tape motor interlock
00C1–00C2	193–194	I/O start addresses
00C3–00C4	195–196	Kernal setup pointer
00C5	197	Current key pressed
00C6	198	# chars in keyboard buffer
00C7	199	Screen reverse flag (0 = off, 18 = on)
00C8	200	Pointer: End-of-line for input
00C9–00CA	201–202	Input cursor log (row, column)
00CB	203	Which key: 64 if no key
00CC	204	Cursor enable (0 = flash cursor on, 1 = off)
00CD	205	Cursor blink delay
00CE	206	Character under cursor
00CF	207	Cursor in blink phase flag (1 = off, 0 = visible)

Table A1 continued

HEX	DECIMAL	DESCRIPTION
00D0	208	Input from screen/from keyboard
00D1–00D2	209–210	Pointer to screen line address
00D3	211	Position of cursor on above line
00D4	212	0 = direct cursor, else programmed
00D5	213	Current screen line length (22,44,66,88)
00D6	214	Row where cursor lives
00D7	215	Last inkey/checksum/buffer
00D8	216	# of INSERTs outstanding
00D9–00F0	217–240	Screen line link table
00F1	241	Dummy screen link
00F2	242	Screen row marker
00F3–00F4	243–244	Screen color printer
00F5–00F6	245–246	Keyboard pointer
00F7–00F8	247–248	Pointer RS-232 receive buffer base location
00F9–00FA	249–250	Pointer RS-232 transmit buffer base location
00FB–00FE	251–254	Operating system free zero page space
00FF	255	Basic storage
0100–010A	256–266	Floating to ASCII work area
0100–103E	256–318	Tape error log
0100–01FF	256–511	Processor stack area
0200–0258	512–600	BASIC input buffer
0259–0262	601–610	Logical file table
0263–026C	611–620	Device # table
026D–0276	621–630	Secondary address or R/W CMD table
0277–0280	631–640	Keyboard buffer
0281–0282	641–642	Start of memory for op system
0283–0284	643–644	Top of memory for op system
0285	645	Serial bus timeout flag (IEEE)
0286	646	Current color code
0287	647	Color under cursor
0288	648	Hi-byte base location of screen
0289	649	Max. size of keyboard buffer
028A	650	Key repeat 128=repeat all keys, 64=repeat no keys, 0=cursor controls
028B	651	Delay before first repeat occurs
028C	652	Delay between repeats
028D	653	Keyboard Shift/Control flag
028E	654	Last keyboard shift pattern
028F–0290	655–656	Pointer: keyboard decode table
0291	657	Shift mode switch (0=enabled, 128=locked)
0292	658	Auto scroll down flag (0 = on, 1 = off)
0293	659	Pseudo RS232 control register
0294	660	Pseudo RS232 command register
0295–0296	661–662	Non-standard bit time (2–100)

Table A1 continued

HEX	DECIMAL	DESCRIPTION
0297	663	RS-232 status register
0298	664	Number of bits sent/received
0299–029A	665–666	Baud rate (full) bit time
029B	667	RS232 end of input buffer pointer
029C	668	RS232 start of input buffer pointer
029D	669	RS232 start of transmit buffer pointer
029E	670	RS232 end of transmit buffer pointer
029F–02A0	671–672	Holds IRQ during tape operations
02A1–02FF	673–767	Program indirects
0300–0301	768–769	Error message link
0302–0303	770–771	Basic warm start link
0304–0305	772–773	Crunch Basic tokens link
0306–0307	774–775	Print tokens link
0308–0309	776–777	Start new Basic code link
030A–030B	778–779	Get arithmetic element link
030C	780	Storage for 6502 .A register during SYS
030D	781	Storage for 6502 .X register during SYS
030E	782	Storage for 6502 .Y register during SYS
030F	783	Storage for 6502 .P register during SYS
0310–0313	784–787	??
0314–0315	788–789	IRQ interrupt vector (EABF)
0316–0317	790–791	BRK interrupt vector (FED2)
0318–0319	792–793	NMI interrupt vector (FEAD)
031A–031B	794–795	OPEN vector (F40A)
031C–031D	796–797	CLOSE vector (F34A)
031E–031F	798–799	Set-input vector (F2C7)
0320–0321	800–801	Set-output vector (F309)
0322–0323	802–803	Restore I/O vector (F3F3)
0324–0325	804–805	INPUT vector (F20E)
0326–0327	806–807	Output vector (F27A)
0328–0329	808–809	Test-STOP vector (F770)
032A–032B	810–811	GET vector (F1F5)
032C–032D	812–813	Abort I/O vector (F3EF)
032F–032F	814–815	User vector (FED2)
0330–0331	816–817	Link to load RAM (F549)
0332–0333	818–819	Link to save RAM (F685)
0334–033B	820–827	??
033C–03FB	828–1019	Cassette buffer

Table A2 – Characters against screen codes and CBM ASCII.

	Screen (POKE)	Screen (PRINT)	Printer (PRINT#)
Set 1	POKE 36869, PEEK(36869) AND 240	CHR$(142)	CHR$(145)
Set 2	POKE 36869, PEEK(36869) AND 242	CHR$(14)	CHR$(17)

Set 1 Upper case + Miscellaneous/Graphics.
Set 2 Lower case + Miscellaneous/Upper case + some graphics.

	Screen (PRINT)	Printer (PRINT#)
Reverse field off	CHR$(146)	CHR$(146)
Reverse field on	CHR$(18)	CHR$(18)

ASCII (American Standard Code for Information Interchange) is a widely used code for representing character data. Normally, it is a 7-bit code allowing 128 characters to be represented. CBM computers store characters in an extended 8-bit version of ASCII format, thus allowing 256 characters to be represented. Within compressed BASIC text bit 7 = 1 signifies a keyword (see Table A5) elsewhere in memory the 8-bit character codes are interpreted as in the following table.

SET 1	SET 2	SCREEN CODE	CBM ASCII	SET 1	SET 2	SCREEN CODE	CBM ASCII	SET 1	SET 2	SCREEN CODE	CBM ASCII
@	@	0	64	Q	q	17	81	"	"	34	34
A	a	1	65	R	r	18	82	#	#	35	35
B	b	2	66	S	s	19	83	$	$	36	36
C	c	3	67	T	t	20	84	%	%	37	37
D	d	4	68	U	u	21	85	&	&	38	38
E	e	5	69	V	v	22	86	'	'	39	39
F	f	6	70	W	w	23	87	(	(	40	40
G	g	7	71	X	x	24	88	)	)	41	41
H	h	8	72	Y	y	25	89	*	*	42	42
I	i	9	73	Z	z	26	90	+	+	43	43
J	j	10	74	[	[	27	91	,	,	44	44
K	k	11	75	£	£	28	92	-	-	45	45
L	l	12	76	]	]	29	93	.	.	46	46
M	m	13	77	↑	↑	30	94	/	/	47	47
N	n	14	78	←	←	31	95	0	0	48	48
O	o	15	79			32	32	1	1	49	49
P	p	16	80	!	!	33	33	2	2	50	50

SET 1	SET 2	SCREEN CODE	CBM ASCII	SET 1	SET 2	SCREEN CODE	CBM ASCII	SET 1	SET 2	SCREEN CODE	CBM ASCII
3	3	51	51	▨	▨	92	124	▤	▤	133	69
4	4	52	52	|	|	93	125	▥	▥	134	70
5	5	53	53	π	✗	94	126	▨	▨	135	71
6	6	54	54	◣	▨	95	127	▦	▦	136	72
7	7	55	55			96	160	▮	▮	137	73
8	8	56	56	▌	▌	97	161	▮	▮	138	74
9	9	57	57	▄	▄	98	162	▨	▮	139	75
:	:	58	58	▔	▔	99	163	▌	▮	140	76
;	;	59	59	─	─	100	164	▦	▮	141	77
<	<	60	60	▏	▏	101	165	▦	▮	142	78
=	=	61	61	▨	▨	102	166	▨	▨	143	79
>	>	62	62	|	|	103	167	▤	▮	144	80
?	?	63	63	▨	▨	104	168	▨	▮	145	81
─	─	64	96	◤	▨	105	169	▨	▨	146	82
♠	A	65	97	|	|	106	170	▨	▨	147	83
|	B	66	98	⊢	⊢	107	171	▮	▦	148	84
─	C	67	99	▪	▪	108	172	▥	▨	149	85
─	D	68	100	∟	∟	109	173	▨	▨	150	86
─	E	69	101	┐	┐	110	174	▨	▨	151	87
─	F	70	102	─	─	111	175	▨	▮	152	88
|	G	71	103	┌	┌	112	176	▨	▨	153	89
|	H	72	104	⊥	⊥	113	177	▨	▨	154	90
\	I	73	105	┬	┬	114	178	▮	▮	155	91
\	J	74	106	┤	┤	115	179	▨	▨	156	92
/	K	75	107	|	|	116	180	▮	▮	157	93
L	L	76	108	|	|	117	181	▦	▦	158	94
\	M	77	109	▎	▎	118	182	▨	▨	159	95
/	N	78	110	▔	▔	119	183	■	■	160	32
⌐	O	79	111	▬	▬	120	184	▦	▦	161	33
┐	P	80	112	▪	▪	121	185	▦	▦	162	34
●	Q	81	113	⌟	✓	122	186	▦	▦	163	35
─	R	82	114	▪	▪	123	187	▦	▦	164	36
♥	S	83	115	▪	▪	124	188	▦	▦	165	37
|	T	84	116	⌐	⌐	125	189	▨	▨	166	38
/	U	85	117	▪	▪	126	190	▮	▮	167	39
×	V	86	118	▪▪	▪▪	127	191	▨	▨	168	40
○	W	87	119	▨	▨	128	64	▨	▨	169	41
♣	X	88	120	▨	▨	129	65	▨	▨	170	42
|	Y	89	121	▨	▨	130	66	▨	▨	171	43
♦	Z	90	122	▨	▨	131	67	▮	▮	172	44
+	+	91	123	▨	▨	132	68	▨	▨	173	45

SET 1	SET 2	SCREEN CODE	CBM ASCII	SET 1	SET 2	SCREEN CODE	CBM ASCII	SET 1	SET 2	SCREEN CODE	CBM ASCII
		174	46			202	106			230	166
		175	47			203	107			231	167
		176	48			204	108			232	168
		177	49			205	109			233	169
		178	50			206	110			234	170
		179	51			207	111			235	171
		180	52			208	112			236	172
		181	53			209	113			237	173
		182	54			210	114			238	174
		183	55			211	115			239	175
		184	56			212	116			240	176
		185	57			213	117			241	177
		186	58			214	118			242	178
		187	59			215	119			243	179
		188	60			216	120			244	180
		189	61			217	121			245	181
		190	62			218	122			246	182
		191	63			219	123			247	183
		192	96			220	124			248	184
		193	97			221	125			249	185
		194	98			222	126			250	186
		195	99			223	127			251	187
		196	100			224	160			252	188
		197	101			225	161			253	189
		198	102			226	162			254	190
		199	103			227	163			255	191
		200	104			228	164				
		201	105			229	165				

Table A3 – CBM ASCII codes 192 to 255.

These codes are not normally used on the VIC-20 and are included only for interest's sake. It is a curious fact that whichever character set is selected and regardless of whether reverse field is on or off PRINTing these codes to screen or printer will give the characters listed below.

	CBM ASCII		CBM ASCII		CBM ASCII
–	192	×	214	▮	236
♠	193	○	215	∟	237
|	194	♣	216	¬	238
–	195	¦	217	–	239
–	196	♦	218	⌐	240
–	197	+	219	⊥	241
–	198	▓	220	⊤	242
¦	199	¦	221	⊣	243
¦	200	π	222	|	244
`	201	◥	223	▌	245
\	202		224	▮	246
⌐	203	▌	225	–	247
∟	204	▪	226	▪	248
\	205	–	227	▬	249
/	206	_	228	⌐	250
⌐	207	¦	229	▮	251
¬	208	▓	230	▫	252
▮	209	¦	231	⌐	253
–	210	▓	232	▪	254
♣	211	▶	233	π	255
¦	212	¦	234		
/	213	├	235		

Table A4 – CBM ASCII screen control codes.

CBM ASCII 0 to 31 and 128 to 159 are reserved for special use, mostly as screen or printer control characters, e.g. PRINTCHR$(147) is equivalent to SHIFT + CLR/HOME. See Chapter 5 for a complete table of printer codes; the control codes listed below refer to the screen.

CBM ASCII CODE	CONTROL		CBM ASCII CODE	CONTROL	
0	–		128	–	
1	–		129	–	
2	–		130	–	
3	–		131	–	
4	–		132	–	
5	PRINT WHITE	"▇"	133	FUNCTION KEY F1	
6	–		134	FUNCTION KEY F3	
7	–		135	FUNCTION KEY F5	
8	–		136	FUNCTION KEY F7	
9	–		137	FUNCTION KEY F2	
10	–		138	FUNCTION KEY F4	
11	–		139	FUNCTION KEY F6	
12	–		140	FUNCTION KEY F8	
13	RETURN		141	SHIFT & RETURN	
14	SWITCH TO LOWER CASE		142	SWITCH TO UPPER CASE	
15	–		143	–	
16	–		144	PRINT BLACK	"▇"
17	CURSOR DOWN	"▨"	145	CURSOR UP	"▢"
18	REVERSE FIELD ON	"▨"	146	REVERSE FIELD OFF	"▣"
19	HOME	"▨"	147	CLEAR	"▨"
20	DELETE		148	INSERT	"▐"
21	–		149	–	
22	–		150	–	
23	–		151	–	
24	–		152	–	
25	–		153	–	
26	–		154	–	
27	–		155	–	
28	PRINT RED	"▨"	156	PRINT PURPLE	"▨"
29	CURSOR RIGHT	"▐"	157	CURSOR LEFT	"▐"
30	PRINT GREEN	"▐"	158	PRINT YELLOW	"▥"
31	PRINT BLUE	"▨"	159	PRINT CYAN	"◣"

Table A5 – CBM VIC-20 Basic keyword codes.

Code (decimal)	Character/ Keyword	Code (decimal)	Character/ Keyword	Code (decimal)	Character/ Keyword	Code (decimal)	Character/ Keyword
0	End of line	66	B	133	INPUT	169	STEP
1–31	Unused	67	C	134	DIM	170	+
32	space	68	D	135	READ	171	−
33	!	69	E	136	LET	172	•
34	"	70	F	137	GOTO	173	/
35	#	71	G	138	RUN	174	↑
36	$	72	H	139	IF	175	AND
37	%	73	I	140	RESTORE	176	OR
38	&	74	J	141	GOSUB	177	>
39	'	75	K	142	RETURN	178	=
40	(	76	L	143	REM	179	<
41	)	77	M	144	STOP	180	SGN
42	*	78	N	145	ON	181	INT
43	+	79	O	146	WAIT	182	ABS
44	,	80	P	147	LOAD	183	USR
45	−	81	Q	148	SAVE	184	FRE
46	•	82	R	149	VERIFY	185	POS
47	/	83	S	150	DEF	186	SQR
48	0	84	T	151	POKE	187	RND
49	1	85	U	152	PRINT#	188	LOG
50	2	86	V	153	PRINT	189	EXP
51	3	87	W	154	CONT	190	COS
52	4	88	X	155	LIST	191	SIN
53	5	89	Y	156	CLR	192	TAN
54	6	90	Z	157	CMD	193	ATN
55	7	91	[	158	SYS	194	PEEK
56	8	92	\	159	OPEN	195	LEN
57	9	93	]	160	CLOSE	196	STR$
58	:	94	↑	161	GET	197	VAL
59	;	95	←.	162	NEW	198	ASC
60	<	96–127	Unused	163	TAB(	199	CHR$
61	=	128	END	164	TO	200	LEFT$
62	>	129	FOR	165	FN	201	RIGHT$
63	?	130	NEXT	166	SPC(	202	MID$
64	@	131	DATA	167	THEN	203–254	Unused
65	A	132	INPUT#	168	NOT	255	π

Bibliography

The single most useful book covering all aspects of CBM BASIC, reference sections on CBM ROMs and containing innumerable useful 6502 machine code programs is

> Raeto West, *Programming the PET/CBM*, Level Ltd., P.O. Box 458, Hampstead, London NW3 1BH, 1982.

Although it does not deal specifically with the VIC-20 this encyclopaedic text contains a wealth of interesting material for anyone working with a PET or VIC.

> Two useful books concerned with 6502 machine code programming are

> Lance A. Leventhal, *6502 Assembly Language Programming*, Osborne/McGraw-Hill, 1979.

> Rodney Zaks, *Programming the 6502*, Sybex, U.S.A., 1981; available from The Computer Book Shop, 30 Lincoln Road, Olton, Birmingham.

The standard VIC-20 specific references are

> A. Finkel *et al. VIC-20 Programmer's Reference Guide*, Commodore Business Machines, Inc. 1982.

> Nick Hampshire, *VIC Revealed*, Computabits Ltd., P.O. Box 13, Yeovil, Somerset.

Index

Index to figures and tables